ERMAN 2.0

Waterman 2.0: Optimized Movement for Lifelong, Pain-free Paddling & Surfing
Dr. Kelly Starrett with Phil White

Copyright © 2018 Dr. Kelly Starrett and Phil White

All rights reserved. This book may not be reproduced in any form, in whole or in part (beyond the copying permitted by US Copyright Law, Section 107, "fair use" in teaching or research, Section 108, certain library copying, or in published media by reviewers in limited excerpts), without written permission from the author.

Hardcover ISBN: 978-0692070659
EBook ISBN: 978-0-692-14952-2
Softcover: 978-0-692-17103-5

Images © their respective owner
Generic water images throughout © Shutterstock

Book cover and layout design by *the*BookDesigners
www.bookdesigners.com

This book is licensed for your personal enjoyment and education only. While best efforts have been used, the author and publisher are not offering legal, accounting, medical or any other professional services advice and make no representations or warranties of any kind and assume no liabilities of any kind with respect to the accuracy or completeness of the contents and specifically disclaim any implied warranties or merchantability or fitness of use for a particular purpose, nor shall they be held liable or responsible to any person or entity with respect to any loss or incidental or consequential damages caused, or alleged to have caused, directly or indirectly, by the information or programs contained herein.

The discomfort described in this book relates to the normal range of stress reactions. If you believe for any reason that you have physical or mental symptoms that require medical attention, get proper help immediately.

WATERMAN 2.0

OPTIMIZED MOVEMENT FOR LIFELONG, PAIN-FREE PADDLING & SURFING

DR. KELLY STARRETT
PHIL WHITE

FOREWORD BY
LAIRD HAMILTON

1	**Foreword by Laird Hamilton: The Way of the Waterman**
5	**Introduction**
19	**Kelly's Story: Confessions of a River Rat**
37	**Chapter 1: Becoming a Lifetime Waterman**
45	**Chapter 2: Mobility 101**
56	**Chapter 3: Meet the Standards**
62	**Chapter 4: The Spine and Hips**
65	Standard #1: Can you achieve and maintain a stable spine?
78	Standard #2: Can you hinge from the hips without sacrificing trunk stiffness?
94	Standard #3: Can you maintain trunk stability while squatting?
105	**Chapter 5: The Shoulders**
109	Standard #4: Do you have full overhead capacity?
124	Standard #5: Can you achieve and maintain a stable shoulder and spine in the press archetype?
136	Standard #6: Can you achieve optimal shoulder positioning in the hang archetype?
144	**Chapter 6: The Feet and Ankles**
152	Standard #7: Are you standing, walking, running, stepping and jumping with neutral feet?
159	Standard #8: Can you perform a lunge and master Warrior Pose II?
165	**Chapter 7: The Hands, Wrists, Elbows and Arms**
166	Standard #9: Do you have full wrist flexion?
171	Standard #10: Can you fully articulate your hands when your elbows are extended?
183	**Chapter 8: Preparation and Recovery**
184	Standard #11: Do you have an appropriate hydration and fueling strategy?
195	Standard #12: Are you physically prepared to get on the water?
205	Standard #13: Are you recovering effectively?
214	**Conclusion**
215	**Mobilizations Appendix**
253	**Waterman Wisdom: Tips from the Pros**
390	**Resources**

THE WAY OF THE WATERMAN

To me, the term "waterman" is rich with meaning. From a physical standpoint, it means being a well-rounded individual who has the skills to perform multiple disciplines with a variety of boards, boats and your own body. Mentally, a waterman needs a deep understanding of the ocean that allows him to read the conditions so that he can excel in any situation. Then there's the relational aspect. My wife Gabby has said that the ocean is the only woman she will share me with and that shows how meaningful my relationship with the water is. There are also the friendships that are forged with others who have the same love of the water. These are built through all the highs and lows that being out on the water presents—having fun, being scared and sometimes risking our lives. We have a mutual reverence for the ocean and the activities we partake in.

Waterman culture also has a spiritual component. I'm a better person after I've been out surfing or paddling than when I left the house. When you're in harmony with the water you develop a sensitivity to it that goes beyond the physical. We can become so self-important in life and I welcome the honesty of the water and how being out in the most dynamic setting nature has to offer reminds me of my true insignificance. The magnitude of the ocean gives me a sense of perspective, which is amplified when it unleashes a little of its power. If it's possible to learn spirituality, then the majesty of the sea is the ultimate teacher. People sometimes ask me how I "conquered" a certain wave and I find that peculiar. When you surf a wave there's no conquest involved—if you behave well and with respect, then you make it through.

To experience the full benefits that being a waterman offers, you don't just need that kind of knowledge. Your body also needs to be up to the challenge. Kelly's work represents an opportunity to better understand yourself and how you move, so that you can fix errors and become more efficient and resilient. This book will not only help you improve your performance, but also make you more durable by offering a counterbalance to the repetitive motions that can wear you down otherwise. If I had known Kelly earlier, I believe that I would've avoided a lot of the injuries that came from being in compromised positions and not knowing how to fix myself. When issues arise, I can go to Kelly in full confidence, trusting that he can help solve the problem and get me back to enjoying the ocean.

As you'll discover when you read his story, Kelly's vocation comes from the purest intentions. He needed a better way to heal himself and once he'd done so, became determined to use what he had learned to help as many people as possible. Then you add in his first-hand experience on the water and continual pursuit of knowledge and you have something really special. He's determined to make a positive difference and you can only benefit from that. I've incorporated Kelly's techniques into my daily life to help me move better on and off the water, improve my recovery and reduce the chance of getting hurt in the future. In the following pages, you'll find tips and tools that are highly applicable to your life and are effective in the real world. Kelly has helped me to become a more sustainable waterman—I know this book will do the same for you.

Laird Hamilton
KAUAI

THE WAY OF THE WATERMAN

INTRODUCTION

"You must be shapeless, formless, like water. When you pour water in a cup, it becomes the cup. When you pour water in a bottle, it becomes the bottle. When you pour water in a teapot, it becomes the teapot. Water can drip and it can crash. Become like water my friend."
—*Bruce Lee*

Do you remember the way you felt the first time you caught a wave, stood up on your SUP or peeled out of an eddy? "Stoke" doesn't even come close, right? The glide across the water, the spray on your face, the sense that this was *it*, the thing you'd been searching for, and that you'd do forever. From that moment on, you lived for getting back out on the water, knowing that sensation was accessible again and again.

So where did it all go wrong? Maybe it was the day you woke up with a lower back so sore you felt like you couldn't get out of bed. Or perhaps it was that horrible burn in your shoulders that wouldn't go away, no matter how many ibuprofens you swallowed. It might've been when your hand suddenly cramped up when you were driving back from the beach. Something had changed, and the lifetime you were once certain you'd spend on the water was now in question.

That's why we wrote this book. We believe that you can indeed spend the rest of your life enjoying the water sports you love without the pain, move-

ment restrictions and tacked down tissues that have become the norm. That you can access free power, strength and endurance that will take you to the next level. And that you can do it all without special equipment, thousands of dollars in medical bills or the painkillers that one veteran paddler told us had become her "second religion."

If you've spent any time with Kelly, watched his MobilityWOD videos or listened to him at a mobility seminar or on a podcast, you'll know that his main reason for being a teacher is to help and empower as many people as possible. He possesses a contagious zeal for educating men, women and children of all ages and abilities about how to move, perform and live better.

Kelly believes that each of us is engineered to move well for 110 years. As much as he enjoys trail running, Olympic lifting and many other land lubber sports, he is a waterman at heart. Through his years of competing at the highest level in whitewater slalom and rafting, he found out first hand

photo by Tom Servais

WATERMAN 2.0

that although surfing and paddle sports have reached astonishing new heights in performance during recent years, they remain primitive when it comes to developing movement, mobility and strength and conditioning practices and remedying soft tissue and joint issues.

From bum knees to torn rotator cuffs to herniated discs, even the best paddlers, rowers and surfers are finding that just because they're not pounding the pavement doesn't mean they're participating in a "non-impact" sport. As Laird shared in the foreword, the repetitive motion of millions of strokes taken in bad positions can mess you up. The trouble is that very few paddlers or surfers know how their body works, what correct positioning looks like or how to perform even basic maintenance to prevent and treat injuries and restore soft tissue health. Multiply this lack of knowledge across the millions of people who take to the water each year, and you have a massive, systemic problem. And a tremendous opportunity for change.

Before we start exploring how you can help yourself perform better, stay in the water longer and enjoy water sports for life, let's quickly take the pulse of the industry. Surfing is the logical place to start, as the most culturally, socially and economically significant water sport of the past 100 years. According to the latest research, it's a $7.4 billion business, with 1.7 million Americans hitting the waves at least once a year.[1]

When you look at surfing as a truly global phenomenon the numbers skyrocket, with an estimated 23 million surfers worldwide. And while surfing hit a revenue road bump a few years ago, it's on the rise again, thanks to a growing middle class in developing nations and the availability of

---

1 Allan Edwards, Keith Gilbert, James Skinner, *Some Like it Hot: The Beach as a Cultural Dimension*, 20.

cheaper boards. Not to mention the development of wave pools by the likes of Kelly Slater. Plus, the sport will get a global boost with its inclusion in the 2020 Olympics.[2]

Though it still trails its paddle-less cousin in participation stats and the revenue rankings, SUP is catching up fast. In the past 10 years there have been a lot of new fleeting fitness trends, but 2 sports have continued their strong growth and become part of mainstream culture: CrossFit and standup paddling. *Outside* magazine's most recent "Best Places to Live" issue mentioned SUP access just as much as running, and if you browse almost any outdoor or lifestyle magazine you'll likely see several ads of smiling families on SUP boards (even if, annoyingly, their paddle blades are often the wrong way round!). No longer just a fixture in surf shops, SUP boards are now available everywhere from REI to big box stores like Costco and Sam's Club. Hollywood is even getting in on the act, with everyone from Will Smith to Rihanna to Matthew McConaughey being snapped on their boards.

The Hawaiians of old were the first to grab a board in one hand and a paddle in the other. Later, legendary surfer Duke Kahanamoku and his peers took on Tongg's and other hallowed breaks with a paddle in the 1920s, 30s and 40s. But it wasn't until Laird Hamilton started looking for something different to do on the water when Peahi wasn't breaking big that the sport was reborn in the 2000s. When Hamilton, Dave Kalama and company started getting the word out about the versatility of SUP between 2008 and 2010, it was quickly introduced to California by the likes of Rick Thomas and boom! The standup revolution began.

Almost overnight it seemed like SUP boards were everywhere. Sure, novices dropping in on longboards with 7 foot spears irked a lot of surfers, who couldn't stand the recklessness of these newbies that had no concept

---

2 Nic Couchman, "Why the £10bn Surfing Industry Deserves its Introduction as an Olympic Sport in 2020," *City A.M.*, available online at http://www.cityam.com/247308/why-10bn-surfing-industry-deserves-its-introduction-olympic.

of pecking order or lineup etiquette. Some even tried to ban standup from their beaches. But despite this clash of old and new schools—which led to Hamilton launching a line of "Blame Laird" apparel—it quickly became apparent that SUP wasn't going anywhere. By 2011, participation had ballooned to 1.2 million people. According to the Outdoor Industry Association, 60 percent of these—almost 3 quarters of a million—were trying it for the first time. In the years since, SUP participation has grown to over 2 million.

One of the reasons for standup's popularity is the versatility of the craft. Surfing's growth in the US was limited once it reached saturation on the coasts, but you can use a SUP board on any reasonably sized body of water, from the ocean to rivers to lakes. This versatility opened up the chance to glide to millions of landlocked Americans, many of whom had never so much as tried to pop up on a surfboard.

A few short years ago people in any of America's landlocked states would look at a person with a longboard on their car like they were nuts. But now that the non-coastal states have gone SUP crazy and recreational paddlers are taking to lakes and rivers in droves, SUP is no longer a fringe activity. And it's not just one-off newbie paddlers who have become pervasive away from the coasts, but also systematized SUP-focused fitness programs like Brody Welte's PaddleFit. At the site of the Pacific Paddle Games, Doheny State Beach, The Paddle Academy has created a formalized practice for the first SUP generation that is already producing elite athletes like Shae Foudy. So too has Performance Paddling. Clearly, SUP is here to stay.

Standup manufacturing is booming in unlikely destinations such as Austin, Texas, and one of the nation's largest retailers, Paddleboard Specialists, has built a thriving business in Waunakee, Wisconsin. And as SUP continues to increase in popularity on both coasts, standup boards, paddles and equipment are revitalizing surf shops in traditional hot spots.

The SUP racing and performance scene has become just as diverse as the industry that supplies it. From the first SUP surfing event at Pipeline to The Pacific Paddle Games in California to canal races in Europe to gnarly whitewater courses at the GoPro Mountain Games—yep, that's the Vail

Mountain Games to us old timers—SUP competitions are stretching the limits of organizers' imaginations and participants' skill sets.

Meanwhile, endurance fiends like Shane Perrin are completing ultramarathon river races previously limited to canoes and kayaks, such as the Texas Water Safari and MR340, not to mention tackling long distance expeditions through the Belize jungle and Amazon rainforest. And iconoclasts like Ken Hoeve and Kelly's longtime friend Dan Gavere are scaring the pants off of everyone with daredevil rides down rapids and on river waves.

Standup paddling has arguably also increased participation in OC1, surfski, prone paddleboarding and other water sports that have been foundering for the past few years. Indeed, a report sponsored by the Outdoor Foundation found that 19 million Americans participate in water sports. Of these, 3.7 million went rafting, 9.8 million canoeing and 10.3 million kayaking. When we're looking at 202 million outings on the water, it seems that rumors of paddling's death have been greatly exaggerated![3]

It has certainly helped canoeing and kayaking that inter-disciplinary competitions like The Ultimate Waterman see SUP world champions Zane Schweitzer, Danny Ching, Kai Lenny and Connor Baxter test their versatility in these other sports. Meanwhile, increased media focus on banner SUP events like the grueling Molokai 2 Oahu (M2O) channel crossing has encouraged greater participation in the other disciplines at these races. As we were starting to write this book, Kelly subjected himself to the horrors of long sessions on the water and the Concept2 Ski Erg to prepare for the OC1 event at Molokai.

Gear outfitters have taken note of standup's rise and the resurgence of other aquatic activities and upped their game accordingly. Finally, equipment has begun catching up to ergonomics and the unique needs of different paddling demographics, with mad scientists like Jim Terrell and Dave Chun creating specialized paddles for women and kids, adding double dihedrals and creating new shaft shapes that encourage efficiency.

---

3 "Outdoor Participation Report," *The Outdoor Foundation*, 2017, available online at https://outdoorindustry.org/wp-content/uploads/2017/05/2017-Outdoor-Recreation-Participation-Report_FINAL.pdf.

Likewise, board manufacturers have finally realized that not everyone is 5' 9" and 150 pounds, and master shapers like Joe Bark are creating high performing boards tailored to everyone from groms to heavy hitters like Kelly (who is 6' 1" and 230 pounds). These quantum leaps in design have also made their way into other water sports, with crazy light OC1s, bulletproof slalom canoes and feather-like paddles now the norm.

All these advances have made SUP, surfing and paddle sports more accessible than ever before, from elite pros to recreational paddlers to the special needs/adaptive community, and more. And really, that's the prevailing mindset for most of us who love to be on the water, isn't it? We just want to get out there and lose ourselves in the glide, flow, stoke, gnar or whatever cliché you'll hopefully forgive us using.

The trouble is that no matter how experienced we are on the water, many of us aren't adequately prepared to be in the kind of flow state Steven Kotler describes in his seminal book *The Rise of Superman*. That's all well and good if we've been taught and have reinforced proper technique in a formal movement practice, and default to this while moving unconsciously across the water (most people aren't thinking about those knees collapsing inward while crouching in a wave barrel, but sure feel it the next day).

Unfortunately, practice makes permanent and if we're merely ingraining faulty motor patterns on land and over thousands of hours and millions of strokes on the water, we're going to get messed up eventually. How much stoke is there when you're lying on a physical therapist's table? As someone who's been in the role of both wrecked patient-athlete and orthopedic medicine practitioner, Kelly knows the answer is "not a lot."

This has been confirmed by the dozens of paddlers, surfers and rowers we've asked about their injuries, aches and pains. Across all the different water sports disciplines, a familiar story emerges—chronically sore lower back and hips, sore shoulders, tight wrists. But the more disturbing thing is not the injuries and pain themselves, but what athletes are doing about it.

Or not. The most advanced response we got about a movement and mobility practice was, "I use a foam roller." Most of the other watermen

and women we talked to just take it easy when they feel that angry back flare up, perform the same ineffective static stretches every day or take a bunch of painkillers and hope for the best. And these aren't amateurs, but some of the biggest names in the water sports world. Clearly, something has to change.

The purpose of this book is not to dilute the purity of your on-the-water experiences, or to discourage you from participating if you're not moving correctly. If anything, we would like you to spend *more* time on the water. Yet we don't want you to wait until your lumbar spine detonates, your shoulders seize up or you can't feel your hands before you start to make change.

To advance our thinking, we need to examine the impact of simply getting out of the car, grabbing our gear and charging headlong toward the river, ocean or lake. To take a long hard look about what we're doing once we get into or onto the water. And to evaluate why drying off and going back to sit at the office, at home or at a bar for a few hours afterwards is not exactly ideal recovery. Oh, and before we forget, to address the fact that many of us are chronically dehydrated, make poor nutritional decisions and walk around in a zombie-like, sleep-deprived state.

Once you've read Kelly's river rat story, we're going to (pun alert!) dive right in to how you can transform yourself as a waterman or woman. Though each water sport obviously has its own technical nuances, there are more commonalities than differences. For starters, all require us to achieve and maintain a stable spine and trunk, to generate torque from the hips and shoulders and to apply this through the water or off of a fixed object (hands, paddle, oar, etc.). Most water sports also ask us to perform work in an overhead position.

Fortunately, the hips are the hips, the shoulders are the shoulders and the spine is the spine for every person and in and on every water craft. This means that if we can learn how to adopt correct positioning in one discipline and reinforce it on land we can apply the same principles to any and every water sport. The results? Less injuries, higher performance and the fullest expression of your human potential on the water.

YOU MUST BE FORMLESS. YOU BECOMES THE CUP. WATER. YOUR WATER IN A BOTTLE BECOMES THE BOTTLE. YOU POUR NOT THE WATER CRASH.

WATERMAN 2.0

Whether you're a pro, a seasoned recreational athlete or a beginner, our goal is to help you enjoy paddle sports, rowing and surfing for life without the range of motion restrictions and pain many of us have come to take for granted. Over the coming pages, we'll break down basic movement patterns and positions that apply to all water sports, address common mechanical and lifestyle errors and give you a blueprint for healthy and sustainable movement and mobility practices.

We will also walk you through 13 standards that you can work toward to improve your performance and durability and help you overcome your limitations. Plus, you'll discover tips and tricks from some of the world's best surfers, paddlers and rowers. It took a career-altering injury for Kelly to stop hiding behind his weaknesses and start fixing himself. Don't wait that long to upgrade yourself to Waterman 2.0!

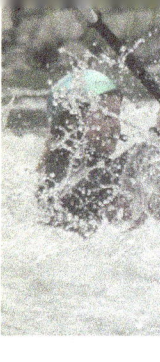

KELLY'S STORY:
CONFESSIONS OF A RIVER RAT

If it's true that we become what we behold, then I had little choice in becoming a river rat. When I was six years old, my Mom and I moved from Seattle, Washington to Garmisch in southern Germany, where she was to be a psychology professor for the University of Maryland's satellite campus and a teacher at the local international school. An idyllic, heavily wooded mountain town located in the shadow of the country's tallest peak, Zugspitze, Garmisch is just a stone's throw from the Austrian border. To a kid who loved the outdoors, it was paradise.

The best way to describe my newly adopted hometown is as a German mash-up of Durango, Telluride and Aspen. Garmisch hosted the Winter Olympics in 1936, which was the first Olympiad to feature alpine skiing, and the World Alpine Ski Championships in 1978 and 2011. It's also famous throughout Europe for the New Year's Day ski jumping competition.

But it'd be wrong to limit Garmisch by calling it a ski town. The Partnach Gorge is one of the most renowned whitewater spots in Germany, with the roiling current pushed at a frantic pace through a perilously narrow gap between towering limestone cliffs. Remember horses charging through the Elven river in Lord of the Rings? That's Partnach Gorge. So it's no surprise that in addition to hosting its fair share of mountain guides and ski instructors, Garmisch was also home to some fanatical kayakers. Since the 1972 Munich Olympics, the sport had blown up across

Germany, and Garmischians (like Ron Burgundy's San Diegans) were nuts about whitewater kayaking.

That's why for me, water sports were the background noise of my childhood. My Mom's friends were watermen and women and I saw what looked like impossibly small boats hurled down the Partnach as I rode my bike around town. The 10th Mountain Division sent its troops for kayaking 101 in Garmisch, and as my Mom and I swam in the lakes nearby during the summer, the kayakers zipped across the water until the sun failed them by dropping behind the mountains.

So it was kind of inevitable that I enrolled in my first kayak camp at age 12. Sure, the minimum age was 15, but when you're buddies with all the instructors, little rules like that are easily forgotten. I showed up on the first day of camp as the only kid, and a kid who had no idea what to expect, at that. But although I may have initially felt out of place among this group of adults, any lingering doubts soon vanished in the rush of my kayak flitting over the lake like a water bug.

If I learned some valuable paddling tips on that bright, sunny day, they were secondary to the confidence boost I got from mastering a simple safety procedure: a capsize roll. Sure, the coaches told us that the chances of successfully rolling our kayaks if we were upended in a raging river were slim to say the least, but for the first time I realized something about my newfound sport: I could do this.

The exhilaration was gone by the next morning. In its place was a head-to-toe soreness like I'd never experienced. For a brief moment I questioned whether I could even push the pedals on my bike, but the pull of the water would not be denied. So I got in the saddle and rode back to camp, my legs protesting loudly every inch of the way.

My instructors may not have been as technical as those I'd encounter in the next few years, but they were certainly fearless. A group of them were the first kayakers to run the Middle Earth—er, I mean Partnach—Gorge and it was considered extreme. These were the days when there were just a handful of boat builders and Prijon was king in Europe. You didn't have today's luxury of browsing extensive collections from dozens of paddle manufacturers, either. Perhaps the lack of gear options made these river runners even more fanatical, as it was all about the water.

On that second day of camp, I was well on my way to joining them in the latter stages of addiction. With that successful roll under my belt (or boat, I guess), I charged headlong into the drills, and the following day got to try out what I'd learned on the lake in more challenging conditions. I certainly wasn't ready for the rigors of running the Gorge, but as a 12-year-old rookie, a Class II section of the Partnach may as well have been the Black Canyon of the Gunnison.

As the river carried us through town, my instructor was focusing on a lady who, despite being at least 20 years older than me, was at least 100 times as scared. So while they did their thing, I was left on my own to see how far my 2 days of training would take me. The answer was not very far. I screwed up my line going into an eddy and boom, the boat flipped! I still remember how time slowed to a crawl, and as I watched the rocks beneath me and the bubbling water all around I thought, "OK, it's time to roll." I instinctively did what I'd been taught less than 48 hours before and just like that I was back in business. The instructor was more relieved than I was, as she hadn't let the underage kid she was meant to be watching drown.

Now that I'd aced my first barrel roll, I felt bulletproof. The rest of the summer I kayaked my ass off, and the following year became an unofficial assistant coach to a local pro, Patty, whose husband Scott was on the U.S. national whitewater team at one point. Until this youth adventure camp I'd been the only kid paddling with a bunch of adults, but as soon as my friends were exposed to kayaking, everything changed. Suddenly, the sport had context because this was what we did, what we talked about and how we related. We were paddlers.

The next summer I signed up as a counselor at a Boy Scouts high adventure camp. The instructors were the same people who'd spent so much time teaching me, and as they knew how far I'd come, they promoted

me to a full instructor. We took campers out for a 3-day session, with 2 days on the lake and 1 on the Partnach. People often ask me how long I've been teaching and when I tell them "32 years" they stare at me like I'm either insane or really bad at math. But that summer was indeed my first formal teaching experience, and leading my own groups for 8 weeks set me up well for a career in coaching complex skills in an accessible way.

It turned out that it was to be my last summer in Germany, as my Mom remarried and moved us to Washington, D.C. Going from a mountain town to a bustling city and leaving my friends behind was quite a jolt, but the biggest challenge was the loss of the waterman culture I'd been embedded in. Nobody I knew in D.C. paddled whitewater, so for the next year I logged some serious hours on the flatwater of the Potomac.

While I enjoyed those sessions, it just wasn't the same high I'd become hooked on while slaloming in Garmisch. So my attention drifted and I started trying other, landlubbing sports, going out for track and playing football. Just when I could've lost the water sports bug for good, we made another move, this time to Carmel, California. In my senior year, my best friend Chad Hawker was a surfing fiend. He took me out to the Lover's Lane break and I got my ass handed to me by a big closeout set.

I forgot to mention that while he was on his surfboard, I was in my kayak. Even though he talked some serious smack about my unusual choice of craft, Chad was pretty impressed when I managed to side surf the last few waves of the day in my big, unwieldy yellow Perception Dancer. As I prepared to go to Colorado University in Boulder that fall, I started paddling around by the beach in just a few feet of water, trying to figure out these unfamiliar ocean conditions.

Later that summer I got to try something a bit more challenging as a flood took the Carmel River to the sea for the first time in years. My friends and I, being dumb kids, took a canoe down the torrent and saw 4 other boats wrapped around trees on the way. Somehow we made it to the ocean safely.

That was just the start of me taking bigger risks. Once at CU, my friend Brian and I rode our mountain bikes down gravel roads to slow flowing sections of Boulder Creek and then had a heck of a job getting the bikes back as the water washed them downstream. Later that year we taped the sleeves of our windbreakers to our wrists, ran a 10K section of the river in a canoe and became hypothermic. We only thawed out because it was a 4 mile bike ride back to campus. It didn't occur to us until afterwards that stunts like this could've gone badly wrong.

That first semester I joined CU's kayak club and met my future best man Shane Sigle. The next summer Shane and some other friends got jobs as guides on the Arkansas River, while I was stuck building fences. I'd get off work early each Friday, hurriedly load up my car and drive to meet them. We'd kayak until it got dark, then go out on the river all day Saturday and Sunday. And with my forearms so tight I could barely grip the steering wheel, I'd high tail it back so I was ready for work the next day.

We might have been students, but classes were just an afterthought—paddling was what we did. We worshipped guys like Corey Nielsen who were just a few years older, but were doing some really crazy stuff in big Class IV and V water. In 1992, paddling was still a fringe thing even in Boulder, but it was on the verge of blowing up and entering that decade-long heyday where people started pushing performance further than we'd thought possible and the equipment started to catch up. For us, paddling had become our whole identity. We *were* watermen.

Each winter there'd be a huge release of water into Boulder Creek from the snow melt. My friends and I waited for it obsessively, like surfers staring at Surfline waiting for a storm to break. When that day finally came, we'd show up with our kayaks at 4 or 5 AM and just go at it.

In my sophomore year, Shane and I were elected co-presidents of CU's canoe club. We organized a spring break trip to Cataract Canyon on the Colorado River, held daily roll sessions in the pool to supplement our river running and got the university to pay for an advanced water safety course. We'd then do things that many people would think are profoundly unsafe, like charging through "The Widowmaker," a section of Boulder Creek where the water just disappears. In the summer, unsuspecting tourists would come down in inner tubes and get stuffed into the hole. We ran it again and again for fun. Another great time was when permit season for Westwater Canyon ended on October 1st. 300 of us would show up the next morning and stay out on the water all day.

Races at venues like Gore Canyon popped up, which was 25 minutes of chaos, pure gnar. The Vail Mountain Games was just getting going, and you could win $500, which seemed like a fortune to us broke students. The money was a minor thing though, compared to the racing, training and river rat lifestyle that had sucked me in. When I changed my major from biology to water resource management, I believe my parents threw up their hands. They thought they were losing their son!

That year I also got a job as a rafting instructor, which helped me pay for school. But the real benefit was being around a bunch of advanced, fearless paddlers. I'd been exposed to very technical conversations when I was a kid and went to ski camps run by people like World Cup winner Andre Arnold. Now I was geeking out on technique again with some of the best watermen in the country—testing and re-testing new things, practicing the heck out of them, recording videos to share with my friends. Then we'd go out at the weekends and apply what we'd learned as we tried to take on every Class V run in Colorado. This was my foundation and my education for what later became MobilityWOD.

It was also an excuse to see the world. The next summer I took an amazing trip to Nepal as a guide with Ultimate Descents and got to paddle rivers in breathtaking postcard scenery. After turning 21 in Kathmandu, I flew back to Boulder, all excited to share my photos and stories with my friends.

That enthusiasm quickly turned to shock when I learned that a good friend had died on the water. That really shook me up because it brought home that what we were doing was real. We'd always considered even the sketchiest runs to be safe because we'd spent thousands of hours practicing the micro-steps needed to become advanced paddlers. With that accident, I recognized that while I couldn't eliminate risk, I'd try to further minimize it by honing my boating skills even more.

And by my senior year, that meant transferring what I'd learned kayaking to a new discipline: slalom canoe. At that time, it was hard to get into, but Shane and I found a spring break junior development camp at Nantahala Outdoor Center, which *Outside* has since rated the nation's best canoe and kayak school. The camp was run by 2 Olympians and as well as being eager to learn from them, we wanted to buy their spare boat. Before Craigslist, eBay and online gear forums it was really hard to get top level equipment.

So off we went to Bryson City, North Carolina with just enough cash to buy the boat, but no real clue about the ins and outs of whitewater slalom. We had a blast and on the drive back to Colorado decided that we'd go all out for C2. When we were done working as rafting guides during the day, we'd fetch our boat and get back on the water until it got dark each night. On the weekends, we entered every slalom race we could find.

We soon moved to Durango so we could be near the sport's center for excellence. There was an incredible slalom community there and Shane and I were battling for a spot on the national team. At the trials we'd usually end up as the fifth boat because the other guys had been all about C2 for years. We still got to compete in the World Cup in Wausau, Wisconsin.

By this time I was paddling 5 or 6 hours a day, at least 300 days a year. And suddenly those millions of strokes started taking their toll. My lower back was trashed, and my right hand would suddenly go weak so I'd lose my grip.

One time I was using a friend's espresso machine and my hand pumped out for no reason and I couldn't grip the portafilter handle.

After a heavy training session one day, I was carrying my canoe away from the river and a friend was messing with me. He jumped up and pushed down on the boat and it depressed into my right shoulder. It wasn't like he put his full weight on it, but pain shot up my neck and down my right arm like I'd been bitten by a rattlesnake. I dropped the canoe in a panic and knew right then that this wasn't just another overuse injury, like the ones I'd been powering through for years. This was serious. My hopes of a pro career were done.

I couldn't turn my head for weeks afterwards, even though I got on the usual sports-medicine carousel—going to chiropractors, physical therapists and acupuncturists. Though I'd done everything I could to paddle in correct positions, I had no clue how to untack the soft tissues that had locked down from the millions of burn cycles I'd subjected them to each year. It wasn't just my neck and shoulder that were wrecked. I also discovered in my journey down the sports medicine rabbit hole that I had no cartilage left in my right wrist because of all the times I'd slammed it shut, hour after hour, day after day. And that black spot on my MRI? Probably not good.

Basically, I was screwed. Years of hard work had vanished in a moment, and I was critically poor because I spent my meager instructor's paychecks on boats, paddles, gas and food. I had geared everything toward being a pro waterman, and now that goal was as ruined as my shoulder, neck and wrist. No amount of chiropractic adjustments, cortisone injections or ibuprofen was going to fix my broken down body. It was panic time.

All through this traumatic season, my coaches acted like it wasn't a big deal. "That's just what happens," they told me. My reaction was, "WHAT?!" I couldn't get my head around their blasé attitude. How was the kind of system shutdown I experienced the norm? And what about all the shoulder surgeries girls on the team were having? Or all those blown-out backs? Again, just par for the course when you amped up training volume. Torn rotator cuffs, herniated disks, neck spasms. No biggie, we've seen it all before.

That didn't sit well with me. Sure, I was putting my body through a lot. On

the day of my accident I'd done a 10K bike ride to the pool, followed by a 2 hour workout. Then I'd cycled another 10K home and lifted weights, followed by paddling in the evening. But even with that kind of intense daily routine, it just didn't seem right that I'd suddenly blow up and be unable to move properly, let alone train and race. Or that nobody—not even my national team coaches—had any clue what had gone wrong or what to do about it.

Our teammates thought Shane was nuts when he started doing hamstring stretches to try and loosen up his tight lower back. They looked at me funny when I smashed my burning forearms on the inside of my car door. That was the culture I'd made my Faustian bargain with. Just paddle more and paddle harder in faulty positions until something breaks, take a bunch of painkillers and keep going or get surgery. Repeat until your body can't take it anymore.

Though that insane mindset had ruined whatever chances I had of breaking through in whitewater slalom, I just couldn't kick the boating habit. The fall after the accident, I became a sales rep for a leading canoe company. The territory was Montana to Texas, and I learned a lot talking paddling every day. My C2 days were done, but once I recovered enough function in my right shoulder, I got right back into kayaking and rafting. It was a simple life: selling canoes during the day, paddling in the evening. Just living in my van with my dog, eating gourmet fare like cottage cheese and apple sandwiches.

Shane and I were still fit and pretty good technically, so we did well on the growing race circuit, even winning the Camel Whitewater Challenge in 1999. It was 30 to 40 minutes of craziness, heartrate at 180, trying not to die. We also held our own in the annual Beer Slalom race, the water sports equivalent of today's Beer Mile track races. You'd slam a beer, go through a few gates in your kayak, down another beer and complete the same course in a canoe. Scott Shipley just killed it because he was so proficient in canoeing, as well as being a kayaking world champ and Olympian. To say nothing of his beer drinking prowess (totally kidding, Scott).

The following February, Shane and I went to Chile for the 2000 Whitewater World Championships and placed third. Something else happened that week that was far more important: I met my future wife, Juliet. She'd rowed at UC Berkeley, won 2 whitewater world titles and had been a river guide. Finally, I'd found a girl who was not only beautiful, smart and athletic, but also didn't roll her eyes when I lapsed into boating talk.

Soon enough, I was done with a memorable decade in Colorado, moving out of my van and into an apartment in San Francisco where Juliet was in law school. I was managing the Sports Basement, bartending in the evenings to make extra money and getting out in the ocean as much as possible in between. One day I was surfing a heavy set at Ocean Beach letting my mind wander. Suddenly, I had an epiphany, a moment of satori, and saw myself owning a gym and going to physical therapy school. Water sports had given me my wife, lifelong friends and a passion for paddling, and now it had, unconsciously, provided a vision for my future.

Right away, I got a job as a physical therapist's aid and started cranking through my pre-requisite courses. Over the next 2 years, any time I wasn't spending with Juliet, working or studying was channeled into a new challenge on the water, outrigger canoe. My friends and I had talked about it for a long time, but as whitewater nuts we'd always kind of pooh-poohed flatwater paddling. But the first time I got into an OC1 I was hooked. Now I could apply all the techniques I'd learned in whitewater to an endurance discipline.

The gym I went to was right under the Golden Gate Bridge, so I'd work out and then have immediate access to the open ocean. I started riding the waves from tankers in the bay and entering races up and down the California coast, everywhere from San Francisco to Catalina Island. While my body could no longer withstand competitive slalom canoeing, I soon knew I could do OC1 forever.

Once I'd got 40 credits and started PT school in 2006, I forced myself into a new discipline. It was fun to mess around in the waves in my surf kayak, but it wasn't the right craft for the conditions. I kept getting caught inside and it just wasn't maneuverable enough. So I bought a surfboard and took it out 3 or 4 times a week until I was at least competent. In addition to longboarding, I soon discovered the pleasures of prone paddleboarding.

So when SUP blew up in 2010, I was fully primed. The first time a friend got me on his standup board in Hawaii, it just felt like "aahh, this is home!" I'd had a paddle of some sort in my hands my whole life, had the sliding sports experience with surfing and skateboarding and now here was a chance to enjoy the ocean from this new, elevated vantage point. I paddled out on my knees and then stood up all the way back in. And that was it—I was hooked on yet another water sport.

Fast forward a few years and I'm sharing this passion with Juliet and our daughters. We go on float trips, mess around on our SUP boards and get out on the ocean, river or lake every chance we get. To me, that's the fullest expression of a lifestyle sport, something you can do with your family at any age. For 10 years, Juliet and I also introduced teens with HIV/AIDS to the joy of paddling at the Liquid kayak camp on the American River. Some of the kids can't even swim, but once they've been out on the water for a few hours they just light up. It's a transformative experience for them and for us.

While it's fun to be back in a kayak for the camp, I'm spending much more time these days in my OC1, which gathered too much dust while Juliet and I were busy raising kids, building my orthopedic medicine business and growing our gym. While I'm never going back to those crazy days of paddling 6 hours a day, Juliet and I are doing long sessions on the water in OC1s and our OC2 and taking a beating from the Concept2 Ski Erg, which I think is the best land-based training tool for any paddler (and no, I'm not paid to say that). The goal is completing races like Molokai 2 Oahu, and seeing how far we semi-reformed river rats can push ourselves. Anytime I get ahead of myself, Juliet reminds me there's only *one* world champ in our house, and it isn't me!

As part of getting back into outrigger canoeing, I've been amazed by the advances in equipment. 10 years ago there were just a few big manufacturers who maybe had a couple of different paddles and boats. Now we're in the middle of an outfitting revolution, as equipment and ergonomics come closer together. That's great to see, but while innovations such as the wing blade and double dihedrals can boost efficiency by up to 3 percent, what good is that if you're missing 80 percent internal rotation in your shoulders and 60 percent hip extension?

WATERMAN 2.0

We've got to start applying what we've learned about positioning, movement patterns and mobility to water sports. There may not be as many injuries as in some other activities (step forward, running), but there is evidence that paddlers, rowers and surfers are tearing up their bodies on an epic scale. One survey of Hawaiian outrigger canoeists found that 62 percent had at least one overuse injury, while 73 percent of elite junior rowers surveyed by the US team physician reported similar chronic problems.[4]

Some water sports injuries are caused from catastrophic events such as being rag-dolled by a wave, capsized in a canoe or thrown from a raft, but 98 percent of them result from poor mechanics, tacked down soft tissues and the inability to create and maintain stable body shapes. If every stroke you take is in a poor position that means you're hammering your joints and soft tissues between 1,800 and 3,000 times an hour (if you're taking 30 to 50 strokes per minute). Paddle 3 times a week? Then we're talking 5,400 to 9,000 bad strokes a week and 280,800 to 468,000 a year. Almost half a million duty cycles. If you're a competitive or elite paddler, it's far more.

No wonder your shoulders hurt, your lower back is bombed and your elbows are on fire! With a new generation getting into SUP and other water

---

[4] Jo A. Hannafin, "Common Rowing Injuries: Prevention and Treatment," *World Rowing*, 2011, available online at http://www.worldrowing.com/uploads/files/Prevention_of_Rowing_Injury_2011.pdf.

KELLY'S STORY: CONFESSIONS OF A RIVER RAT

sports without any formal movement practice, these problems are only going to grow, unless we take decisive action.

We've gathered more than enough data to do just that. Over the past 12 years at San Francisco CrossFit, our coaches have observed how people move through more than 140,000 training hours. I've also accumulated thousands of additional hours as a water sports guinea pig, and paid a heavy price for it. Then there are all the watermen and women I've trained with, raced and treated. As a result of all this information harvesting, we now understand what the barriers are to efficient, high-performance and injury-free surfing and paddling and how to tear them down. It's time to put this knowledge into action and to finally run a stake through the unacceptable mindset that career-ending and life-altering injuries are inevitable if you spend enough time on the water.

Back when I was rafting and racing whitewater slalom, our idea of a warmup was "no hard strokes for 5 minutes." After that we'd go all out for a few hours, then carry the canoes out of the water and continue with the rest of the day. No cooldown, no mobility, no rehydration. When pain came you just pushed through it and toughed it out. Everyone was hurting and we used to think that if we took a day off maybe we'd lose our edge or place on the team. I ignored the warning signs for years—the random nerve pain shooting down my right arm, the hand

pump outs, the neck and shoulder cramps—until my body's defense mechanism kicked in and shut me down. And no one really knew any better.

These excuses are no longer valid. The internet enables us to gather and disseminate ideas from the top athletes, coaches, therapists and exercise scientists. We've spent more than enough time studying the best watermen and women on the planet to diagnose the common movement faults, lifestyle errors and training holes that keep them from being even better. And above all, to see the compromised positions they're defaulting to under stress—like the chin on the chest and rounded, C-shaped spine for canoeists and kayakers, collapsed arches and valgus knees for surfers and SUPers—and how to fix them.

We've helped many of these elite athletes, like Laird Hamilton, Nic Vaughan, Erin Cafaro Mackenzie and others you'll read about in the book, get past their self-imposed limitations and reach even greater performance heights. If world and Olympic champions can still improve and fix themselves, so can you. It's time to spin these lessons backwards so everyone who participates in water sports, at every age, and at every skill level, can stop destroying their bodies and start achieving everything they're capable of. Otherwise, water sports are just a circus or, even worse, a gladiatorial contest in which our watermen and women are thrown to the lions of pain and injury.

My goal is that by the end of this book you'll have the know-how to achieve full positional capacity, to diagnose and fix soft tissue restrictions and to develop strength and conditioning, movement and mobility practices that support a healthy life spent on the water. Whether you're a pro, a recreational athlete or a newbie, you'll also benefit from tips and tricks that keep Dane Jackson, Emily Jackson-Troutman, Kai Lenny and other world-beaters at the top of their game.

By the time you reach the final page, you'll have mastered universal archetypes and technique cues that enable you to tap into power and endurance you never knew you had and to take millions of strokes a year without the wear and tear that can leave you stuck on dry land. And you'll have learned how to live a fuller existence by eating and hydrating smarter, getting better quality sleep and avoiding the dreaded "couch potato athlete syndrome." Are you ready to become Waterman 2.0?

MY GOAL IS THAT BY THE END
OF THIS BOOK YOU'LL HAVE
THE KNOW-HOW TO ACHIEVE
FULL POSITIONAL CAPACITY,
TO DIAGNOSE AND FIX SOFT
TISSUE RESTRICTIONS AND
TO DEVELOP STRENGTH AND
CONDITIONING MOVEMENT
AND MOBILITY
THAT SUPPORT
LIFE SPENT

photo by Donald Miralle

CHAPTER 1
BECOMING A LIFETIME WATERMAN

"The biggest sin in the world would be if I lost my love for the ocean."
—*Laird Hamilton*

The primary goal of this book is to empower you to spend a lifetime on the water. Your body's structures are designed to do just that, but moving poorly, failing to prepare and recovering inadequately can jeopardize such longevity. In this chapter, we'll explore some of the reasons that surfing, paddling and rowing present unique challenges, and how these push us into injury-prone positions in which we can't move safely, efficiently or powerfully.

While understanding how we should move is essential, it's useless if our soft tissues are so stiff that we can't get into them. This, in turn, is pointless if we don't have the motor control to retain stability throughout the movement. Which is even worse if we're also sabotaging ourselves with lifestyle maladaptation—see poor nutrition and hydration, lack of sleep and non-existent recovery. First, let's examine why doing water sports right is so darn hard.

In *Ready to Run*, TJ Murphy and I explored how running is a foundational skill the body is designed to perform. To Christopher McDougall's point, we are indeed born to run and hardwired to put ourselves in motion from the time we could stand upright. Yes, there are some technique cues that we need to run efficiently, effectively and without boring holes in our knees, hips and feet, but for the most part running is a natural, foundational movement.

Paddling, surfing and rowing? Not so much. For the intermediate or advanced waterman or woman, these disciplines feel like they're second

37

nature. But the flow states some of us are able to obtain—in which we're moving almost unconsciously across the water—are not a reality the first few times we try a new water sport.

When you're a beginner, your brain and body are struggling to get and keep your craft in motion, let alone focus on movement sequencing, positioning and force generation. Did you pop-up and carve down the face of a 10-footer the first time you went surfing? Did you run a Class V rapid without catastrophe on day one? Could you keep that ludicrously narrow shell

steady as you dipped those oar blades in during that junior rowing initiation? Heck no!

So what on earth is going on? Why is it so hard to paddle, surf or row well? Before exploring anything else, we've got to consider the torrent of sensory input that bombards you during each and every stroke. I believe whitewater kayaking is the hardest sport to teach adults because of the overload their brains experience. When you're a kid, you've got more neuro-plasticity than Stretch Armstrong's limbs, and your fast-learning brain can start adapting to the ever-changing river environment very quickly. Not so with our more slowly reacting adult noggin, which freaks out with everything your body and the water is throwing at it when you get in your kayak and hurl yourself downriver.

The water slapping on your board or boat. The spray in your eyes. The foam in your nostrils. The roar of the rapids or waves in your ears. Trying to balance on an unstable, constantly moving surface. All with the small matter of generating power off of a fixed object (your paddle) that you have little to no idea how to wield. It's not much different for rowing, canoeing, standup or prone paddleboarding, surfing or any other water-centric discipline. Just dealing with the barrage of stimuli is, quite literally, mind boggling, and compromises our ability to move well.

TACKLING TECHNICAL DISCIPLINES

Even those disciplines that don't feature an oar or paddle, like surfing and prone paddling, still require you to control your movements across multiple planes and to manipulate your joints through full ranges of motion while also maintaining trunk stiffness. Add in a paddle or oar and you're also asking your hips and shoulders to create power using an object that you're fighting to control against the fluidity of the water and the rocking of your board or boat.

Have you ever watched how hard it is for a beginner on a SUP to move across a placid lake without fish-tailing, how difficult it is to even stand on a surfboard in itty bitty waves or how quickly a newbie flips a rowing shell or OC1? Then you get the idea. Just staying afloat and moving in a straight line is hard enough, but when you're trying to carve tight turns, duck through narrow slalom gates or avoid swirling eddies, things become even more difficult. And you're not trying to do these things slowly, but in a split second with speed and control. And while every water sport has commonalities, there are technique nuances—spins, rolls, aerials and so on—that require many hours of practice to perfect.

The technical complexity and sensory overload make it all too easy for us to try and make do with faulty positions, which is why we see so many standup paddleboarders with their knees caved in, surfers with their backs hyperextended and kayakers with their shoulders hunched. There's so much else going on that we've got little to no opportunity to focus on how we're moving across the water. It's only later when your knees are creaky, your back is bent and your shoulders are stiff that you consider the possibility that maybe you're doing something wrong.

That's why it's vital that we start our journey by addressing basic human positions that we all should be able to achieve and maintain. If you can replace bad mechanical habits with optimal positioning in the gym, you will automatically get into and sustain the best possible shapes when you're on the water. This will leave you free to focus on fine tuning technique and enjoying the sports you love at the highest level of performance that you're capable of.

RECKONING WITH ROTATION

Another challenge for us water junkies is the unnatural way in which our bodies propel us down the river, into the waves and across the lake. It's when we start adding rotation that things get sketchy. Now, tennis and any sport that involves throwing an object—think football, baseball, rugby, lacrosse and the shot put—require rotation. But these are one-off torso twists that are interspersed with running, jumping and other movements that don't place as much demand on our spines and supporting tissues.

Then along comes paddling, with its never ending rotation. Coil, recoil. Twist left, twist right. Clockwise, counter-clockwise. And with this rotation comes a whole host of movement pattern problems and mechanical challenges that only water sports present. When these are hurled at a body that lacks full range of motion, has restricted soft tissues and is often chronically dehydrated and under rested, we've got trouble. Add into the mix a brain lacking deeply grooved blueprints for safe, efficient motion and things can start to go wrong really fast.

We were designed to move in all directions quickly and fairly effortlessly. The trouble with rotation is that it makes it even more difficult to balance a surfboard, SUP board, canoe or whatever our craft is on a profoundly unstable surface that's always changing—i.e. water. Everyone sucks at reactive balance, so when you throw in rotation it's even worse, not to mention the neurological overload we've created with all the stimuli we mentioned earlier. And we're not just trying to balance, right?

Rather, we want to create power and speed through rotation that will allow us to move and steer ourselves as nimbly as possible, for as long as possible, without wearing ourselves to a nub. This can certainly be achieved, but is not sustainable long term without a stable spine and torso, or without full capacity in the shoulders and hips.

ALL THE GEAR AND NO IDEA: OVER-RELIANCE ON EQUIPMENT

Here's a newsflash: your paddle/oar is YOUR tool, not the other way around. So why do we conform our bodies to the paddle in an effort to create stability? The prime example is when I observe the junior rowing teams I work with. You see these kids slumped over their giant, adult-sized oars as they pull away in a desperate attempt to create torque off the blade. No wonder we see such a high injury rate in competitive rowing!

Part of the problem is that we're trying to hide behind our equipment. Sure, that huge 120 square inch paddle doesn't flutter as much as a slimmer SUP blade as you pull it through the water. But why aren't you first looking to create a stable upper body to protect your spine? And then checking the shoulders and hips to see if they're working optimally?

Yep, that double bend shaft reduces stress on your wrists and forearms. But they're still misaligned as your elbow flares way out to the side on each pull. Today's advanced equipment certainly offers the promise of efficiency, but what good is a 2 percent gain if that mid-spine hunching is costing you 50 percent power output?

I'm not telling you that you shouldn't get the best equipment you can afford, but to achieve optimal performance and alleviate the scourge of injury and pain we've got to first look at our own bodies, not to our board, boat or paddle manufacturers. If you can commit to mastering basic positions, the strength and conditioning practice needed to support them and some daily mobility work to give you full capacity, you'll make much better use of your body's capabilities. Then you'll be ready to make the most of the latest and greatest gear.

YES, YOU CAN!

When you're dealing with injuries, pain and compromised performance, the situation can seem hopeless. I know because I went from national team-level training to not being able to turn my head in an instant. And as you start exposing the underlying positional faults, movement and adaptation errors and range of motion limitations, it'd be all too easy to throw up your hands and say, "Forget it!"

That's not why you're reading this book, and I'm here to tell you from personal experience that you *can* fix yourself, reach your full potential and enjoy the water sports you love for the rest of your life. The human body has an astonishing ability to self-correct. As one of my mentors puts it: "Muscles and tissues are like obedient dogs." Regardless of how beat up, broken down or burned out you feel right now, you can heal, improve and become Waterman 2.0. And all it's going to take is a few minutes a day.

CHAPTER 2
MOBILITY 101

"The fishermen know that the sea is dangerous and the storm terrible, but they have never found these dangers sufficient reason for remaining ashore."
—Vincent van Gogh

Traditionally, the so-called "solution" for mobility has been static end-range stretching after you cool down. The trouble is that this approach is inadequate. It doesn't work because it only addresses the muscle rather than all of the bodily structures and systems involved in movement. The static stretching approach doesn't take into account joint position or function, ignores motor control and thumbs its nose at how your sliding surfaces—muscles, skin and nerves—work together.

Another dirty little secret of static stretching is that lengthening the muscle doesn't help performance and often hampers it. If you pull on a t-shirt from both ends for long enough, you get a stretched out, misshaped shirt, right? Static stretching does the same thing to your muscles. Yes, it may lengthen them. But have you done anything to improve your motor control so you can handle that new end-range position? No. And if all of these "pull your leg up behind you and hold it for 30 seconds" stretches are working so well, then why are we still seeing sky-high injury rates?

So if we've concluded that static stretching isn't the way to go after you cool down, then what is? <u>A comprehensive, systems-based approach to mobility</u>, which addresses every aspect of your physiology. This includes tight and short muscles, joint capsule and soft tissue restriction, motor control limitations and missing end range capacities. My mobility and movement system is a proven method that enhances joint mechanics, muscle dynamics and sliding surface function. The good news is that you don't need a PhD in some fancy discipline to access its benefits—just a few minutes a day, every day, using the techniques in this book. The results will include improved tissue health, reduced pain and injury risk and, most importantly, enhanced recovery and performance.

I'm hoping you brush and floss your teeth. If so, do you just do it once a week, once a month or once a year? No! You know that if you took an on-again, off-again approach to your oral health, several things would happen. One, you'd have Austin Powers-style yellow teeth. Two, you'd develop gum disease, cavities and all kinds of other problems. And three, your dentist would yell at you (hint: never provoke the person standing over you with a drill).

To avoid these dire consequences, you make brushing and flossing a daily practice that keeps your teeth and gums healthy. It's the same principle when it comes to mobility. By devoting at least 10 minutes a day, every day, to de-gristling soft tissues, improving range of motion and correcting movement dysfunction, you will greatly improve on-water performance, alleviate pain and reduce injury risk.

Remember that you don't need to reach superhuman standards, but rather get back to a baseline level of functionality. In short, the goal is always to try and reclaim normal. Due to our constantly changing activities and lives, this is a moving target. Listen to your body and go to where you're tight, restricted and compromised. And then stay there until you make change.

Despite the amazing increases in range of motion that daily mobilizing can provide when you first start, my friend, frequent MWOD collaborator and founder of Tune Up Fitness Jill Miller maintains that it can take 2 years to make meaningful and lasting change in the fascia. And as I'm hoping you'll keep paddling,

MOBILITY 101

rowing and surfing (plus developing or enhancing a strength and conditioning practice), your soft tissues will continue to be under load and get short and stuck down as you exercise. Then there are the biomechanical demands of daily life. This means that you can't just do a couple of weeks of mobility and then quit. It has to be a daily commitment from now on.

I can't tell you the number of times someone has come to my practice and asked, "What's the one mobilization that will fix my shoulder/back/hip/whatever issue?" And my standard response is, "I have no idea." This invariably leads to a look of puzzlement and sometimes panic, because the patient assumes that I've got a magic mobility bullet for them. This is partly due to our cultural expectation of a quick fix for every issue, partly because most people have no idea how their body works and partly because the sports medicine-pharmaceutical industrial complex often promises such an instant cure-all.

The trouble is that YOU know your body far better than I ever will. So sure, I'll give you a range of techniques that can improve your positional capacity, remove your restrictions and alleviate your pain. But it's up to you to explore each of them to see which is most useful and has the biggest positive impact on your surfing, paddling and rowing. While I'm here to help, it's ultimately your responsibility to make yourself better. Eventually, as our good friend Gray Cook says, "We're going to send you out in the woods with a tent, a box of matches and a flashlight, and you'll have to figure it out on your own!"

A primary motivation for mobilizing daily is to address the restrictions we create through activity and by going about our daily business. But we're not just mobilizing for its own sake. Cultivating a daily mobility practice not only alleviates stiffness, but also allows you to get into optimal shapes and move more efficiently.

Many people have spent so long in faulty, unsustainable positions that their tissues will no longer enable them to get into the archetypes we will explore in the standards. But if we restore full function and range of motion, we're suddenly able to get into better shapes in which we can create maximum force, move across the water safely and efficiently and apply our conditioning without being mechanically compromised.

A key principle at MobilityWOD is to make things observable, measurable and repeatable. With regard to this chapter and the mobilizations appendix, this means testing your range of motion before performing a certain mobilization for a few minutes, and then re-testing it before moving on. Doing so will enable you to see how effective each exercise is in freeing you from restriction and increasing capacity.

- One of the things we like to do to demonstrate this in our Daily RX video series on MobilityWOD.com is to have a guinea pig (often yours truly—I'm not afraid to test this stuff on myself because I know it works) show how tight they are in an archetypal position, such as with arms overhead in full external rotation.

Then I'll perform a mobilization, such as the banded bully you'll see later on, on one side. Next, I'll raise both arms above my head again, and it's immediately apparent that I've dramatically increased my range on that side compared to the other, un-mobilized one. I encourage you to do the same as you move through each exercise to make sure that you're making change. If you don't notice a difference, spend a few more minutes repeating it, or attack the restricted area with a different mobilization or from a different angle. Then re-test again. Remember, we're not making change unless something actually changes.

The front and back of your body are in a constant tug of war, fighting against themselves as you attempt to establish and maintain positions of stability. When you're short on one side—such as in the scapula, trapezius and rhomboids on the posterior side, or the pecs, deltoids and abs on the anterior side—the opposing side has to increase tension to maintain equilibrium.

So what happens? It gets tight and stiff. Same goes for left versus right sides and medial versus lateral seams. It's a vicious cycle of asymmetrical push and pull that not only tacks down your tissues, but also wastes energy, limits force production and reduces endurance.

By mobilizing full systems and regularly going head-to-toe rather than the traditional approach of only targeting the same old muscles (hamstrings, quads, etc.) again and again, you can limit the stress you're placing on yourself with the tissue tug of war, tackle your imbalances head on and fast track your progress to elevated performance.

When we put our body under tension, one of the first things our sympathetic (fight, flight or freeze) nervous system does is mess up our breathing patterns. Either we start taking a lot of short, panting breaths that don't involve our diaphragm, but rather express themselves at the chest or neck, or we just stop breathing altogether. The same goes during mobility work. Even

people who are world class athletes and devoted Supple Leopards who don't realize that they're not breathing right when mobilizing.

Over the past couple of years, in large part thanks to the work of my friend Brian Mackenzie with his Art of Breath seminars, we've started prioritizing full mechanical ventilation efficiency in all situations. This doesn't just mean when you're paddling like crazy, but also when you're stationary or performing mobilizations. Why does it matter? Because if we're going to restore full range of motion and glide to your soft tissues, we need oxygenated blood to be flowing to them.

One of the reasons we recommend soft tissue work after activity and again in the evening is because it helps move your body from its high alert sympathetic state into the "chill out" parasympathetic one. To speed these transitions, you simply must breathe slowly, deeply and through your nose, or you're just giving yourself mixed "get going/relax" signals.

A third reason that I say, "Deep breath in, exhale all the way out," about 900 times a day is that your ability to breathe optimally, or not, in any given position is one of the ways we use mobilizations in the diagnostic process. If you can't take a full, deep and controlled breath from your diaphragm in a banded distraction (i.e. when you've hooked one end of a band to an anchor, the other to yourself and are applying load to a body part or joint), it likely means that you've pulled the band too far away from the anchor point and can no longer exhibit full motor control.

If you can't breathe properly when using an implement like a lacrosse ball to smash a certain muscle, you're obviously super matted down at this spot and need to spend longer than the minimum 2 minutes ungluing it.

Finally, breathing is another way for the tissues to contract and relax, which enhances any of the mobilization methods we'll explore. Even just breathing deeply while on an implement like a ball or roller is a legit technique by itself. Or better yet, use a protocol Brian Mackenzie and I came up with and do a 4 second nasal inhale, 4 second hold and 8 second nasal exhale during each mobility exercise. So try to focus on your breathing during each and every mobilization, so that you get the maximum benefit from your time investment.

You always get what you always got. It's a good strategy to go after the areas you constantly struggle with when mobilizing—any muscle group that fires off a pain flare when you touch it, any joint restriction that's preventing you from meeting a movement standard and any area where you've had surgery or persistent injuries. For me, that's my diaphragm, right shoulder complex, first rib and right wrist. You can certainly hit each of these trouble spots once or twice a day to make early and lasting improvements. But don't fall into the temptation that many of us succumb to on the water and in the gym, namely just doing the same old thing.

As Quickblade mad scientist and Olympian Jim Terrell rightly says, "We tend to do what we're good at." That's certainly true in mobility. If you feel like you're making progress with your hip range by using the couch stretch, you'll likely want to do it every day.

I'm totally cool with that, but to ensure you keep progressing, you should also explore other positions and stimuli for the hip, such as the banded distractions you'll find later in this book. That way you'll accelerate change and stop your body from turning off. Just as in a workout and while surfing, paddling and rowing, the body won't adapt if you keep subjecting it to the same demands. You need new stimuli to prompt adaptation and change.

It's the same with mobility. That's why you should try to mix things up. A systemic approach will help make the invisible visible and show you new areas where you're tacked down and didn't even know it. By finding and attacking them, you'll become better able to create and maintain optimal shapes and overcome the soft tissue concerns that are stopping you from reaching your full athletic potential.

You can also use each mobility exercise as a diagnostic that informs which one you do next. So, for example, if you can't get up into the top position of the couch stretch (see The Spine and Hips section of the mobilizations appendix), then you know that your quads and the front of your hips are tight. Try doing the quad smash for 5 minutes a leg and then doing the couch stretch again—an example of our "test and re-test" philosophy. You'll probably find that you unglued the tissues so that your hip flexion is improved and will have also eliminated the tightness that might be causing your quads to pull on your knee. If not, try some more quad smashing and then do the couch stretch a third time.

In the realm of athletic performance, there's always a premium on speed. But when it comes to mobility, slower is better, for several reasons. The first is that when you're taking tissues to end range, they're under massive tension and therefore at greater risk for damage. Instead of rushing out to the finish point, get there cautiously and under control.

Another reason that we don't push the pedal when mobilizing is that going fast when smashing the soft tissues creates a sympathetic fight, flight or freeze response. With post-exercise mobilizations, this is the opposite of the parasympathetic relaxation stimulus we're going for. Rushing can also cause damage to the muscles, fascia and other structures—again, the very opposite of what we're trying to do. So take it easy with all the mobilizations and your own "informed freestyle" variations.

Unless your adrenals are completely burned out and you've lost proprioception, you often know when something in your body is going to pop during exercise. The same goes for your mobility practice. If a joint feels like it's going to dislocate, then it's going to dislocate. If it feels like you hit a nerve, you hit a nerve. If a muscle feels like it's going to tear…you get the idea.

Basically, if something feels sketchy, it is sketchy and you need to stop what you're doing, switch to a softer tool or reduce the pressure to prevent doing yourself more harm than good.

For too long, people have had a very narrow view of injuries and soft tissue restrictions. If my knee hurts, it must be a problem with the joint, right? Not necessarily. Certainly, you could've damaged the cartilage, bone or other structural elements. But the tacked down muscles and fascia above and below the joint are likely a contributing factor, if not the root of the problem. If you attack those brutally tight quads and hamstrings, open up the front of your hips and restore glide to your calves and ankles, that knee ache may well disappear because the soft tissues will stop tugging on the knee.

We call this feeding slack into the system, and it applies to every part of the body. If you clear restrictions all the way along a fascial sheet, restore optimal function to the muscles and alleviate tightness in the tendons, you will be amazed at how much range of motion you can reclaim and how much you can improve tissue health.

Combine the improved positioning and increased movement efficiency we'll cover in this book's standards (for example, stopping yourself defaulting to the ducked or pigeon-toed feet positions that lead to knee misalignment) with mobilizing upstream and downstream of problem areas and you'll restore biomechanical function, boost power output and alleviate pain.

One of the lessons I've learned from observing thousands of hours of human motion is that you have to mobilize the position of restriction. So if you're having trouble getting into a deep squat, hang out in the bottom position of the squat for 10 minutes a day. Does your shoulder hurt when you paddle or overhead press? Then try some of the overhead movements in the mobilizations appendix such as the trap barbell/PVC pipe mobilization. You'll not only recapture missing range of motion, but will also re-educate your body about what normal capacity feels and looks like in the shapes you're struggling to achieve and maintain.

When you're warming up for a water session, the goal is to get hot and sweaty, increase blood flow to the muscles and prime yourself for activity. You shouldn't be trying to reclaim range of motion at this time. Think about kids coming out of the classroom to go to recess. Are they spending 20 minutes on a foam roller before they run at top speed? Nope, and neither should you. Save the soft tissue work for after your workout. You should not be using your pre-workout routine to reclaim function.

Another reason for not rolling out before you hit the water is that exercise requires the sympathetic nervous system to be in high gear. As I've mentioned, soft tissue mobilizations activate the parasympathetic system that tells us to relax and recover. Think about how you feel after a massage. Ready to jump on your board or in your boat? I doubt it. Instead, you're likely a little sleepy, because the massage has stimulated nerve endings in your fascia. Not ideal before charging waves or running rapids, right?

Rather than doing soft tissue work before you exercise, spend 5 to 10 minutes with a light aerobic warmup (jogging, slow rowing or paddling, etc.) and then another 5 to 10 minutes on dynamic exercises like air squats, mountain climbers and push-ups. Also, add in the shoulder warmup and the 3-position carry that you'll see in standard #12. If you're going to also do some mobility work, the banded distractions in the mobilizations appendix that don't involve putting pressure on your soft tissues are the way to go. They will improve capacity while keeping your core temperature up and will avoid triggering a parasympathetic response that will compromise your performance and make you feel sluggish.

One of the best things about the water sports community is how open and inclusive it is. You should apply the same aloha spirit to what you learn in this book. You have a responsibility to not only be able to diagnose and fix yourself, but also to pass on your increasing knowledge to coaches, friends and yes, even competitors.

When we lived in the pre-internet information dark ages, it was difficult to disseminate information. Now we don't have that excuse. If you have a buddy who's struggling with plantar fasciitis, tell him about how the foot exercises in the mobilizations appendix have helped you fix your feet. Know that your friend is struggling to come back from shoulder surgery? Then show her some of the mobilizations for that joint. We're all busy, but taking just a few moments to share and teach can make a big impact.

CHAPTER 3
MEET THE STANDARDS

"The best dividends on the labor invested have invariably come from seeking more knowledge rather than more power."
—Wilbur and Orville Wright

This is kind of like meet the Flintstones, except with less dinosaurs, less foot-powered cars and more caveman-approved movement patterns. Here we'll introduce you to the standards that you'll find throughout the book. Each of them is a basic benchmark that you should be able to meet to perform at your best on the water. And if you can't meet a standard, don't despair. I'll give you some mobility exercises and positional pointers to get you to where you need to be. I'm not asking you to pretzel yourself like a Cirque du Soleil performer or to reach some Olympian level of positional awesomeness. Rather, the standards are here to show you what normal and abnormal look like, progress from potentially damaging positions into safe ones and fix yourself when you break down.

Now, that's not to say that meeting every standard will be easy. We've set up progressions so they give you nowhere to hide and become harder as you move onto the next step. Do OK with a fixed object like a bar, paddle or PVC pipe? Good job. Now we'll try a similar movement in a more challenging context, like swinging a kettlebell, pressing a dumbbell or doing a push-up on the TRX Duo Trainer or gymnastics rings. And let's see how you hold up with a little speed or load, moving your body in different directions and adding some water-mimicking instability. We haven't designed these standards just to torture you. Instead, they will help you learn or re-learn the fundamental skills and sustainable movement patterns needed to be a resilient, high-performing waterman or woman.

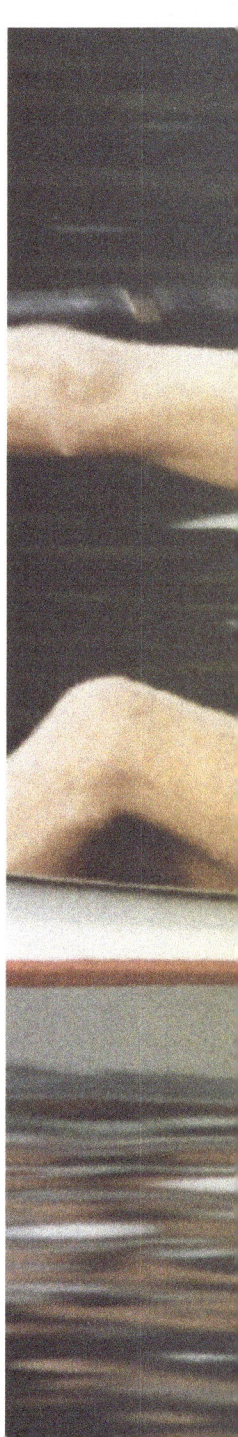

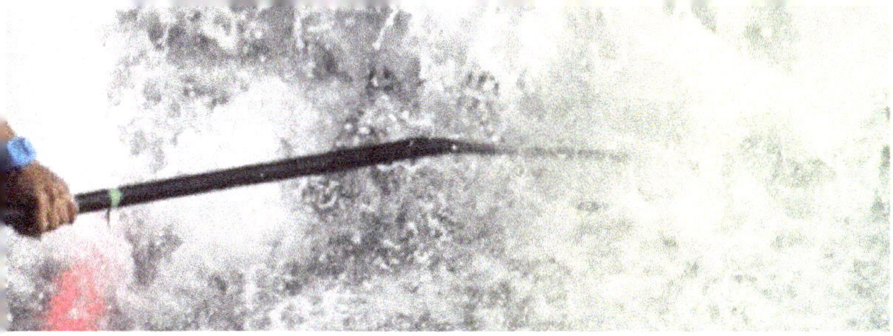

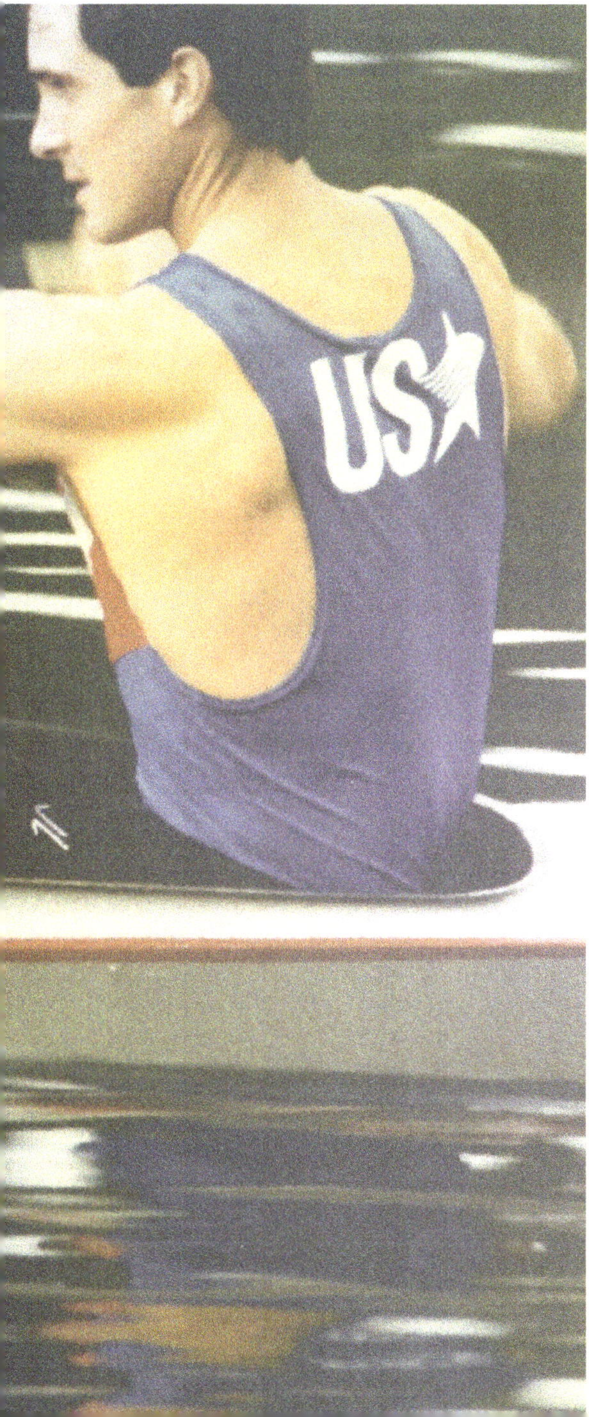

As you move through the book, we want you to continue surfing, paddling and rowing. When people find out what I do, they often mistakenly think, "Oh, so you just spend all day rolling around on a ball?" Not at all! Just like you, I have positions to tune up, grisly tissues to unglue and the consequences of old injuries to address. Despite these challenges, I'm still living life and training 5 to 7 days a week.

While progressing through the standards, please keep doing your sport. That way you will put what you're learning to the ultimate test: how does what you're doing on land positively impact what you do on the water?

It might be tempting to rattle through the book and rush headlong into achieving all the standards simultaneously. That's possible, but I recommend you start with tackling the first one. Each of the standards is important, but we've also prioritized them in order of significance. Like binary code, every standard is either a 0 or a 1. You either make the grade or you don't.

You simply cannot start addressing issues with your hips or shoulders without taking aim at your spine. And there's no point in speeding to sort out those aching wrists or messed up feet until you've started upstream at the shoulders and hips. I promise, there is a method to the madness!

To improve how you move and perform, you'll need to grasp the ideal body positions we'll explore in the upcoming standards. Then make an effort to practice them throughout the day, whether that's in your boat/on your board, in the gym or in any other environment.

Try to make your fight stance your everyday stance—i.e. to apply what you're learning in all situations—and you'll make early and sustained progress toward not only achieving the standards but also reclaiming full capacity, ungluing tacked down tissues and, ultimately, unlocking your full potential as a paddling/surfing ninja. This means that if you're keeping your spine in a good position while doing a quick test at home, make an effort to do the same on the water.

There's plenty you can do on your own to improve your range of motion, develop or improve a daily movement and mobility practice and diagnose and fix your body's issues. But your troubleshooting will be even more effective if you pull in a coach, training partner or friend. In return, you'll be able to provide them with invaluable feedback that will help advance their journey.

Seeing how your body moves through someone else's eyes will help you pinpoint problems that might have eluded you for years. When there's something wrong with a car, you take it to a mechanic. This professional doesn't start yanking parts out of a car engine until he's run a full diagnostic on it. Similarly, you won't be your best without fully analyzing your difficulties and areas for improvement and seeking input from your fellow surfers, paddlers and rowers.

Your self-care and improvement process shouldn't stop when you put this book back on your bookshelf. You should be continually seeking to gain greater knowledge about your body, how it moves and what you need to do to reach optimal function on any given day. The journey toward sustainable excellence never ends.

WATERMAN 2.0

THE STANDARDS

Now we've examined the core principles anchoring this book, let's take a look at the standards themselves. They are:

1) Can you achieve and maintain a stable spine?
2) Can you hinge from the hips without sacrificing trunk stiffness?
3) Can you maintain trunk stability while squatting?
4) Do you have full overhead capacity?
5) Can you achieve and maintain a stable shoulder and spine in the press archetype?
6) Can you achieve optimal shoulder positioning in the hang archetype?
7) Are you standing, walking, running, stepping and jumping with neutral feet?
8) Can you perform a lunge and master Warrior Pose II?
9) Do you have full wrist flexion?
10) Can you fully articulate your hands when your elbows are extended?
11) Do you have an appropriate hydration and fueling strategy?
12) Are you physically prepared to get on the water?
13) Are you recovering effectively?

CHAPTER 4
THE SPINE AND HIPS

"When I'm 50 I want to be a better surfer than I am now—for me it's a lifelong journey."
—Kelly Slater

There are half a million spinal surgeries in the US each year. 50 percent of office visits to doctors are for musculoskeletal issues. 80 percent of people will experience back pain some time in their lives.[5] And as an experienced waterman, I'd bet good money that every water athlete has had or will experience some kind of back issue (hey, something to look forward to, newbies!)

When we talk about runners' overuse injuries, it's mind boggling to consider how many foot strikes occur in each training session (thousands), month (tens of thousands) and year (hundreds of thousands or millions for the high mileage crowd). We know that all these duty cycles lead to shin splints, runner's knee, plantar fasciitis and all manner of other problems if the runner in question is performing each foot strike in a ducked or pigeon-toed position, doing little to no self-maintenance and recovering poorly.

So why don't we ever apply the same analysis to water sports? Just like the pavement pounders, you're putting your body through potentially millions of strokes each year. And while it's mostly the runner's lower body that bears the brunt of repeated lousy movement patterns, for we water folk it's the upper body and, as the stats show, specifically the spine. From disc herniation to spondylolisthesis to stenosis and fractures, continually defaulting to improper spinal shapes has severe consequences for the water athlete.

Back when I was on the national team in whitewater slalom canoe and rafting, back pain wasn't something that just affected a few people—all of us dealt with it daily. But just like the displaced ribs, the torn rotator cuffs and

---

5 "Low Back Pain Fact Sheet," NIH, available online at https://www.ninds.nih.gov/Disorders/Patient-Caregiver-Education/Fact-Sheets/Low-Back-Pain-Fact-Sheet.

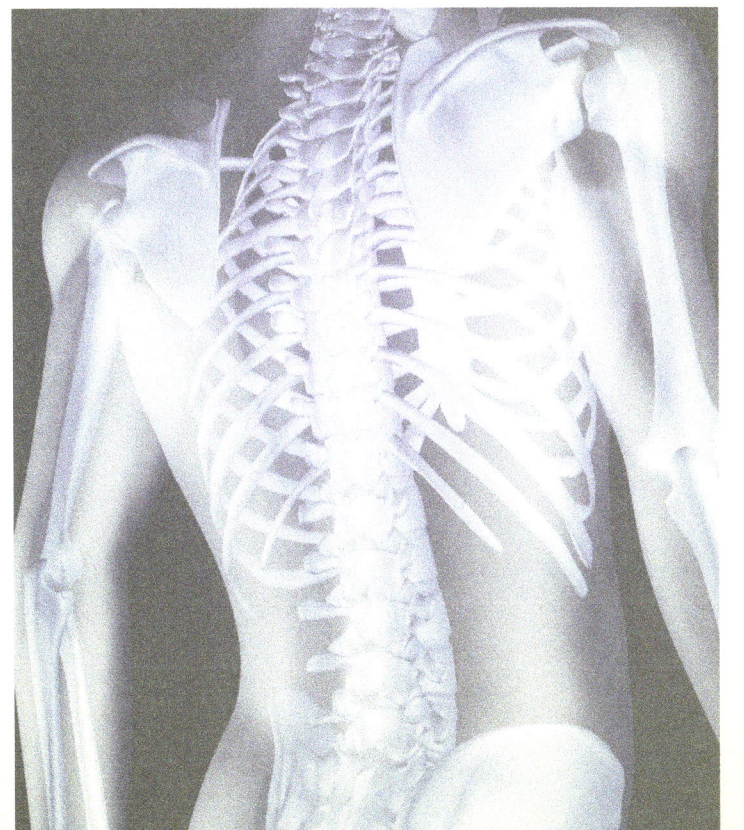

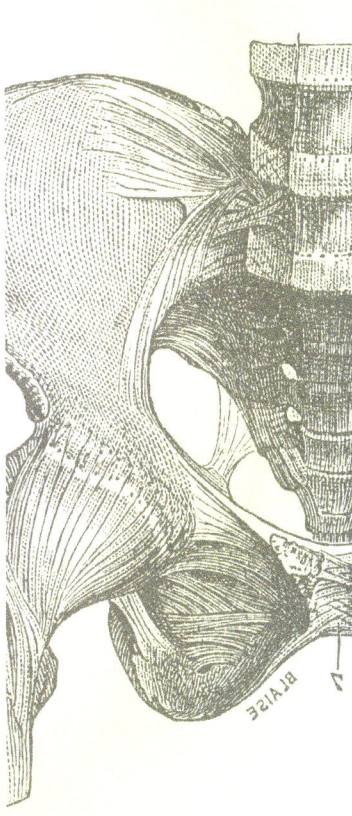

THE SPINE AND HIPS

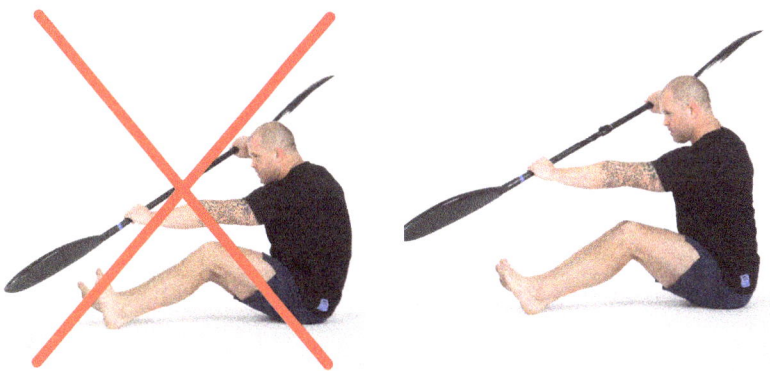

the jacked up wrist ligaments, it was just something you were expected to fight through. Sometimes it was more than pain, but also locked down facet joints, sciatica and/or herniated discs. Sound familiar?

The coaches' mindset was: "You're paddling 300 days a year, several hours a day, so you're gonna get messed up." OK, adding intensity and volume certainly has its risks, but I'm here to tell you that back injuries are NOT inevitable and neither is throwing back handfuls of ibuprofen and adding to those surgery stats. However, we can't just wait around for something to snap. It's time to take action. Now.

STANDARD #1
CAN YOU ACHIEVE AND MAINTAIN A STABLE SPINE?

MOTIVATION

Water sports place unique stressors on the spine, and you can only maintain peak power output, avoid injury and pain and protect your central nervous system if you can achieve a stable trunk from first stroke to last. In this chapter, we'll explore how you can maintain a stable spine when standing, sitting and paddling/surfing/rowing. You'll also develop the ability to preserve this position under load using some simple movement progressions.

WATERMAN 2.0

BRIEFING

It turns out that the writer of the old song "Dem Bones" was on to something, as none of our body's systems work in isolation. In fact, we're designed for them to be interdependent and if you've got positional issues in one spot, chances are it's going to negatively impact other areas. Nowhere is this truer or more significant than at the trunk, which we should think of as the chassis for the entire vehicle of the body. It doesn't matter how big your aerobic engine is if your frame can't support it.

Our brain exists to help us move through and experience the world. And the main power line to this command center runs through the spinal cord. When your brain perceives a threat to your central nervous system (CNS), such as when one section of your spine hinges and presses on a nerve root, it takes action by contracting the surrounding soft tissues to restrict motion in this potentially dangerous position. This limits force production locally and starts a cascade of negative consequences throughout the body.

The peripheral nerves that connect the CNS to your limbs and organs also freak out as the weight of your upper body slams that local hinge shut. The resulting neural tension reduces the capacity of your hips and shoulders to create the torque that should power your paddling, surfing and rowing. It also has a lingering effect on your tissues—stiffness and restriction among them—once you get off the water.

So when you lack the ability to achieve and maintain a stable trunk it's not just the spine's vertebral segments and nerves that are compromised, but also the very power centers that are supposed to drop you into a wave, propel you across a lake or spin you around in a freestyle run down a river. If your shoulders are in a poor position, you must also make changes in the spine, hips, arms and legs in an effort to compensate, which can contribute to further diminished performance and injury.

Let's do something about it.

If you place one thumb at the top of your pelvis and the other at your sternum, you should be able to hinge at the hips without the distance between your thumbs increasing or decreasing. You can use this quick test of trunk integrity when sitting, lying, kneeling or standing.

BRACING SEQUENCE PROGRESSION #1: SUPINE

During this chapter, I'll take you through several basic spine shapes that you must understand and master to become a better waterman. First, let's explore the most versatile one: braced neutral. This is an essential athletic position, as it gives us the trunk stiffness required to keep the spine straight and, therefore, to protect the central nervous system.

The braced neutral shape also allows us to transmit maximum power and force through the hips and shoulders without the horrendous shearing loads that occur during rowing, paddling and surfing when the spine is in a compromised shape (usually local flexion or extension). In fact, I believe that the braced neutral position can increase range of motion by up to 40 percent throughout your body by reducing neural tension.

We're going to take you through a simple, multi-part progression that will test your ability to get into and hold the braced neutral shape in various positions and with different anatomical demands. Satisfying this standard will not only help you move through the world with a safer spine, but will also be directly translatable to your favorite water sports.

First up is achieving a braced neutral spine while lying supine with your back on the floor. This eliminates the force of gravity that we'll deal with in the second progression, and also the anterior load that we'll encounter in the third progression.

WATERMAN 2.0

1) Lie on your back with your feet together and your arms by your sides

2) Squeeze your butt as hard as you can to put your pelvis into the correct alignment

3) Contract your abs and take a deep diaphragm breath in, which should make your belly button move out. This pulls your rib cage down into a neutral position.

4) Take a couple of seconds to exhale, while maintaining 20 percent tension in your abs. This may seem impossible at first, either because you're not used to breathing from your diaphragm or because you're brutally tight in the musculature of your lumbar and thoracic spine and abs. Keep at it until you can breathe under control and still maintain that 2 out of 10 ab tension that will protect your back and nervous system by maintaining a solid connection between your lumbar spine and pelvis.

5) Lift your legs a couple of inches off the floor, while still breathing from the diaphragm and holding the 20 percent ab tension

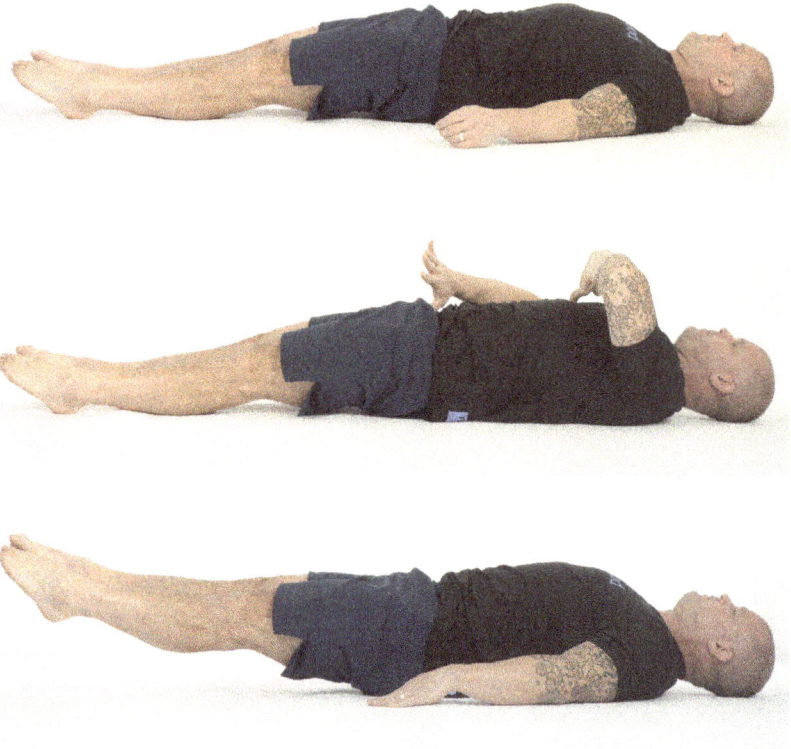

If you found it difficult/impossible to maintain a braced neutral spine while nasal breathing from the diaphragm, chances are that this crucial pump is not only underused, but also underdeveloped. If you've been neck and chest breathing for years or decades, your diaphragm has likely forgotten what it's like to pull large amounts of air into your lungs and push it out again in the most efficient manner, particularly under the demands you're putting on your cardiovascular system on the water. As a result, you probably pant in a stress breathing pattern, which comes at a massive energy cost and inhibits your ability to be your best.

Enter the almighty diaphragm vacuum exercise, which will not only supercharge your lung capacity and maximum ventilation efficiency, but will also help reawaken your body's natural breathing patterns during activity and at rest. I tip my hat to my good friend Jill Miller, author of the indispensable book *The Roll Model*, for this one:

1) Lie on your back with knees bent, feet on ground. Practice a few rounds of nasal inhales and exhales.

2) Take a deep nasal inhale as you reach arms overhead and clasp your hands onto corners of a mat or against a wall

3) Exhale completely until there is no air left. After exhaling (do not allow ANY air in) take a half breath into your ribs. This expands them laterally while the diaphragm stretches into the vacuum created by the expanded ribs. Simultaneously, pull the mat apart and stretch it overhead (or push into the wall to elevate your shoulders) in order to maximize tractioning of your rib cage away from the pelvis. This exaggerates the length of the diaphragm.

4) Maintain the vacuum as long as you can. Reset your arms down by your side. Then take a few complete nasal breaths before beginning another round.

BRACING SEQUENCE PROGRESSION #2: STANDING

You may think you know how to stand right. It sounds so simple, doesn't it? But though you've been able to stand since you were an infant, that doesn't mean you're doing it correctly. And in fact, once you know what standing in an organized position looks like and start to see how others stand at the coffee shop, the grocery store and just about anywhere else, you'll see all manner of positional faults that contribute to postural issues, cause pain and compromise performance. Step into my world!

The ability to get into and maintain an organized standing stance tells me a lot about your ability to sequence basic coordination from your head down through your trunk to your hips. And then, also further downstream through the knees, ankles and feet. If you can't achieve a braced neutral position on a stable surface on land, you're certainly not going to do it on the water.

That's why our second progression for achieving and holding a braced neutral position couldn't be any simpler: standing with your spine in an organized position. To do so, follow these steps:

1) Stand with your feet facing straight ahead (neutral feet) and shoulder width apart

2) Squeeze your butt as hard as you can to put your pelvis into the correct position (hint: if your pelvis shifts, you were standing incorrectly)

3) Take a deep nasal breath initiated with your diaphragm—which means your belly button should push out. Engage your abs and exhale slowly. This will pull your rib cage down into the neutral position.

4) While keeping your feet pointing straight ahead, screw them into the ground as if they were spinning outward on dinner plates. Even if you have flat feet, you should feel your arches engage.

5) Set your head into a neutral position, i.e. aligned over your center of mass. If you have a tight cervical and thoracic spine and deal with forward rounded shoulders, this might be difficult. We'll work on this

later. For now, just do your best to not have your head jutting out in front of your trunk.

6) When you're standing for extended periods, such as at the standing desk you should really invest in (see the Get Up, Stand Up section), reset your position every 15 to 20 minutes by starting again at #1 in this list. Eventually, this braced neutral position will become automatic.

WATERMAN 2.0

BRACING SEQUENCE PROGRESSION #3: KNEELING

Now we're going to see how you do in another position that will further test your spinal positioning and stability. The kneeling stance is common to several water sports disciplines, including prone paddleboarding, canoeing and sprint canoeing. Kneeling is often hard to do correctly in your water craft because we frequently drop into over-extension in the lumbar region, which then puts an unholy burden on the hamstrings and musculature of the lower back, such as the QL and psoas, to keep us upright.

If you're tight along the quads and the front of the hips, it can be difficult to maintain a functional, pain-free kneeling position during daily activities, let alone in a canoe. Have you ever knelt beside the tub while giving your toddler a bath? If so, maybe you can recall how quickly your lower back started screaming at you (maybe even louder than that kid who hates taking a bath). If this sounds all too familiar, you know how challenging this next part of the standard is going to be.

1) Kneel down on the floor or on a mat
2) Squeeze your butt and abs and breathe from your diaphragm

To reach full potential in any water sport, we need to create powerful rotation around a solid central axis, as our bodies work from core to periphery and trunk to sleeve. To do so, it's vital that we minimize kinks in the nervous system, which not only place us at risk of pain and injury, but also lead to the body limiting force production to safeguard itself.

One of the most common kinks we see is a "forward head on neck" fault. Rounding in the thoracic spine (middle back) creating a localized hinge at the C7 and T1 vertebrae at what we call the cervicothoracic junction—i.e. where the cervical and thoracic spine converge. This not only places a massive shearing load on these spine segments, but also leads to an extension compensation in the upper cervical spine. We've already created a neuro-muscular freakout in the tissues around the mid-back hinge, and now we're adding in even more tension to our already overtaxed nervous system in the upper back and neck.

Every inch the head moves forward of this midline creates an extra 10 pounds of weight to lug around, on top of the 10 to 12 pounds the head already weighs. It's not uncommon to see paddlers, surfers and rowers with their heads 6 inches in front of the midline—effectively carrying a 70 pound head!

This has consequences for other parts of the body. The t-spine is where we typically get slack to feed into the back and shoulder complex. But with the flexion hinge here and resulting extension compromise, we lose that. So we start looking for a way to relieve all that extra neural tension that our positional faults have created. With watermen and women, this typically manifests itself in one of two ways.

The first is tilting the head up. True, this mechanical default does buy us some slack. But it comes at a high price, as it encourages the shoulders to translate to the front of their sockets, where they can't produce the external rotation torque needed for either stability or force production. With this shoulders-forward position, we're putting a vice on the nerve complex at the base of the neck, which leads down through the arms. This is a key contributor to numbness, tingling and the kind of "pump out" (where you lose the ability to grip your paddle) that I used to get while on the rafting and slalom national teams.

A head-up tilt further compromises the scapulae and places more load on the ribs, which is one of the reasons we're seeing more fractures than ever before in our rowers. We regularly observe a head tilt of up to 50 degrees, placing massive load on your soft tissues and nerve tunnels, which are already struggling to deal with the performance-sapping, nervous system-endangering kinks in your middle and upper back.

Another way in which people add a kink into the system at the neck is by tilting the chin down. I've often shared a picture of an Olympic slalom kayaker who's going through a gate with a horribly rounded back and his chin almost on his chest. If this is happening at the highest level, you can bet it's also common among recreational athletes. Tilting your chin down is your last ditch attempt to bring the head more in line with the rest of your upper body when you're hinging in the middle back and your shoulders are internally rotated and hunched forward.

It lengthens the thoracodorsal fascia in an attempt to both create artificial stability and purchase some black market slack, but again, there's a cost. This time it's brutally tight neck flexors, fried traps and rhomboids and overextended neck extensors. Getting tension headaches after you paddle or dealing with neck pain? Hmm. I can't think why.

To avoid these head position-related issues and keep your noggin in a neutral position that protects your nervous system and helps enable maximum force production at the shoulder, follow these steps:

1) Practice the bracing sequence until you're familiar with how to stand and sit with a neutral head atop an organized trunk that only hinges at the hips and shoulders

2) Tackle t-spine stiffness and that knotted neck with the mobilizations in The Spine and Hips section of the mobilizations appendix

3) Continually assess your head position when paddling, rowing and surfing. Of course you'll sometimes have to look down or sideways to check water conditions and your surroundings, but for the most part make sure your gaze is fixed straight ahead. Try to reset your position at least every 10 to 15 minutes to make sure your head is properly aligned over your shoulders. Another way to recognize undue tension is by being aware of your face. Are you scrunching it up like Dizzy Gillespie belting out a jazz trumpet solo? Then most likely that extra tension is coming from an overly clenched jaw and/or forward head position. If you recognize your face feeling tight, it's time to reset.

4) Try swallowing occasionally when you're on the water. In fact, try it right now with a neutral head position. Nothing could be easier, right? Now try again with your head tilted up. I'll bet it feels like someone has their hands wrapped around your neck. Try one more time with your chin on your chest. Yikes! Now you can see what a head up/head down position does to your neck musculature. If you have trouble doing the "swallow" test while on your board or in your boat, you know you need to sort out your head alignment.

Unless you have some major motor control or range of motion issues, you likely found it fairly easy to get through the steps of the bracing sequence for standing. But it's when we ask you to change your body's shape—extend your arms overhead or hinge at the hips, for example—that we might see holes in your bracing strategy. Add a little load, such as an overhead squat with a paddle or PVC pipe or hip hinging while swinging a kettlebell, and we may find out that you can't keep your trunk stiff throughout the movement. This can be because of tissue restrictions that limit capacity and/or because you lack the required motor control to preserve a neutral spine.

As we further challenge your organizational strategy with basic movements that involve the hips and shoulders, keep this simple "one joint rule" in mind—you should only see movement at these and other joints (such as the elbow in the push-up and the knee and ankle in the squat), NOT in your spine. This doesn't only apply to the tests, standards and progressions in this book, but also to your water sports of choice. As Jim Terrell has found through testing the world's best paddlers in his flume at Quickblade HQ, each extra hinge requires soft tissue contraction to correct and stabilize, wasting valuable energy and reducing stroke efficiency.

When you drive your paddle into the water in the catch phase of your stroke, you should be hip hinging, not rounding the middle of your back. If you're rowing, you shouldn't be bent over the oar or erg handle like the Hunchback of Notre Dame. And when you're digging in to make a wave, you can't have your head tilted skyward and your lower back over-extended (see The Dread Pirate Pop-Up section later in this chapter for a better way).

Another important component of the one-joint rule is that the hips and shoulders are functionally very similar. Both have a ball-in-socket structure, the capacity to internally and externally rotate and the ability to flex and extend. But while these joints and the surrounding tissues are designed to generate massive amounts of torque, the spine is not. The trunk is meant to be the stable platform that enables these engines to kick out all the horsepower they're capable of, and if we compromise it with local flexion and extension, we're trading the output of a Ferrari for an American Motors Gremlin (Google it if you want a chuckle).

STANDARD #2
CAN YOU HINGE FROM THE HIPS WITHOUT SACRIFICING TRUNK STIFFNESS?

MOTIVATION

If you've been involved in water sports for longer than 5 minutes, you'll likely understand why you have to be able to long sit in a safe position, and maintain an organized spine for the duration of your paddle. For canoeists, kayakers and rowers of all variations, this is a fundamental shape. And yet so many of the spine issues we see are caused by the complete inability to perform the long sit with a braced neutral spine. Exhibit A: how many times have you come off the water and felt like your lower back was on fire? That's because you either lack the range and motor control to keep your trunk stiff as you paddle from a seated position, or your bracing sequence breaks down as you fatigue.

BRIEFING

In this section, we'll test your capacity to not only long sit, but also to hip hinge from a standing position. Then, just for kicks, we'll see if you can hip hinge effectively with a braced neutral spine while generating force through the hips and shoulders. OK, it's not for kicks. Really it's a land-based mirror of what you do anytime you stick your paddle or oar into the water.

HIP HINGE PROGRESSION #1: LONG SIT

One of the reasons that it's hard to long sit is because we're adding a posterior load, and also asking our body to achieve global flexion, with the hip acting as a hinge. If you have poor motor control in your lumbar spine, your dorsal thoracic and dorsal lumbar fascia, glutes and hamstrings are too tacked down or you're compensating for stiffness in the cervical and thoracic spine, you're going to have issues getting and keeping your torso upright in the long sit.

Instead of globally flexing, you're likely going to commit a local flexion or extension fault somewhere along the spine, as your body tries to compensate for lack of range at the hips and the inability to maintain trunk stiffness while adding flexion. If there's a problem doing this with no load or rotation on dry land, imagine the trouble you're going to have when we add fast-moving current and a few thousand strokes into the equation!

Some athletes who hip hinge from a locally flexed back position are able to somewhat flatten out, which can trick them into thinking that they're getting into an optimal shape. In fact, this athlete is cheating by using the Four Horsemen of the Hipocalypse—the rectus femoris that runs down the middle of your quads, the quadratus lumborum (QL) that goes from the bottom of the rib cage to the top of the pelvis, the iliacus that attaches on the front of the pelvis, the femur and the psoas that inserts on the front of the pelvis and lumbar spine—to compensate for their inability to open the hips and hinge there.

So they have to reckon with competing vector loads coming from multiple directions in the lower back and abdominal region, which will further inhibit their ability to explode out of a hip hinge position, whether that's when swinging a kettlebell or paddling. When you're doing the long sit, single leg hip hinge/Romanian deadlift and kettlebell/dumbbell variations of this progression, don't just pay attention to whether you can achieve the shape, but also if you can do so without feeling like your muscles and supporting soft tissues are pulling you apart with shearing forces like you're hungrily tearing apart a grilled cheese sandwich.

Now, enough about sandwiches. Let's see if you can nail the long sit, or if it nails you!

WATERMAN 2.0

1) Sit down with your legs out in front of you and extend your arms in front of your chest

2) Point your toes and squeeze your butt

3) Hinge at the hips and lean forward

4) Can you maintain an upright position while nasal breathing? Or do you round forward by hinging in the middle of your spine?

5) Remember that this is NOT the old gym class "sit and reach" test, aka the worst movement assessment of all time. Trying to hinge forward and then reach as far as you can won't tell us a darn thing, other than the fact that you can put yourself into a wretched position with zero stability and place a crazy load on your spine. We hinge, we don't sit and reach.

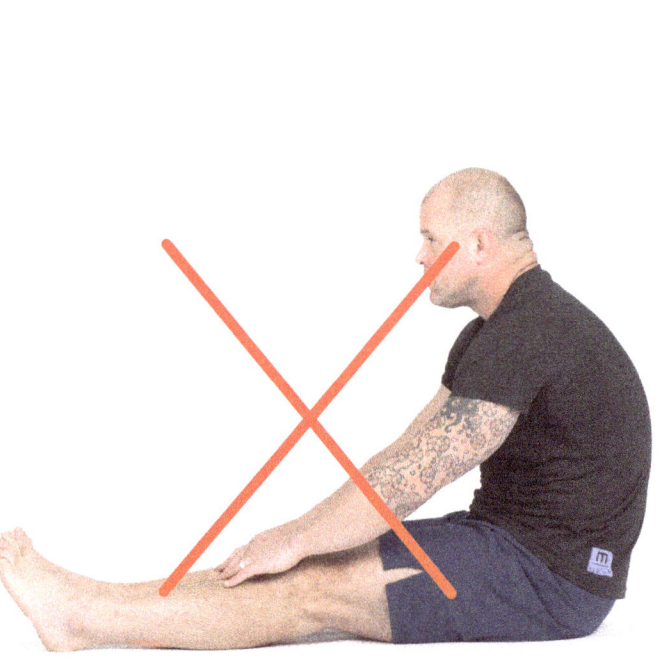

HIP HINGE PROGRESSION #2: SINGLE LEG HINGE/ROMANIAN DEADLIFT

1) Stand on your left leg
2) Fold forward at the hips and extend your right leg behind you
3) Keeping your left leg almost straight with just a slight bend at the knee, lower your torso until your right hand almost touches the floor, maintaining a flat back
4) Return to the starting position
5) Repeat on the other leg

HIP HINGE PROGRESSION #3: STANDING HIP HINGE

To reiterate, you must develop the ability to achieve and maintain a braced neutral spine if you want to reach your goal of enjoying the water for life, and need the capacity to simultaneously achieve full flexion at the hip. So bear with me as we take just a few more steps in this progression.

Next, we're going to apply the principles of the long sit to a standing hip hinge. If you've ever been in a fancy restaurant or watched your fair share of Downton Abbey, you'll understand why we also call this the "waiter's bow" (humbly, m'lord). It's a classic test of your range of motion along the posterior chain, and will help illuminate tightness in the glutes, hamstrings, abs, lower back and more.

If you're going to paddle in any way, you simply must have the capacity to <u>achieve at least 90 degrees of flexion at the hip and ideally 120</u>. And before we can go about digging a blade into the water (or, for that matter, setting up for all manner of exercises such as the deadlift, clean, snatch, RDL and kettlebell swing), we must first check to see if you're missing this ability to flex at the hips while maintaining—yep, you guessed it—a braced neutral spine.

When paddlers are missing this normal range of motion or get fatigued, we see that they start developing a local flexion fault part way up the spine, typically at the thoracic junction. This not only inhibits the ability to generate torque through the hips and shoulders, but also places spinal vertebrae and discs at risk by combining the toxic combination of local flexion and rotation.

Remember that when the trunk twists, 50 percent of the protective rings around each disc disengage. This is OK if we're in a braced neutral, global extension or global flexion shape. But when we also add in local flexion or extension faults, all bets are off and you're in the danger zone. If you take thousands of strokes, something bad is bound to happen sooner or later. Now let's see if you can avoid such an issue by hip hinging correctly.

1) Stand with neutral feet shoulder-width apart

2) Squeeze your butt, clench your abs and keep your legs straight

3) Screw your feet into the ground. This creates torque at the hips and helps other areas of your glutes—i.e. the most powerful muscles you have—to fire and connect your pelvis to your lower back throughout the movement.

4) Keep looking at the floor as you maintain 20 percent squeeze in your abs and hinge at the waist. You should be able to get to 90

THE SPINE AND HIPS

degrees without your spine doing something funky. If you can't, then we've got to address your motor control challenges and tightness in the posterior chain.

5) Don't hang on your hamstrings and push your butt back, as this will encourage a local over-extension fault in your thoracic spine (mid-back), which inevitably pushes the shoulders forward

6) To use the hip hinge as a diagnostic tool, you can also incorporate the two thumb/hand test (see the subhead craftily named Learning the Bracing Sequence/Two Thumb Rule back in standard #1) and make sure that the

distance between your thumbs isn't increasing or decreasing as you bend over. This is particularly useful if you're hip hinging without a training partner or coach to observe your form.

HIP HINGE PROGRESSION #4: SINGLE ARM KETTLEBELL SWING

Ok, buckle up. Things are about to get really interesting. Now that we've seen if you have full hip flexion and the ability to express this while maintaining a stable trunk, we need to challenge the integrity of your positioning with a little load. In this case, we're going to perform the hip hinge with the added joys of a kettlebell, which will test your ability to develop momentum and power from the hip hinge position while keeping your trunk stiff. The kettlebell swing is also challenging because it adds global extension into the mix.

This kind of swing is a fundamental movement in the strength and conditioning world because it develops power from the ground up, requires engagement in just about every muscle in your body and also reinforces the fundamental hip flexion and extension movement archetype used in paddling. Remember that our bodies and brains are wired for movement, not exercises or muscles, so what we spend our time on when we're off the water should be movements that are transferable to our favorite water sports (curls and calf raises need not apply!).

If you don't have a kettlebell you can also use a dumbbell for this swing. We're not going for world records here, so just use a light KB or DB to start.

1) Repeat the set up sequence from the standing hip hinge, but with the kettlebell or dumbbell in one hand and your legs a bit wider apart. If using a kettlebell, hold it with an overhand grip. If using a dumbbell, hold it with your thumb up and the palm facing your midline to create external rotation at the shoulder. Again, your feet should be facing forward and you should screw them into the ground to create external rotation torque at the hip.

2) Hinge at the pelvis and as you do so, swing the KB or DB between your legs

3) While squeezing your butt and maintaining ab tension and a straight arm, swing the KB or DB up until it reaches eye level

4) Return to the starting position

5) Perform 5 reps for each arm

MOBILITY MOMENT: HIP HINGE MOBILIZATIONS

If you're missing range at the hips and find it hard to keep your spine organized during any/all of the hip hinge progressions, we've got some work to do. Start addressing your issues by doing a couple of these mobilizations each day. Remember, spend a minimum of 2 minutes per side on each exercise. Then re-test the progression sequence. You'll be amazed at the positive impact on your positional capacity. You'll find all of these exercises in The Spine and Hips section of the mobilizations appendix.

- Banded long sit
- Hip capsule mobilization
- Side hip smash
- Couch stretch
- Glute tack and floss
- High glute smash and floss
- Hamstring smash
- Banded posterior chain mobilization
- External rotation hip opener
- Single leg flexion with external rotation
- Hip capsule internal rotation

Developing spinal shape fluency, reinforcing it on land and applying it on the water is crucial to increasing performance, breaking the injury and pain cycle and ensuring your primary engines can function at full power. But if you spend 8 to 12 hours a day sitting in a slouched position you're undoing most of your good work.

Biomechanically we become what we behold, so if most of your time is spent hunched over your laptop and steering wheel during the day and then for a few more hours watching TV or messing with your iPad at night, it's going to be much more difficult to apply the principles of a braced neutral spine to your water time as you're naturally going to conform to a rounded, C-shaped spine.

It may sound dramatic, but in many ways sitting really is the new smoking as I explore in my book *Deskbound*. What I mean is that it is one of the biggest factors in adult and childhood obesity, increases your risk of heart attack, stroke and all manner of other life-threatening conditions and, of course, mats down tissues throughout your posterior chain, in your quads, shoulders, neck and just about everywhere else.

Sitting also makes your body hit the snooze button on many functions, including the lymphatic system that's responsible for flushing out waste products. This is a particularly acute issue after we work out, when we need muscular contraction to pump out the by-products that exercise triggers.

It's pointless to drink your go-to post-workout shake if all those nutrients have nowhere to go because byproducts are blocking up the pathway to recovery like a lymphatic landslide. When we sit, there's very little muscular contraction, which is why we feel terrible if our routine is to rush out onto the water, paddle/surf/row like crazy for an hour, shower and then sit for 4 hours. Can't you hear your back creaking at the thought of it?

In addition to the detrimental impact on the lymphatic system, sitting also douses the flames of our metabolic furnace. A study by Texas A&M School of Public Health found that kids who sat all day in their classroom burned 17 percent less calories than a control group that used standing desks. Other research shows that people with high body mass indexes burn 30 percent more calories by standing most of the day.[6]

Another issue is that continual sitting convinces our tissues that they only need a limited range of motion. For example, sitting requires 90 degrees of hip flexion—30 degrees short of the American Academy of Orthopedic Surgeons'

---

6   Mark E. Benden, Jamilia J. Blake, Monica Wendel, John C. Huber, Jr., "The Impact of Stand-Biased Desks in Classrooms on Calorie Expenditure in Children," Texas A&M School of Public Health, available online at http://www.ncbi.nlm.nih.gov/pmc/articles/PMC3134494/ ; Gregory Garrett et al, "Call Center Productivity Over 6 Months Following a Standing Desk Intervention," *IIE Transactions on Occupational Ergonomics and Human Factors*, May 2016.

"normal" range of 120 degrees. And just think about what me planting my 230 pounds on my hamstrings is going to do to those soft tissues. It's no surprise that most people are chronically short along their posterior chain.

Some of us have no choice but to sit for extended periods, whether it's in business meetings, flying an Apache helicopter or anything in between. But if you work from home or in an office where your employer would rather you don't miss time for PT visits and back surgeries, do yourself a favor and invest in a standing desk or get an add on for your existing workstation.

If you're buying a new desk I advise you to get one with a swinging bar, like the ones we purchased for my kids' school. Or you can use a step stool or one of those cool vintage barrels that are a staple at Restoration Hardware and on Etsy. Adding such an item to your standing set up will allow you to take a load off one foot at a time in the "Captain Morgan" pose, rather than doing what many all-day standers do and throw out the "Hey, girlfriend" hip to one side when they get fatigued. The Captain's hat and beard are optional. Also, make sure that you're taking frequent movement breaks throughout the day.

BUFFERING BAD POSITIONING AND LIFESTYLE ERRORS

Your body and brain are really sneaky. While pain is your body's way of telling you that you're in a compromised position, you unfortunately have an amazing (see: disturbing) capability to ignore these biomechanical tornado sirens and handle years of moving inefficiently without sufficient midline stabilization. We can stay in this state of neuromuscular denial until something goes really wrong, like our nerve canals pinching, a joint dislocating or a muscle shearing off a bone like a salmon fillet being pared by a chef's knife. So take corrective action now before you hit a wall.

THE SPINE AND HIPS

So you've heard there's a big swell coming and have been glued to Surfline since midnight waiting for it to roll in. You pack your gear in the dark, slam some coffee and head for the beach at 5 AM. And who can blame you? Your favorite break is all yours, there are perfect barrels coming in and you've got 3 hours till you need to be at work.

But while you're raring to go, your spine isn't such an early riser. Throughout the course of each day, we lose up to an inch in height as our vertebrae compress. At night, our spinal structures swell and literally stretch us out again. When we first get out of bed they're still full of fluid. That's why so many people tweak their back performing seemingly innocuous early morning tasks such as tying their shoes.

None of the top lifters—we're talking the 1,000-pound squat brigade—I know work out in the morning because they know their spine isn't game. Personally, I take a soak in the hot tub to start each day, which encourages my body to flush out all the fluids that have built up overnight. That sounds gross, doesn't it? But in all seriousness, we need to baby our backs in the morning.

Now, this isn't to say I've never got up for a pre-dawn paddle. Nor am I telling you to stay off the water until lunchtime. But if you are hitting the waves or going to the lake or river within 3 or 4 hours of waking, you should spend a lot longer on a dynamic warmup—as long as 30 to 40 minutes if you can make the time. Sure, this will delay your start a little, but is saving half an hour really worth it if you tweak your back and miss a couple of weeks?

Like the Dread Pirate Roberts, if he had anything to do with popping up on a surfboard. Sadly, unlike *The Princess Bride*, the hyperextension fault we see all too often in surfers is no laughing matter. When a surfer is tight in the front of the hips because the anterior musculature—think the iliacus, rectus femoris and psoas—is all gnarly and tacked down, there's going to be an issue during every pop-up. As this tightness is pulling the pelvis forward and preventing hinging at the hip and safe extension in the lumbar spine, we typically see the athlete trying to create a joint that doesn't exist in the lower back. Kind of like a second hip.

The vertebrae and other small spinal structures don't like this one bit the first time you hyperextend. After a few hundred pop-ups they're ticked off. After a few thousand? Rage doesn't even come close. At best, we see low-grade soreness and at worst, surfer's myelopathy, which can cause paralysis.

Know any fellow surfers who seem to walk around permanently overextended in the lower back? Maybe your own back feels like someone's taken a bat to it after you've been out on your board all day. It certainly doesn't help that many of us sleep in over-extended positions all night because our mattresses are too hard. That means double the back pain the next morning, right when you want to charge back out into those perfect barrels.

So what's a wave junkie to do? Well first, point your toes when you're dropping in before you pop-up. This gives you better triple extension so you can fire your glutes to control the low lumbar position and limit spinal movement. It's not just popping up (or indeed, on land, burpees) that exposes the over-extension, local hinging issues.

Frantic drop-in paddling with your head up and rib cage tilted skyward means you can't control your shoulders as you paddle. Again, pointing your toes, squeezing your butt and loading in a push-up position helps you create a better and safer global extension shape that minimizes spine variability, takes the load off your neck and prevents the horrors of shoulders-forward paddling.

MOBILITY MOMENT: HANDLING HYPEREXTENSION

From a mobilization standpoint, you've got to take the stiffness out of the front of those tacked down hips and the anterior and posterior tissues that are playing tug of war with your spine and pelvis. Here are good starting points. You'll find all of these exercises in The Spine and Hips section of the mobilizations appendix.

- Couch stretch
- Glute tack and floss
- Hamstring smash
- Quad smash
- Gut smash
- Oblique side smash
- QL smash
- Lateral hip opener

In addition, taking a warm bath or jumping in a hot tub before you hit the surf is a surefire way to remove some of that stiffness which is daring you to hyperextend yourself into lower back oblivion.

CREATING GLOBAL EXTENSION: THE WORM/PLANK TEST

As well as removing the restrictions that cause you to be in an overextended, lumbar spine-destroying shape, we've also got to go to the root of the issue and get you into a stable position in which safe, organized global extension is the order of the day. Enter the amazing, death-defying worm to plank test! This will help you to not only improve the speed and explosiveness of your pop-up (and after the push-up part of the burpee), but will also help you transition from a global extension shape into a braced neutral position. OK, let's do it:

WATERMAN 2.0

WORM TO PLANK TEST PROGRESSION #1

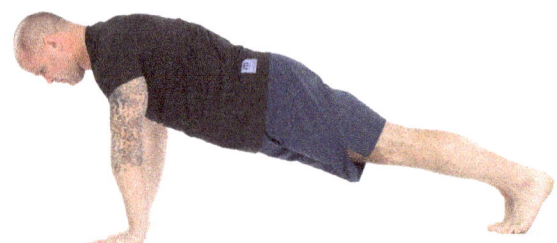

1) Lie on your stomach as if you were prone on your surfboard, SUP board, etc., with your hands by your sides like you were starting a push-up

2) Point your toes and squeeze your butt like your life depends on it. Pointing your toes instead of being in a "feet up" position helps you activate your glutes.

3) While keeping your elbows close by your sides, screw your hands into the ground to create stabilizing torque through the shoulders

4) Explosively push yourself up

5) Instead of jumping to your feet as you would in the water, engage your abs and stop at the top of the push-up position

6) Maintain your ab tension and squeeze your butt again to hold the plank position for 2 minutes

7) Make sure you keep the external rotation in your shoulders turned on, so that your elbow pits face forward. Look down the entire time so you don't get the awful neck crick we often see in prone paddlers and surfers.

8) Remember to breathe from your diaphragm, unless you want to black out

THE SPINE AND HIPS

If you were able to go from the worm position to the plank without collapsing and then hold the plank for 2 minutes, it's time to further test the integrity of your positioning. Any time we raise a body part away from the midline or add a unilateral load (i.e. on one side only), we force the muscles and supporting tissues to work harder. So let's see what this looks like:

1) Repeat the steps from progression #1 and spread your feet apart

2) Raise your right arm off the ground for 10 seconds

3) Return it to the start position and then repeat with the left arm

4) Raise your left leg off the ground for 10 seconds

5) Repeat with the right leg

6) Raise your right arm and left leg simultaneously and hold for 10 seconds. Then return to the starting position and repeat with your left arm and right leg. Complete 3 rounds.

WATERMAN 2.0

STANDARD #3
CAN YOU MAINTAIN TRUNK STABILITY WHILE SQUATTING?

MOTIVATION

Now that we've tested your ability to hinge at the hips while staying organized through the trunk and upgraded your pop-up, it's time to subject your bracing strategy to a different demand with a fundamental exercise: the squat. This progression will not only reveal the gaps in your braced neutral set up and execution, but will also reveal if you're missing range of motion at the hips and ankles.

BRIEFING

While we're exploring the foundational shapes of the spine, your range of motion and your motor control in connecting the upper and lower trunk to the rest of your body, we simply cannot ignore the squat as a uniquely powerful diagnostic tool. Don't squat in the gym? Well, I could yell at you and give you 1,000 reasons why it should be one of the pillars of the strength and conditioning practice you need to support a lifetime on the water. But we'll save that for later. For right now, we're just going to use several variations of the squat to test your capacity.

The squat is one of the most fundamental, universal movements there is. Sitting down in a chair? You're squatting. Bending down to pick up a box? You're squatting. Coming down to eye level to talk to your kid? More squatting. And yet, for all its simplicity, many of us cannot squat without local flexion or extension in the spine, collapsing our knees and feet inwards and internally rotating our hips (just for starters—there are umpteen other movement faults that the squat exposes).

Why is this? One of the key reasons is how sedentary we've become as a society. Sure, you and I like to get out on the water at every opportunity, but what about the rest of our day? Are we spending most of the time standing and much of it moving? Not bloody likely! Too many of us are cramming ourselves into chairs, car and plane seats, living room couches and such, and moving far less than our species has at any other time in history.

All these issues are bad enough when we're stationary. But then we get out onto the water and into the gym and try to move, often explosively, with all these tight tissues and missing rotation, flexion and extension range at the hip. When squatting, this systemic over-tightness inhibits our ability to create trunk stability, which prevents us from generating the external rotation at the hips needed to maintain an upright torso throughout the squat movement. To invoke a positive pessimism, "Your quads and hamstrings are brutally tight, but at least you're missing ankle range of motion."

To be able to function as a human and perform to your potential on the water, you simply must be able to squat. Let's take a look at how you do in these simple progressions, and then address how you can untack your tissues, recapture range and improve spinal, hip and leg mechanics.

SQUAT PROGRESSION #1: BOX SQUAT

At my gym, we use a plyometric box for several reasons when assessing the squat. First, it only requires you to go down until your upper legs are parallel to the ground—the basic minimum for daily function. Second, it exposes motor control issues in the lower back and many people's inability to perform basic load sequencing. Third, after revealing your wonkiness on the way down, the stage in which your butt meets the box allows you to reset to a more upright torso before returning to the starting position.

Finally, the box squat exaggerates the motion of bending over to stick your paddle in the water. If you can't squat in an optimal, organized shape without soft tissue restrictions and tension hunting, you're not going to be able to paddle safely, efficiently or powerfully.

1) Follow the standing bracing sequence—squeeze your butt, squeeze your gut and screw your feet into the ground

2) Pull your shoulder blades back and externally rotate your shoulders. This sets your upper and mid back (i.e. cervical and thoracic spine) in a stable postion.

3) Maintaining tension in your abs and looking straight ahead, push your knees out as you lower your hamstrings toward the box

4) Try to keep your torso as upright as possible as you preserve the tension in the outside of your glutes/hips, in your foot arches and in your abs

5) Once your butt reaches the box, drive your feet into the floor to stand back up

6) Repeat 10 times

SQUAT PROGRESSION #2: AIR SQUAT

Once you teach the box squat who's boss, it's time to move onto the second squat variation: the air squat. This allows us to see if you can get to or below the hip crease (to parallel) without the feedback of the box, and also makes it easier to test the robustness of your squatting mechanics. In this case, we're adding in some speed and metabolic demands in the form of a Tabata squat test.

One of the pioneering exercise physiologists of our time, Izumi Tabata, devised a way to increase baseline conditioning with just a 4 minute time investment—namely, 8 maximum effort 20 second intervals with 10 seconds rest. The first time Power Speed Endurance founder Brian Mackenzie put some of the top watermen and women through a rowing Tabata test on the Concept2 erg, he about killed them, and these athletes have amazingly powerful engines.

For our purposes, we'll stick with an air squat version of the Tabata torture test. The goal is for you to get a minimum of 10 reps per 20 second work interval. That's what we expect of athletes recovering from ACL surgery, so if you're not rehabbing a knee injury, aim for 12 reps plus.

1) Stand with neutral feet shoulder width apart
2) Stick both arms out straight in front of you with your palms facing down to create external shoulder rotation
3) Squeeze your butt, engage your abs and screw your feet into the ground
4) Lower your hamstrings until you get as deep in the squatting position as you can while maintaining a braced neutral spine. The minimum depth is going down until your upper legs are parallel to the floor.
5) Maintaining the tension in your glutes, abs and hips, and keeping your big toes on the ground, drive back up to the starting position
6) Repeat as many times as you can for 20 seconds
7) Rest for 10 seconds
8) Do 7 more 20 second full speed/10 second rest intervals
9) Collapse in a heap and ponder your mortality (kidding, kinda)
10) For an extra challenge, follow Brian Mackenzie's advice and try to only breathe through your nose during the workout to improve your lung capacity and carbon dioxide tolerance. For more tips like this, see his Art of Breath seminars and online materials.

SQUAT PROGRESSION #3: OVERHEAD SQUAT

In the spirit of constant improvement, let's move onto the third and most challenging squat variation in our sequence: the overhead squat. Few movements tell me more about your restrictions and limitations than this, as it requires not only full hip and ankle range, but also full capacity at the shoulder. The reason you should pay particular attention to the overhead squat is because it mimics the paddling and swimming archetype common to just about every water sport. If you can maintain trunk stiffness while extending your arms above your head, you will give your spine every chance of handling the rigors of rotation without breaking down.

1) Repeat steps 1 through 2 from the box squat
2) Your shoulder blades should be pulled back and your armpits facing forward. Another tip for activating your shoulders is to "reach for the sky" with your arms extended overhead.
3) Staying engaged at the shoulders and keeping tension in the abs, glutes and arches, drop into a squat. Go as low as you can without changing your spinal position.
4) Drive with your legs to push yourself back to the starting position
5) Repeat 10 times

MOBILITY MOMENT: SORT OUT YOUR SQUAT

If you encountered any range of motion or motor control issues with the squat progression or had to make compensations (see: cheats) along the way, then we need to address them. Start with these exercises, which you'll find in The Spine and Hips section of the mobilizations appendix:

- Side hip smash
- Couch stretch
- Glute tack and floss
- Quad smash
- Knee Voodoo Floss
- Adductor smash

- Calf smash
- Bone saw
- Knee gapping
- Olympic wall squat
- Trailing leg hip extension
- Medial and anterior smash

A little earlier in this section we examined the importance of maintaining a neutral head position when you're on the water, and the consequences when you don't. We can't just deal with the head or neck in isolation though, as there's a big open circuit in the middle of this complex system: the jaw.

While the human jaw isn't a showstopper like that of the anaconda, which allows it to swallow a whole goat, it's still a powerful mechanism that can be a force for evil when it comes to biomechanics. TMJD, grinding and even arthritis are just some of the issues we see in athletes' jaws and most of these troubles stem for misalignment exacerbated by sporting activity. We even recently consulted with a top decathlete who suffered from lock jaw and had to be on a liquid-only diet for almost a month. True story.

So what's up with the power yawn, gritting and grinding that we see in athletes' jaws? Typically, they're the result of poor head positioning and compensatory tightness in the neck, which we can address by following the steps in the Don't Lose Your (Neutral) Head (Position) section in standard #1. But just as the body can create reciprocal stability—such as an organized trunk stabilizing the shoulders and hips, and organized hips and shoulders stabilizing the trunk—it can also create reciprocal neural tension.

In this case, that means that while head and neck alignment certainly cause jaw issues, these don't exist in isolation, but also lead to further compromises at the head and neck, including tacked down tissue and clamped nerve tunnels. A quick way to fix problems with jaw mechanics is to push your tongue to the roof of your mouth, with the tip touching your top teeth (this should be a light pressure, not like a kid trying to dislodge a loose tooth so they can earn a few bucks from the Tooth Fairy).

You can do it right by exaggerating each syllable in the word "thin." When you get to the "n," that's the right position for your tongue and, therefore, your jaw. Heading down the system, there should be a slight gap between your top and bottom teeth, otherwise you're over-clenching and adding tension where you don't need it.

One of the reasons that paddling, surfing and rowing are difficult to do right is rotation. To create torque through the hips and shoulders, you have to rotate your trunk clockwise and counter-clockwise. The trouble is that rotation puts an added vector load on the spine, which has to transfer power effectively through those engines by maintaining rigidity as your torso turns left and right.

So now you're not only trying to maintain trunk integrity, but to do so with yet another demand added into the mix. And this is why many water athletes suffer a biomechanical collapse every time they get in their shell, on their board or in their boat.

In talking to The Paddle Academy's Mike Eisert for this book, we asked him what his coaches emphasized when it came to the paddling stroke. While reach was certainly key, Mike also told us "rotation, rotation, rotation." When I look at how canoe clubs are teaching beginners now, too many of them are forgetting that lesson, and are just paying lip service to the importance of generating force through the twist. Instead, we see far too many OC1ers, kayakers and SUPers falling apart late in races and defaulting to local hinging in the thoracic spine.

If you have a flexion or extension fault in just one spine segment, the entire structure is compromised. Remember that when we rotate, 50 percent of the protective circular structures around the discs are shut down. This isn't a problem if we maintain trunk stiffness, but the minute you throw in a local flexion fault, these under-protected discs are like a soldier going into battle with no body armor. Do enough twists when you're locally flexed in the t-spine and you may as well book an appointment with your local back surgeon.

To stop things ever getting this far, we need to develop a fluency in the language of spinal shapes. At the most basic level, this means understanding what braced neutral, global flexion and global extension archetypes look like, and then developing the ability to maintain them under load. We also need to test our body's rotational capacity to see if we can apply torque effectively.

ROTATION QUICK TEST

Even if you can achieve full range of motion for rotation, this capacity is useless if you commit the sins of local flexion (hinging at the mid back or tilting the head forward as you round your shoulders) or extension (tilting your head back). So you can fully understand how these local gotchas are impacting your ability to create powerful twists on each stroke, perform the following steps:

1) Get into a braced neutral standing position and put your arms out to the sides

2) Turn your torso as far as you can to the left

3) Return to the starting position

4) Repeat on your right side

5) You should end up looking at around 7 or 8 o'clock (noon being looking straight ahead)

6) Now repeat the test while cranking your head up to look at the ceiling

7) Then do the same but looking down at your feet. I'll bet good money that you only get to 3 or 4 o'clock. This shows how badly we impact rotation when we make the mistake of hinging anywhere other than at the hips. Have a coach or friend video you next time you're out on the water. Then sit down with someone who knows their stuff and examine whether you're hip hinging or doing something funky at the neck or in the thoracic spine.

WATERMAN 2.0

MOBILITY MOMENT: ROTATION FIXES

If you fell short on the rotation test (or the seated version below), pick a couple of the following mobilizations and perform them several times a week (remember, 2 minutes per side, per exercise is the minimum therapeutic dose to make change). You'll find these in The Spine and Hips section of the mobilizations appendix.

- Side hip smash
- Hip capsule internal rotation
- Oblique side smash
- T-spine overhead extension on Gemini
- Lat smash
- T-spine flexion on Gemini

CHAPTER 5
THE SHOULDERS

"The ocean humbles you. You can go and win a world title, but you're never going to beat the ocean."
—Stephanie Gilmore

To say that shoulder injuries are common in water sports is like saying that there are quite a few Ewoks in the Ewok Village—it's a massive understatement. One of the main reasons that shoulder trauma is so prevalent is that the shoulder is a big mystery to most athletes. Many people only ever consider the actual ball and socket, without also taking into account all the forces acting on the joint that originate in surrounding structures in the chest, neck, upper back and arms.

Your shoulders have insertions for all manner of muscles, including the rhomboids, traps, deltoids, lats, serratus, triceps, biceps, pecs and many more. If you have slide and glide in all of these, can organize the scapula and know how to maintain good, stable positions when your arms are in front of you, behind you or overhead, then you're going to be OK. But tightness in just one area, a lack of movement competence or motor control or a left-to-right asymmetry can subject your shoulders to more shearing forces than they can handle.

To generate power in any water sport, you must be able to screw your arm into the shoulder socket and create an external rotation force. In addition to creating torque, this also creates a functionally stable shoulder and minimizes movement variability as you perform your activity. Just as at the hip, there is slack in the shoulder capsule that enables the limb—in this case, the arm—to perform full movement. Evidently, many of us aren't practicing good mechanics, as there are at least 600,000 shoulder surgeries a year in the US.

AS THE SCAPULA GOES, SO GOES THE SHOULDER

To ensure we have full end range capacity, are creating a stable shoulder and are achieving and maintaining optimal positions when we paddle, we must also address how the shoulder blade—aka the scapula—relates to the spine and to the shoulder. Think about the scapula as the steering wheel for your shoulders. If it's out of position, it doesn't matter what your shoulder joint is doing—you'll be going all over the road. And if your steering is off, you've primed yourself to bleed force, lose power and put your shoulder in a mechanically compromised position that increases injury risk.

The shoulder and the hip are very similar, so we can apply many of the same movement principles. But if the shoulder was identical to the hip and we had joint stiffness, we wouldn't be able to move our arms at all. Instead, those clever hands and arms can still function if our shoulder blades are misaligned and as a result, we're still able to paddle and, at a more elemental level, perform basic human functions like feeding ourselves. But let's not make the mistake of confusing our ability to make do for optimal functionality.

Simply put, we have to account for the relationship between the scapula and spine, and then the scapula and shoulder. That's why we have to start our movement and mobility approach with a "spine first" philosophy. If we can address your tightness in the thoracic spine—i.e. the tissues that pull on your shoulder blades—then we can give you back the range of motion and restore the slide and glide needed to get your scapula into a more optimal position.

THE THORACIC SPINE AND ROTATION

You might recall from back in The Spine and Hips chapter that we addressed the mechanical demands of rotation, and discussed why we have to create paddling power from turning our torso instead of hinging in the middle back and trying to generate force from up-down, front-back motion. We also took a look at the importance of creating a stable trunk as a foundation for rotation, and the importance of the hips.

But we can't dismiss the scapula and t-spine when we're talking about rotation. For too long, people have focused exclusively on the lower back when trying to increase rotation speed and power, and in dealing with mobility issues. But the lumbar spine is only capable of 13 degrees of rotation—about the amount it takes for a minute hand to go from noon to 12:02 on the clock (assuming you don't have any soft tissue restrictions in your lower back). Hardly what we need for a powerful trunk twist, right?

Instead, as pioneering physical therapist Shirley Sahrmann writes in her book *Diagnosis and Treatment of Movement Impairment Syndromes,* "The thoracic spine, not the lumbar spine should be the site of the greatest amount of rotation of the trunk." This gives us more motivation for mobilizing the t-spine and liberating those tight tissues between and around your shoulder blades that are preventing you from generating a powerful stroke and a solid shoulder position.

When I was paddling on the whitewater slalom national team, every girl on the squad had been through at least one shoulder injury. One of the reasons was that none of us knew anything about movement and mobility and another is that we were mortgaging our future tissue health for the sake of short term speed gains.

Sore shoulders? Oh well, at least I'm going faster/harder/longer, right? Wrong. In elite sports, such a tradeoff might be justifiable when a gold medal is on the line. But for the rest of us, we need to go back to basics with our mechanics, positioning and mobility to ensure longevity.

If you push your shoulders forward trying to make your chest muscles look bigger, you have a classic case of "douchebag shoulder." Such forward translation can also be accidental, and is usually the result of inadequate scapular control and/or missing internal rotation capacity.

When you slouch over a desk or walk down the street it's bad enough, but on your board or boat it's a full on biomechanical catastrophe. Suddenly, you've lost the ability to set your shoulders in the back of their sockets with external rotation, so now they come forward in front of your chest. This prevents you from choking down on your paddle and puts undue stress on the biceps and the musculature on the side of your body—the serratus anterior and lats.

With collapsed shoulders you're also hampering the powerful traps and rhomboids in your upper back, and adding neural tension at the neck. A quick test to see if you're standing in a shoulders and head-forward position is to ask a friend if they can see your traps and rhomboids (those big muscles that on the Incredible Hulk are 2 lumps protruding from the top of his shoulders) clearly from behind? No? Then you know you're hunched over.

With your head tilted and moved forward of your center of mass, those pesky neck nerves are clamped, leading to the pain and migraines that trouble many surfers, paddlers and boaters. The avalanche of positional calamity and tension continues rolling down your back, locking up your t-spine and causing you to round your lumbar spine. So that's why your back hurts after you paddle!

And the consequences of douchebag shoulder don't stop there. Now that you're in a rounded back position, you've compromised the relationship between your lumbar spine and pelvis. This reduces force production through the hips. Less power at the shoulders + less hip power = a dramatically weakened stroke.

This is not a pretty picture, is it? Luckily, you can easily enter the patented Douchebag Shoulder Recovery Program. It starts by ensuring you maintain braced neutral posture when you sit and stand.

STANDARD #4
DO YOU HAVE FULL OVERHEAD CAPACITY?

MOTIVATION

Whether you're swimming or paddling any type of craft, your arms will be overhead. And if you have restrictions or motor control issues in this archetype, you're just a force-bleeding machine whose primary upper body engines are idling at 2,000 RPM instead of the 10,000 RPM red-lining they're capable of. If this loss of propulsion wasn't bad enough, lack of overhead capability is also a huge contributor to the hundreds of thousands of shoulder and neck surgeries we see each year. With inadequate shoulder positioning, the elbows and wrists are also jeopardized and the hips can't produce as much torque.

We can avoid this domino effect of doom if we set the shoulders in a stable position and open up the capacity corners you've been missing. This standard will test your ability to get into and sustain the fundamental overhead shape and help restore the range you need to be at your best every time you take to the water.

BRIEFING

If I asked you just to put your hands overhead, you'd probably look at me funny. And yet, you might be surprised to discover that at least 75 percent of athletes are missing the ability to do this correctly without altering the position of their spine or allowing the rib cage to come up, let alone sustain a stable position as part of a paddling and swimming stroke (or bear any other kind of load, for that matter).

Is it possible to paddle, swim or do anything else we like to do on the water without full overhead range? Certainly. Our bodies can get creative and find compensatory positions that buy us some slack. You can do a bunch of work overhead with internally rotated shoulders and partial elbow extension (see: rounded shoulders and a partially bent arm) …until you can't. Eventually, something will give and you'll be stuck with an injury that keeps you land-bound. And in the meantime, every stroke you take will be low-powered, not to mention the trickle down impact on your spine, elbows, wrists, hands and more.

Instead of just letting yourself find secondary stability, let's try to get you in a fully optimized overhead shape, in which you can paddle safely, effectively and powerfully for years without ever becoming part of the shoulder surgery club. If you can nail the ideal starting and finishing positions in the overhead archetype while in the gym, chances are you'll do the same on the water. But if you're tight in the t-spine and your scapula is improperly aligned, you're going to run out of room before you reach full end range.

Same goes if your neck is tight on either side, if your chest muscles and anterior or posterior shoulders are matted down or if your triceps, serratus and lats are tugging on your shoulders like a crew pulling on ropes to put up a tent in high wind. Yep, that's a long list of potential trouble areas, but that's the shoulder for you. It is a wonderfully complex system, which is why there can be myriad issues.

Before we go about fixing these problems, we need to understand exactly what we're dealing with. Let's see if you have full external rotation capacity with no load. Full disclosure: there are a LOT of steps in this progression sequence. But please patiently work through them as the overhead archetype is essential to swimming and paddling.

OVERHEAD ARCHETYPE PROGRESSION #1: ARMS OVERHEAD

1) Stand with your feet facing forward and shoulder width apart, with your hands by your sides

2) Squeeze your butt and engage your abs

3) Screw your feet into the ground

4) Maintaining working tension in your abs, raise both arms overhead like you're about to start the backstroke. Stop when your arms are just behind your ears. They should be completely straight with no

THE SHOULDERS

bend at the elbow. Your thumbs should be pointed backwards and your armpits facing forward.

5) Your spine should have stayed in the same position and your rib cage should not have lifted to compensate for incomplete range. If you arched your back, tilted your head or did something else to your spine that falls in the "funky" category, then you either lack motor control and/or are tight in the cervical, thoracic or lumbar spine.

6) If you can't straighten your arms and/or can't get them just behind your ears, then you are missing full extension

7) If you can't get into the armpits forward, thumbs back position—we often see one or both arms coming down into internal rotation—you're missing external rotation

OVERHEAD ARCHETYPE PROGRESSION #2: SINGLE ARM OVERHEAD PRESS

We often train doing bilateral exercises like barbell shoulder and bench presses and these are great for developing strength and power. But some water-based activities are unilateral—i.e. you emphasize one side of your body. From sprint canoe to dragon boats to 6-man outrigger, such disciplines lead to strength, movement and mobility imbalances similar to what we see in other unilateral athletes, such as baseball and softball pitchers, tennis players, football quarterbacks, shot putters and javelin throwers. Other water sports, such as rowing in anything other than single sculls, also place different demands on one side of the body. As both sides are inter- and intra-connected, this puts unusual, off-axis loads on the non-dominant side.

That's why it's essential that we incorporate single-side dumbbell and kettlebell exercises into our programming for water athletes. You're still using power created at the hips and shoulders to propel an object through a full range of motion, but in an open torque situation that challenges your motor control and tests your midline stability more than when using a barbell (as for push presses or squats) or screwing both hands into the ground (such as for push-ups or planks).

From a strength and conditioning standpoint, we can also eliminate the "strong side/weak side" disparities that can wreak havoc on our movement patterns, performance and soft tissue health. Similarly, we can identify and address left-right imbalances that compromise efficiency. Another benefit of using single arm or leg variations is that they give us a clear window through which to see asymmetry, missing ranges of motion and mobility restrictions. In this case, we're going to use the single arm overhead press to further evaluate your shoulder extension and external rotation capacity.

1) Stand with neutral feet shoulder width apart with a kettlebell or dumbbell in your left hand

2) Engage your glutes and abs, and screw your feet into the ground

3) Create a stable shoulder by turning your hand outward so the thumb is facing forward

4) Raise the kettlebell or dumbbell to shoulder level

5) Maintaining working tension in your abs, extend your left arm overhead. It should be straight and your thumb pointed backwards, with no bend at the elbow. If you have full capacity, your left arm should be aligned just behind your ear and within a few inches of the side of your neck. There should be no pain during the movement.

6) Lower the weight back to the starting position. Complete 10 reps and then repeat on the other side. If you're a unilateral athlete, you'll likely see an imbalance on one side. Use the exercises in this chapter's mobility moments to restore full range of motion on both sides.

When we think about rib issues in water sports, our gaze inevitably goes to the bulk of the rib cage. If I asked you to point to where you think most athletes have rib problems, you'd probably indicate the chest and upper abdomen on the front of the body and middle back on the posterior side, right? But when we're talking about overhead mobility, there's an awkward little bugger that often escapes our attention: the first rib.

You can find the upper insertion of this commonly neglected rib by placing your hand just above the collarbone. That's the front of the first rib, with your lower trap covering the back. Dig into either area after a long session on the water and tell me what you feel. Is it nice and smooth in there? No! It's as gristly as a $5 steak! Tacked down tissue in this area adds a boat load of neural tension into the neck and shoulders, and affects the upper pecs.

Add in the tightness caused by "text neck," slumping in your boat and your office chair and the dreaded "forward head" position, and we have ourselves a problem. Restriction around the first rib exacerbates internally rotated, slumped shoulders, impedes optimal breathing mechanics and puts a vise grip around the nerve bundles that lead all the way down your neck to your fingertips. For me, first rib issues exacerbated my asthma symptoms.

A displaced first rib and/or gristly surrounding soft tissues can severely limit our ability to get into a good overhead shape (i.e. achieve full extension and external rotation at the shoulder). This limits our capacity to participate in SUP, swimming, canoeing and just about every other water-centric activity.

Luckily, there are a few quick mobility fixes. Spend a couple of minutes per side on these bad boys several times a week and you'll restore full function to this often overlooked contributor to all manner of shoulder and neck misery. You'll find the following exercises in The Shoulders section of the mobilizations appendix.

- First rib pin and spin
- Trap barbell/PVC pipe mobilization
- Scalenes pin and spin

OVERHEAD ARCHETYPE PROGRESSION #3: OVERHEAD WALKING LUNGE

When we start to add motion into this progression sequence, things can get messy because many people lack the ability to maintain shoulder integrity and postural control of the scapula when another part of their body is moving. Walking lunges with a bar in the front rack position or dumbbells down by your sides are hard enough (or, in Dave Kalama's case, doing several hundred bodyweight lunges forward and backward in sand), but when we ask you to extend both arms overhead and stabilize an object, your center of gravity is raised and you're placing a greater stabilization demand on your torso. Let's see how you get on:

1) Get a 10 pound weight plate and extend your arms overhead so the load is directly over the imaginary midline that runs from your ears, down through your hips and to your heels

2) Perform the standing bracing sequence—screw both feet into the ground and squeeze your abs and butt

3) Maintaining an upright torso and keeping your gaze straight ahead, take a large step forward with your right foot, dipping the left knee down until it gently touches the ground

4) Switch sides. Make sure you're keeping your arms extended and locked into position—don't let them stray too far in front or behind your head. Take 10 to 20 steps. You can increase the weight once you've mastered the exercise and/or add more steps. If you're at the beach, use a rock in place of the weight plate.

Don't get me wrong, I love my carbon fiber paddles, both for outrigger and SUP. But if you're having that mean old pain in the front of your shoulder, your paddle might be part of the issue. Now, with paddles we usually only think about the length in such scenarios. But the real trouble could be that your paddle shaft is just too stiff. A fiberglass option or FG/carbon combo with a lower shaft stiffness index (SSI) might be a better fit, as the greater flex will reduce the forces coursing through the shoulder complex.

You might think this is merely a tip for beginners, but it's just as applicable to advanced paddlers who try to get as much power as they can from each stroke by cranking a stiff top arm down on top of an unyielding carbon shaft. And what happens when a wrecking ball collides with a brick wall? Fragments fly in all directions. So if you're used to an ultra-stiff carbon shaft, try borrowing a buddy's fiberglass paddle and giving that a go for a few sessions. Also try to back off just a fraction with the top arm. Combining the two might help sort out that nagging shoulder pain.

OVERHEAD ARCHETYPE PROGRESSION #4: HANG FROM A BAR (OVERHAND PULL-UP GRIP)

Hanging is a fundamental human discipline and yet unless you have a strength and conditioning or gymnastics practice, when's the last time you just hung from a bar? Well, we're about to remedy this.

1) Stand under a pull-up bar
2) Reach up with your hands slightly wider than shoulder width apart
3) Wrap your hands around the bar. Make sure you get your pinky knuckle over the bar, as this will encourage better rotation and enable greater stability. Hook your thumbs around the bottom of the bar.

4) Try to pin your shoulder blades back and create some tension on the bar with your hands, like you're trying to break it

5) Your feet should be pointed and your legs extended. This mirrors the hollow hold exercise that's a staple of gymnastics programs. Tucking your knees up behind you is a classic movement fault that contributes to an unstable position and poor mechanics.

6) Hang for as long as you can without losing positioning. Rest for 30 seconds and go again. Work up to a total of at least 2 minutes per day.

OVERHEAD ARCHETYPE PROGRESSION #5: PULL-UP (OVERHAND GRIP)

If there's an upper body exercise I see performed incorrectly more than any other, it has to be the pull-up. Some of the common movement faults include trying to get the chin up and over the bar, which people achieve by cranking their head up to the sky. What do you think that's doing to your neck and shoulders? Another classic mistake is tucking the legs behind you, which undoes the role of your abs and glutes in keeping your trunk in a stable position and excessively loads the lumbar spine. And try to avoid adding speed before a coach or friend has validated your form.

1) Perform steps 1 through 5 from the bar hang movement in progression #4

2) Keeping your abs braced, your gaze fixed straight ahead and your body in the hollow hold position, pull yourself up as far as you can

3) Slowly lower yourself to the starting position and repeat

4) Complete 10 reps. If you can't do a full pull-up, have a training partner help you.

 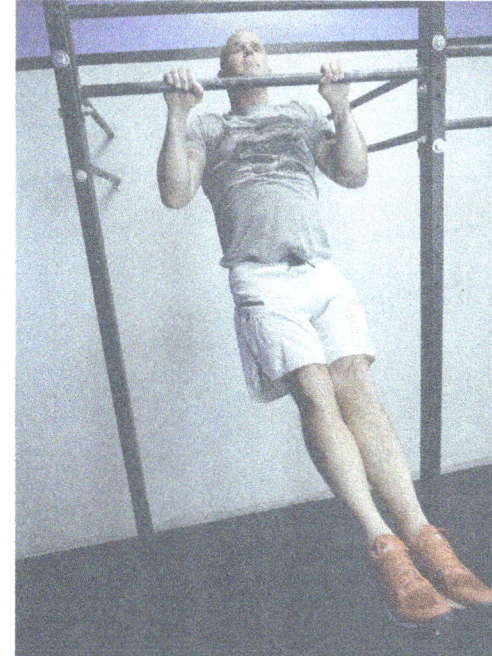

OVERHEAD ARCHETYPE PROGRESSION #6: WAITER CARRY

No, I'm not asking you to literally carry around a waiter, although that might enliven your next dinner date. Instead, what we're talking about here is another way to test your capacity and motor control in the overhead archetype. If you've ever seen a waiter at a fancy restaurant carrying a silver platter laden with enough crockery to sink an ocean liner, you've probably thought, "How the heck are they carrying so much in that position?" The answer is quite simple: by externally rotating to create a solid shoulder platform that can handle an awfully large load, keeping the shoulder, elbow and wrist aligned and preserving scapula control.

Now it's your turn. I don't want you breaking the fine china, so instead of asking you to don a tux and strut around with a silver tray overflowing with plates and bowls, let's just agree that a kettlebell or dumbbell is a better tool.

1) Pick up a kettlebell or dumbbell in one hand

2) With your palm facing your body and thumb forward, press the weight over your head

3) Your thumb should now be facing backwards, with your arm fully extended and your shoulder externally rotated

4) Keeping your abs braced and shoulder blades pinned back and down, walk forward for 20 feet

5) Switch hands and repeat

6) Perform 3 sets. Your shoulder must remain stable at all times. If you feel it buckling, slowly lower the weight.

7) Too easy? Then use a heavier weight or increase the walking distance.

OVERHEAD ARCHETYPE PROGRESSION #7: TURKISH GET-UP

Like Turkish Delight, we can't guarantee that this exercise originated in the birthplace of the Ottoman Empire, but it sounds cooler than plain old "get-up," doesn't it? It's also one of the best ways to test the full expression of the overhead archetype, with the added joys of requiring you to preserve stability while your body moves up and sideways.

When you're paddling, surfing or rowing, your shoulder isn't static. Instead, it's constantly changing orientation. That's why practicing moves like the get-up is so valuable—because they teach your brain to reinforce solid land-based motor patterns through multiple planes in a way that's directly transferable to water sports. The get-up also exposes range of motion deficiencies and positioning faults that, when corrected, significantly decrease your risk of getting hurt while also boosting power output and reducing fatigue.

Mixed martial artists, wrestlers and the like regularly practice the get-up because it allows them to get to their feet using minimal energy, and to generate power from the ground up. For our purposes, the get-up is the most challenging of our overhead progressions because it tests your ability to lock your shoulders in a stable position and then cycle through a full range of motion without the help of generating torque off a fixed object such as the ground or a barbell.

While we do class the get-up as an advanced category 3 exercise in *Becoming a Supple Leopard*, it's performed with minimal velocity, making it a safe way to reinforce the overhead shape for athletes of every skill level. Another bonus is that the get-up also requires the hand that isn't gripping the kettlebell or dumbbell to create stability at the shoulder. Plus, the middle portion of the exercise puts you into a lunge position that's similar to your surfing, paddling or sprint canoeing split stance. Athletes like Nic Vaughan find that get-ups also assist in popping up on their surfboards. In other words, this is a killer exercise for any waterman or woman.

1) Lie on your back with your left leg straight and right knee bent, with your right foot flat on the floor. Then position a kettlebell next to your right shoulder and grip the handle with your right hand.

2) While still gripping the kettlebell with your right hand, use your left hand to help move it toward the center of your body and then extend your right elbow

3) As soon as your arm is locked out, allow your right shoulder to move to the back of the socket. Your right hand and elbow should be in a straight line over your right shoulder. Try to maintain this alignment throughout the rest of the exercise.

4) Roll onto your left elbow, keeping your gaze fixed on the kettlebell

5) With your right arm staying straight, push off the ground with your right leg and extend your left elbow with the left palm flat on the ground and positioned in a straight line down from the left elbow and shoulder

6) Squeeze your butt muscles and drive off the ground with your right foot as you extend your hips toward the ceiling

THE SHOULDERS

7) Use your left arm and right leg to support you as you pull your left leg under your hips. Then place your left knee underneath your torso, making sure that you keep looking up at the kettlebell.

8) Move your bodyweight toward your right side and get your torso upright. As soon as your left hand comes off the ground, pull your left shoulder back and turn your arm outward.

9) Use your right leg to push yourself up out of the bottom position with your torso remaining upright and weight centered over your hips

10) Bring your left foot forward and stand up with your feet facing forward and shoulder width apart. Your right arm should be fully extended overhead and your left arm straight out in front of you.

MOBILITY MOMENT: OVERHEAD ARCHETYPE FIXES

If you can't achieve end range overhead or maintain it under load, we need to liberate those soft tissues surrounding the shoulder girdle. These mobilizations are a solid starting point. You'll find them in The Spine and Hips and The Shoulders sections of the mobilizations appendix.

- T-spine overhead extension on Gemini
- Lat smash
- T-spine flexion on Gemini
- First rib pin and spin
- Subscap tack and floss
- Super front rack
- Banded bully with extension bias
- Banded lateral opener
- Triceps smash

In his excellent book about skill acquisition, *The Talent Code*, Daniel Coyle explains how every time we move in a certain way our brain is reinforcing patterning by wrapping more myelin around the neuron assigned to that movement sequence. The more repetitions we perform, the quicker the brain tells the body to move in that way. To integrate Malcolm Gladwell's 10,000 hours theory, this means that the expert waterman or woman is using a wicked fast Google Fiber connection to surf, row or paddle, rather than the slow dial-up connection of the novice.

That's great if we're automatically creating stable shapes—practice making perfect. But as Coyle's research proves, practice also makes permanent, so if we're unconsciously getting into poor positions and myelinating them over and over, we're going to see sub-optimal performance, torque flowing out like water from a leaky pipe and a destructive pain/injury cycle.

The only way to change faulty patterns is to learn a better way and then practice the heck out of it, so that the brain abandons the old pathway and autonomously starts cueing the new, improved technique. But this only works if we're applying the correct positioning in ALL situations. What we've observed over tens of thousands of hours in the gym is that when you add speed, load or metabolic demand, many people quickly abandon ideal archetypal shapes.

This is particularly common in AMRAP (as many rounds as possible) workouts in which finishing fast is the goal, and applies to high repetition exercises such as box jumps and burpees. We also see it on the water, when coaches are just pushing speed and mileage above all. That's one of the main reasons my body shut down and that I'm still missing full range in my right wrist and shoulder.

It is certainly of some benefit to create a stable shoulder with armpits forward and the head of the humerus screwed into the socket when we're on the water and performing slower movements such as the overhead squat. But if we then do a "movement hack" to a faulty position in fast, high rep exercises, we're cheating ourselves and confusing our brain by reinforcing more than one way to move.

Now the autonomous response is delayed because of the "either/or" movement decision, so we're reacting more slowly and performing below our potential. So if I see you finishing a burpee with shoulders internally rotated and elbows flared or a push-up where you've lost midline stability for the sake of banging out a few more reps, I'm going to yell at you! Help your brain and body out by applying correct positioning to ALL situations. It will make you a better athlete on and off the water, and help reduce injury risk.

STANDARD #5
CAN YOU ACHIEVE AND MAINTAIN A STABLE SHOULDER AND SPINE IN THE PRESS ARCHETYPE?

MOTIVATION

As with the spine, there are several basic, universal shapes that we must be able to achieve if we're going to derive maximum performance from the shoulder, while also coming off the water unharmed. The second of these is the press archetype.

"But my paddling/surfing/rowing is about pulling, not pressing," I hear you say. Really? In fact, every time you rotate your body in the reach phase of your paddling stroke or between the recovery and catch stages of your rowing stroke, you ARE working in the press archetype.

Similarly, when you pull your paddle/oar/hand back toward you and, if you have the capacity, behind your trunk, you're expressing extension and internal rotation at the other end of the press shape. So despite your initial hesitation, the mid-range shoulder is in fact the heart and soul of every paddling stroke.

That's why top level rowers don't just perform Olympic lifts and work on pulling, but also bench press and do dips and push-ups. You need to be efficient and have full capacity at every stage of the stroke to be your best, and just pulling effectively isn't enough—not even for the likes of world-beaters like Laird Hamilton, Erin Cafaro Mackenzie and Lina Augaitis. So embrace the press archetype!

BRIEFING

To improve your mid-range shoulder positioning and power output, we're going to test your ability to establish a stable shoulder with varying demands and loads applicable to pressing. As with the other exercises in our standards, the movements in this progression are merely part of the lab work you can do at home or in the gym. The enhanced sequencing and improved motion control are then directly transferable to your water time.

The press progressions are also useful diagnostic tools. If you're missing external or internal rotation at the shoulder, it's going to be very readily apparent.

THE SHOULDERS

Don't have full elbow flexion? That's going to show up too. And each stage of this progression places more demand on the integrity of your spinal positioning. If you can't keep your carriage in a stable position during a plank, push-up or ring row, you're certainly not going to do it while on the water. If you fail to achieve and maintain a stable shoulder in the pressing archetype, you'll likely default to an unsustainable, shoulders forward, elbows out position when you're rowing or paddling.

PRESS ARCHETYPE PROGRESSION #1: 2-MINUTE PLANK

A lot of people spend time doing "core" workouts that see them contorting into all sorts of shapes, using various implements and incorporating unstable surfaces. But to me, the plank is still the best of all the so-called "core" exercises because it tests your ability to create external torque at the shoulders while using the abs and glutes to preserve spinal integrity.

However, even those people who recognize the plank as both a valuable strengthening exercise and diagnostic tool often do it wrong. Their hands are in odd positions, they don't fully extend the arms or they can't engage their trunk musculature to keep a flat back. As a result, we see multiple local flexion and extension faults, minimal to no torque at the shoulder and a largely ineffective motor pattern being reinforced again and again. Let's see if you can nail the plank (pun intended).

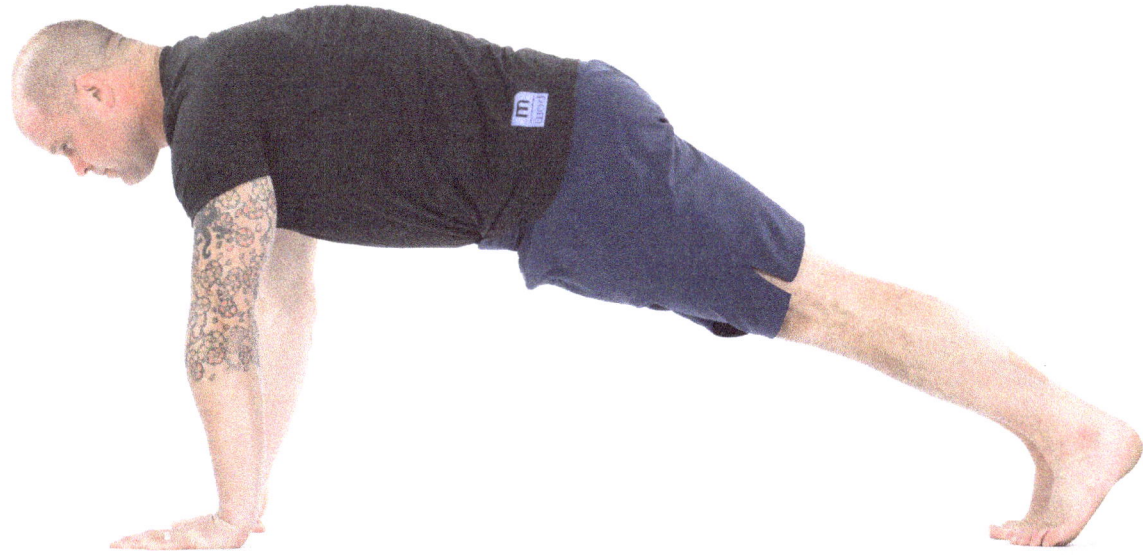

1) Get into the push-up top position—feet a couple of inches apart, hands shoulder width apart, forearms vertical (i.e. directly below your shoulders), head looking down at the floor

2) With your fingers pointed straight ahead, screw your hands into the ground by rotating them as if they're on spinning plates (but without turning them outward)

3) Squeeze your butt as hard as you can

4) Contract your abs

5) Maintain the external rotation in your shoulders so that your elbows stay pointed forward. Keep your butt muscles and abs tight and hold the position for 2 minutes.

6) If you feel your hips start to drop or shoulders go rubbery, slowly lower yourself to the floor, keeping your hands in place and elbows in. Rest for a few seconds and then resume the plank position. Once you can hold a solid plank for 2 minutes, you can work several sets into your workout a couple of times a week, with a minute to 2 minutes rest between sets.

PRESS ARCHETYPE PROGRESSION #2: PUSH-UP

Got the plank down? Great. Now let's mix things up a little bit by testing you with some movement. If the squat is the king of lower body movements, then the push-up is the queen of upper body exercises. It is a lot less risky than the bench press for inexperienced or ill-coached athletes, and yet provides most of the same benefits. And in fact, as you're not supporting part of your weight on a bench, but instead relying on your musculature, fascia, ligaments and tendons to keep your shape throughout the press archetype, it's arguably superior in some ways.

In addition to testing your ability to generate torque at the shoulder while staying organized through the trunk, the push-up also provides added insight

THE SHOULDERS

into motor control deficiencies and range of motion limitations by adding the demands of movement to the archetype. If you're missing capacity at the wrist or elbow, it's going to show up more clearly than in the plank.

1) Assume the top position of the push-up, with your elbows extended. Screw your hands into the ground (turn your left hand counter-clockwise and your right hand clockwise until you feel tension in your shoulders, without actually moving your hands on the ground).

2) Maintaining external rotation at the shoulder and ab/glute engagement, lower yourself to the floor

3) As you do so, keep your elbows in and your forearms vertical

4) Get as low as you can while maintaining a braced neutral spine, and then, keeping those wannabe-flaring elbows in tight to your sides, press back up to the starting position

5) Repeat for 10 reps

6) If you can complete each rep with perfect form, add some speed and/or more reps

PRESS ARCHETYPE PROGRESSION #3:
TRX DUO TRAINER/RING PUSH-UP

Doing planks and push-ups on the ground provides valuable insight into your torque system and spinal mechanics. But doing them on a stable, flat surface is only testing you in a low torque environment, as you have a solid platform (i.e. the floor) to create and maintain a stable shape. To take the progression a step further and increase the load, we're going to add some instability.

Using a TRX Duo Trainer or gymnastics rings makes it difficult to go through a full push-up with sub-optimal mechanics because it's an unstable, open torque environment in which you have to resist your shoulders' desire to internally rotate. The benefit is that it reinforces the need for a proper movement pattern, which is transferable to the plank, push-up and other land-based expressions of the pressing archetype, as well as to water sports.

The instability of the TRX Duo Trainer and rings tells your body that it has to work harder to stabilize you. The best way to stay balanced is to align your hands under your shoulders, keep your forearms vertical and turn out your hands to create the external rotation torque needed to create stiffness.

If the forearms stay vertical, it's easier to keep the elbows tucked in and avoid the nefarious flare out. If you're missing internal rotation, your hands will turn inward and those elbows will fly out, causing your arms to shake and placing an undesirable load on your elbows, shoulders, biceps, forearms and wrists. As stimuli go, it's a pretty unmistakable reminder that something's wrong.

1) Set up the TRX handles or rings so they're a few inches off the ground and shoulder width apart

2) Kneel on the ground and form your grip around each one

3) Walk your legs back until you're balancing on the front of your toes. This will allow you to point your toes which, as you'll know if you read The Dread Pirate Pop-Up section in The Spine and Hips chapter, encourages greater spine-stabilizing glute activation.

4) Create a stable shoulder by externally rotating your hands outward until your thumbs point away from your body (imagine your left thumb being at 11 o'clock and the right at 1 o'clock)

5) Squeeze your butt and engage your abs

6) Maintaining active abs and glutes and external rotation at the shoulders, lower into the bottom position

7) Fight your hands trying to turn inward

8) Still turning your hands out and preserving our old friend the neutral spine, press up to the top position

9) Repeat 10 times with correct form

10) If you're struggling, try breaking the move down into components, working on the set up/top position first and then slowly lowering yourself into the bottom position

PRESS ARCHETYPE PROGRESSION #4: BURPEE

The burpee requires you to create stability coming out of the press archetype, while you simultaneously generate enough force to power yourself into the next phase of the movement. As most people usually do a lot of burpees as part of a CrossFit WOD or HIIT class, people try to speed them up at the expense of correct form—the exact same problem we see in SUP, canoe, kayaking and rowing races. The result? An entire catalog of positional errors.

WATERMAN 2.0

Instead of you trying to blast out 20 burpees as fast as you can, I want you to focus on doing one slowly and correctly. Just as with every other movement in this book's exercise progressions, you can have a training buddy watch, evaluate and even video your form. Also, listen to your body's feedback—if something feels funky—like your shoulders are going to spontaneously combust, for example—then it is funky and you need to stop and evaluate your technique.

THE SHOULDERS

1) Stand with your feet straight. Then squeeze your gut and butt.

2) Pull your hamstrings back and hinge forward at the hips, placing your palms flat on the floor. Try to keep your back flat.

3) Hop your feet backward and get into the top position of the push-up

4) Keeping your butt squeezed, abs tight and elbows tucked in, lower yourself into the bottom position of the push-up

5) Extend your elbows as you jump your feet forward, pulling your knees toward your chest

6) As your feet come underneath your upper body, try to land them where your hands were as you get into the bottom of the squat position. Your arms should be extended in front of you parallel to the ground.

7) Jump up out of the bottom position of the squat with your legs together and arms extended overhead

8) Land in the start position from step #1, ready for the next burpee

PRESS ARCHETYPE PROGRESSION #5: BAR DIP

The dip is like the squat of the upper body. It not only develops your triceps, pecs, biceps and the musculature of the shoulders and upper back, but also tests your mechanical competence in achieving and maintaining internal shoulder rotation. Some handy hints before you get started: go slow, don't lean too far forward or tuck your legs behind you and keep looking straight ahead.

1) Place your hands on dip bars so that they're slightly behind your shoulders. Your forearms should remain vertical (think of the forearms as the equivalent of your vertical shins in the squat).

2) Brace your abs and slowly lower yourself until your upper arms are parallel to the floor. Just like a person that's afraid of heights going up in a gondola—don't look down (or indeed up)!

3) Push yourself back up to the starting position. Keep your elbows tucked into the sides throughout the movement.

4) Complete 10 reps

PRESS ARCHETYPE PROGRESSION #6: TRX DUO TRAINER/RING DIP

When you move from doing a parallel bar dip to a TRX Duo Trainer/ring dip, you're transitioning from a closed to open torque environment. This means it's harder to stabilize because you're not generating force off a fixed object. For this dip variation, check out Carl Paoli's excellent progression at freestyleconnection.com to make sure you've got the basics down. Hopefully, these directions will see you right:

1) With the TRX Duo Trainer handles/rings positioned about shoulder width apart and your elbows tucked in to your sides, grip the rings with your palms facing each other

2) Push yourself up into the starting position by extending your arms. Turn your left hand to 11 o'clock and your right hand to 1 o'clock to generate external rotation and set your shoulders into a stable position.

3) Point your toes and extend your legs a few inches in front of your body (the hollow hold)

4) Stay looking straight ahead as you lower your body until your upper arms are parallel to the floor

5) Resist your shoulder's temptation to rotate your hands inward, and push yourself back to the starting stance. You should finish with your hands back at the externally rotated position.

MOBILITY MOMENT: PRESS ARCHETYPE FIXES

If you can't perform all or any of the press archetype progressions correctly with full range of motion, we need to help you remove the restrictions that are holding you back. Here are some mobilizations that will do just that. Find these exercises in The Shoulders section of the mobilizations appendix.

- Super front rack
- Banded bully with extension bias
- Triceps smash
- Shoulder internal rotation on lacrosse ball
- Sink mobilization
- Biceps barbell smash
- Pec wall smash

"JUST GET STRONGER ROTATORS" WON'T CUT IT

Have you ever seen that guy or girl in the gym who spends half an hour rotating their shoulders every which way with light dumbbells or cables? They're likely following the "Protect Your Rotator Cuff" program from some fitness magazine, which promises injury-free shoulders for life if you'll just beef up those pesky rotator cuffs. Not to be too cynical, but come on!

Our shoulders, just like the rest of the body, are wired for movement and so we shouldn't try to isolate certain muscles with the kind of exercises personal trainers are so fond of. If you've been sedentary for years or have experienced a period of inactivity after an injury, then strength training will be beneficial in providing baseline stability. But perfecting compound movements that are transferable to rowing, surfing and paddling and force your shoulders to stabilize in good positions—like ring rows, push presses and push-ups—are going to be far more beneficial than any fancy exercises that try to isolate the muscles of the rotator cuff.

It's better to focus your time on achieving correct positioning through full internal and external rotation, flexion and extension and applying a systems approach to removing restriction with mobility work than chasing the unicorn of unbreakable rotator cuffs with umpteen sets of the shoulder fly.

DON'T NEGLECT THE NECK

Text neck. Forward head position. Neck breathing. Hours on the water. Rounded shoulders and back. All of these create neural tension and stress in your poor old neck. In turn, the tight muscles, tendons, ligaments and fascia in your neck (including the neck flexors, scalenes, levator scapulae and multifidus) start tugging on the shoulders, chest and back, creating yet more tension in these areas. This limits range of motion in the shoulders, thereby reducing force production. It also puts you at greater risk of rotator cuff and pec tears.

And that's not all. The pre-tensioning in your neck when your head isn't aligned with your shoulders in a neutral position constricts your airway. As forward head on neck is usually paired with a rounded upper back and local hinge in your thoracic spine, you've already made it virtually impossible to breathe from your diaphragm.

So now you start chest and neck breathing, which uses 30 percent more energy. And the very place your body is now trying to breathe from—the upper chest and neck, is awash with added neural tension from trying to stabilize your misaligned head and cervical spine. This means that metabolically costly stress breathing becomes even more demanding.

Going upstream from the neck, many watermen and women suffer from tension headaches, migraines and TMJD that originates in tight tissues above the collarbone. And yet, when people are thinking upper body mobility, the neck is often last on the list, if it makes the list at all.

In contrast, it's vital that you regularly untack the neck tissues that are responsible for holding your head up and bridging your brain and spinal cord. It also pays to un-mat some of the sliding surfaces in your jaw, head and face. Try out the neck mobilizations a couple of times a week and see what a difference they make in improving your paddling, getting rid of those pesky tension headaches and improving your shoulder capacity and head position (don't forget to also mobilize downstream at the thoracic spine, chest and shoulders, too!).

MOBILITY MOMENT: NECK MOBILIZATIONS

If your neck is being unruly, we need to do something about it. Here are some exercises to help, which you'll find in The Shoulders section of the mobilizations appendix.

- Neck tack and floss
- Supraclavicle scrub

STANDARD #6
CAN YOU ACHIEVE OPTIMAL SHOULDER POSITIONING IN THE HANG ARCHETYPE?

MOTIVATION

The hang archetype is a fundamental athletic position. In the gym, we see the hang in the set up for the clean and snatch, and at the beginning and end of the deadlift. On the water, any time you're in the pull phase of your swimming or prone paddling stroke, that's the hang archetype. If you're missing internal rotation, the on-water implications include your elbows flaring out and your shoulders slumping forward.

During a short session you might not feel anything, but remember that pain is a lagging indicator. For endurance prone paddlers—Kai Lenny propelling himself 32 miles across the Channel of Bones or Joe Bark completing yet another Catalina Classic—they're sure going to know about it when they wake up with shoulder and elbow pain the next day. Same goes if you've paddled into pumping surf all day.

BRIEFING

So often when we're thinking about the function and challenges of the shoulder, we focus on your ability to create external rotation. But if you're missing internal rotation, this is just as much of a problem, as it reduces your overall rotation capacity.

We find that almost all our athletes have internal rotation issues, which encourages them to round their shoulders. This means they have an inability to preserve the hang archetype. In everyday life, you're in this shape when your arms are relaxed down by your sides and when you're carrying grocery bags back from the store or suitcases at the airport.

Before we start reinforcing a sustainable hang shape, let's first run a diagnostic check to assess your shoulders' internal rotation capacity.

THE SHOULDERS

SHOULDER INTERNAL ROTATION TEST #1: BASIC HANG SHAPE

1) Standing with your feet neutral and shoulder width apart, let your arms hang by your sides

2) Raise your elbows to shoulder height with your arms bent to 90 degrees. Your forearms should be parallel to the floor.

3) Keeping your elbows at shoulder height, swing your palms down and back while keeping your torso upright

4) If you feel like you have to change your head position, roll your shoulders forward or tilt your rib cage back, it's probably because you have some soft tissue stiffness. Deal with it using the exercises in The Shoulders section of the mobilizations appendix.

5) Try this exercise lying on your back

6) If either shoulder lifts off the ground, you're missing internal rotation

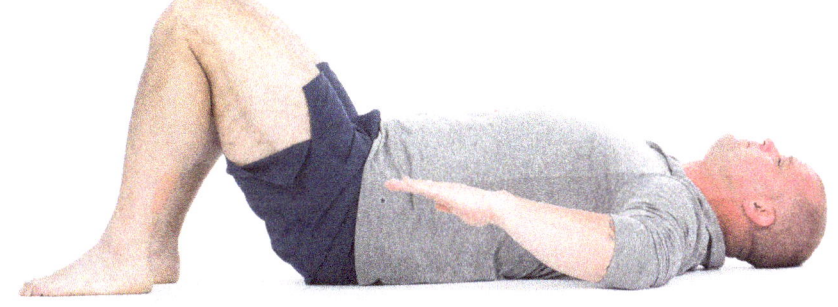

SHOULDER INTERNAL ROTATION TEST #2:
BRIDGE + INTERNAL ROTATION

1) Lie flat on your back

2) Bridge up by driving your hips toward the ceiling while keeping both feet flat on the floor

3) Put your hands together in the small of your back

4) Slowly lower your hips to the floor while keeping the back of both shoulders in contact with the ground

5) If you can't keep your shoulders on the floor (i.e. they raise up) or you feel pain or discomfort in the front of either shoulder, you're missing internal range. Don't feel bad—more than 90 percent of the athletes I work with are in the same boat.

THE SHOULDERS

SHOULDER INTERNAL ROTATION TEST #3: KETTLEBELL BEHIND THE BACK

1) Stand up straight with both arms behind your back and hands close together, with your palms facing backwards
2) Have someone place a light kettlebell in your hands and grip the handle as they do so
3) Hold it behind the middle of your lower back for a few seconds
4) Do you feel pain or discomfort in either or both shoulders? Then you're likely missing internal rotation.

So now that we've assessed your internal rotation capacity, it's time to further explore the hang archetype and work on undoing your restrictions.

As we've seen, it's important to go after the soft tissues surrounding the t-spine. But if we neglect the other musculature that attaches to the shoulder, we're going to severely limit progress. One of these muscles is the pec minor. If our chest muscles are tight they're going to tug on the front of the shoulder. That's why we advocate opening up the chest and anterior deltoid.

It's also a good idea to address the matted down tissues above the collar bone. The first rib is located here and the traps attach to the clavicle itself. So try using the first rib exercises in the mobilizations appendix such as the trap barbell/PVC pipe mobilization and the first rib pin and spin to buy yourself some slack in this area.

We can't just look at the front and back of our trunk when tackling shoulder restrictions, but also need to examine the musculature on the sides, too. Try the banded bully with extension bias variation that anchors around the elbow, and make friends with the lat smash (see the mobilizations appendix). Your poor paddling shoulders will thank you.

WATERMAN 2.0

HANG ARCHETYPE PROGRESSION #1: KETTLEBELL/DUMBBELL DEADLIFT

The deadlift is one of the go-to strength exercises because it builds power from the ground up and develops just about every muscle group in your body. For this section, the KB/DB variation also serves as a diagnostic for your internal rotation capacity and the integrity of your hang archetype. Can you pick an object up off the floor and stand up with it while maintaining a stable trunk and shoulder? We're about to find out.

1) Place a kettlebell or dumbbell on the floor in front of you
2) Perform the standing bracing sequence
3) Squat down to grip the weight. Make sure your feet are neutral, shoulder width apart and screwed into the ground. Your trunk should be in the braced neutral position and your abs and lats tight.
4) With your arms fully extended, slowly stand up. Keep the weight close to your legs on the way up, and clench your abs and butt as you pull the weight upward.
5) Once you're in the standing position, slowly lower the weight to the floor. Your gaze should follow the path of your trunk to keep your neck and head in an optimal position.
6) Perform 10 reps

   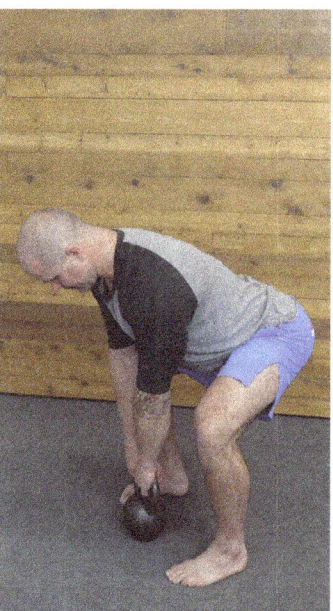

THE SHOULDERS

HANG ARCHETYPE PROGRESSION #2: HANGING KETTLEBELL/DUMBBELL SNATCH

For watermen and women, the snatch should be a staple exercise. It not only allows you to assess your internal rotation capacity and generate force from a hip hinge, but also your ability to transition quickly between the hang and overhead archetypes.

1) Pick up a kettlebell or dumbbell in one hand. Your feet should be in the same position as for the KB/DB deadlift.
2) Squeeze your butt to set your trunk to pelvis position, and contract your abs
3) Perform a quarter squat (don't let those knees cave in!) and as you quickly push your feet away and extend your legs out of the bottom position, squeeze your glutes hard
4) Shrug your shoulders and use this and the leg drive to pull the weight upward as fast as you can
5) As the weight approaches chest height, drop your body under it as you continue pulling your arm upward
6) Finish with your arm fully extended above your head
7) Complete 10 reps on each side

MOBILITY MOMENT: HANG ARCHETYPE FIXES

If you can't perform all the hang progressions and/or the internal rotation tests came back with a failing grade, you need to spend some time cleaning up the tacked down soft tissues that are holding you back (or, in this case, pushing your shoulder forward and encouraging you to tilt your rib cage backwards). Mix and match these mobilizations a few times a week and you'll reclaim some serious end range. You'll find all of these exercises in The Shoulders section of the mobilizations appendix.

- Banded bully with extension bias
- Shoulder internal rotation on lacrosse ball
- Sink mobilization
- Lower rib smash with internal rotation
- Shoulder capsule reset

When dealing with shoulder hot spots and formulating a plan of attack for improving end range, it's all too tempting to only focus on the shoulder capsule area itself. But as we've already explored, this ball-in-socket structure doesn't exist in isolation, but rather in a network of systems. Just as power and stability can be transferred across these intra- and inter-dependent systems, so can undue neural tension and restriction. That's why when we're tackling shoulder mobility, we need to also look upstream and downstream to the chest, arms, neck and, in particular, the thoracic spine.

A study by Michael Voight and Brian Thompson found that scapular instability is a contributing factor in 68 percent of rotator cuff problems and 100 percent of instability in the glenohumeral capsule (in layman's terms, where the shoulder socket ball sits).[7] If you've ever felt tightness along the

---

[7] Brian C. Thompson and Michael L. Voight, "The Role of the Scapula in the Rehabilitation of Shoulder Injuries," *Journal of Athletic Training*, 2000.

THE SHOULDERS

inside of your shoulder blade after a long session on the water or the erg, you'll understand just how involved the scapula is in every stroke.

That's why it's wise to mobilize this criminally undervalued area at least twice a week. My go-to move is placing the MWOD Gemini or 2 lacrosse balls taped together lengthways along the inside of my shoulder blade as I lie on my back. Then I slowly backstroke with my arm on that side, reaching behind my head as far as I can and preferably until my hand touches the floor.

I usually aim for 50 to 100 "strokes" per side. To create more side-to-side shear, start each stroke with your hand on the opposite thigh. Reposition your mobility tool of choice several times to hit the upper and lower t-spine musculature.

CHAPTER 6
THE FEET AND ANKLES

"There is wisdom in waves. Some surfers see it right away, others never do. To find success in surfing, we must learn to be in harmony with nature."
—Gerry Lopez

In our mobility and movement system, we always prioritize spine first, as you'll have seen earlier in the book and on mobilitywod.com. But if your foot dexterity is lacking and positioning is off, so is everything else. A ducked out foot with a collapsed arch causes all kinds of problems upstream, from a caved in knee to internally rotated hips and shoulders to a wonky trunk. In the previous chapter we explored how important head and neck integrity is to proper paddling, surfing and rowing. Well the feet are arguably even more vital.

The feet are meant to be sensory organs when we're on the water. They can't do their job if you've deadened them with years of wearing overly thick and restrictive shoes, letting them get weak from too much sitting and doing nothing to liberate them when they get tight. Eastern cultures understand that the feet are the lightning rods that connect the rest of the body to the ground and, for our purposes in this book, to the craft that propels you across the water. Have you ever had a killer foot massage? Then you'll likely recall how much better your entire being felt afterwards. You don't have to pay a professional to get such a feeling or the associated soft tissue benefits. Instead, spend a few minutes a day gently rolling each foot across a tool like my MWOD Foot Roller.

And we can't look at the foot without the ankle, as it's part of the same complex. If your ankles are missing full capacity, you can't get into the archetypal shapes that water sports and life demand. Lack of range at the ankle gives you less movement options and forces you to make bigger corrections further upstream, such as by collapsing inwards at the knee, doing funky things at the hip or sticking your butt out when you standup paddle.

THE FEET AND ANKLES

Not to mention leaning too far forward, which not only stresses the lower back, but also sends undue tension back down to the feet and ankles and sets your calves on fire. Such over-compensations put excess stress on your joints, stiffen your soft tissues and send trouble all the way up your body. So clearly, we need to go after your ankles, too.

Continual misuse and abuse of the feet can lead to the calcaneus—aka the heel bone—getting locked into place. Lack of motion in this area of the foot manifests itself in lots of nasty ways. It can lead to you overloading the Achilles tendon when you point your toes down. This not only agitates the rest of the foot, but can also cause bone spurs on the back of the heel.

We also see that when you're in a crouch stance on your board and lack full range of motion in the calcaneus, you can't generate a good line of force through the lower leg. So over time you start to get tendonitis issues and matted down tissue along the posterior tibialis and the other structures on the inside of the shin.

Restriction around the heel also compromises the eversion and inversion your feet need to run the rails on your board and make micro adjustments to the constantly changing stimuli that waves present. So if your calcaneus is glued down, you can't be as reactive or make all those nifty turns you've been trying so hard to master. Oh, and it can also contribute to forefoot issues like bunions and dialup that pesky plantar fasciitis.

To see how much play you have in the calcaneus region, plant your feet on the floor in a neutral stance. While keeping all your toes (especially the big toe) on the ground, initiate left to right movement in your hip and knee. You should be able to see your foot rolling inward and outward without pain. If you can't, then your calcaneus is locked in place. Try this quick mobilization to liberate it:

Calcaneus/Lateral Malleolus Liberator

1) Sit down on the ground with your shoes and socks off

2) Take a Yoga Tune Up Ball and place it in front of the ankle bone on the outside of your foot (or lateral malleolus to we orthopedic medicine folk), while placing your knee on the ground

3) Use one hand to pin the forefoot and push down with the other on the inside of the heel, as if driving it to the floor. Do at least 2 minutes on each side and then repeat on the other foot.

4) If the skin on the inside of the ankle is tacked down, use the ball to twist the skin and then give it a whack. Repeat for 2 minutes.

5) The test/re-test for this is to go into a deep squat and see how much more motion you have in the ankle, and how much easier it is to keep your big toe on the ground

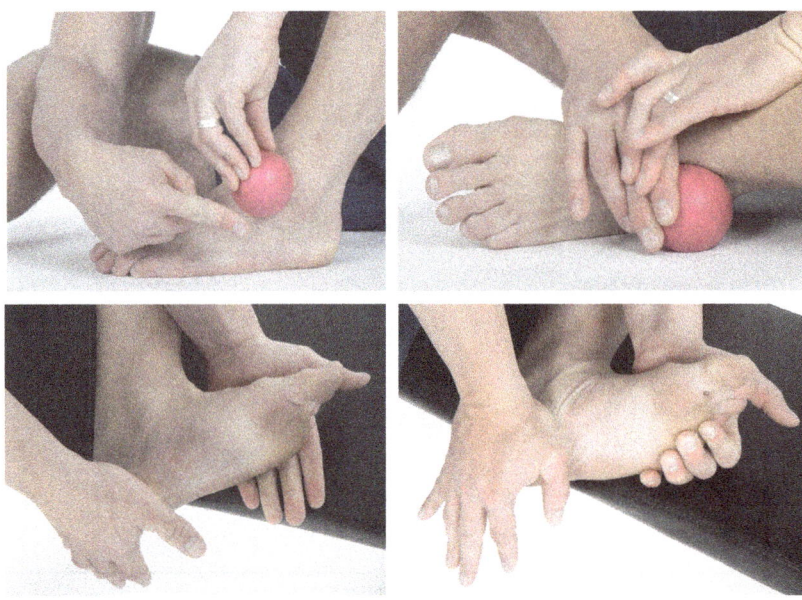

THE FEET AND ANKLES

Far too many of us pay little to no attention to our feet. What did you do with your feet last time you got off your board or out of your boat? I'll wager that the answer is nothing. Ok, clever clogs, maybe "put shoes back on" was your answer. In which case, were they flat, flexible and minimal shoes that allowed your feet to function normally? Or a heeled shoe? Maybe flip flops? If it was either of the last two, we need to talk!

Yes, I know flip flops are technically flat. But because of the design, they also require the ligamentous structures of your feet to be permanently turned on to stop them sliding off as they flit around. The result? You mess up the Windlass Mechanism responsible for supporting your arch. Over time the navicular bone drops toward the floor, permanently collapsing the arch and giving you "island feet." As a result, your feet hunt for artificial stability by ducking outward and collapsing inward. Your knees and hips follow suit, which then messes up the relationship of your pelvis and spine. Now your lower back is under increased tension. A seemingly innocuous foot issue has suddenly become a whole-body problem.

On the other end of the scale are heeled shoes. These cause you to tilt forward as you walk, which moves your body in front of its natural midline and introduces neural tension throughout your system. Heels—and we're not just talking stilettos, but ANY significant heel over about 4 mm—also shorten your heel cords, increasing your risk of an Achilles tear. The bottom of your calf then starts tugging on your plantar fascia, and suddenly your feet hurt all the time. As the soleus and gastrocnemius (the major muscles in your calves) are under non-stop tension, they lock up too, which can start pulling on your knees.

Another stress on the knees is that when you're in heeled shoes you need to counterbalance the instability caused by the exaggerated wedge under the back of your foot. So many times people start letting their knees come forward to keep the see-saw level. The pelvis also tilts forward, which reduces your hip extension—a similar impact to sitting. In addition, the tilting puts pressure on the forefoot and toes, which you've already ticked off by forcing them into a narrow toe box.

Once again, a simple lifestyle or environmental choice—i.e. what you put on your feet most of the day—has a massive mechanical impact. Instead of wearing heels or flip flops, try to go barefoot as much as you can. When you can't (bare feet at school or the office are probably not socially acceptable), choose flexible shoes with zero or minimal heel to toe drop and a wide toe box that allows your toes to splay without hindrance. This is one of the most important things you can do to start restoring your feet to their naturally functional state.

WHAT KIND OF BIRD ARE YOU: A DUCK OR A PIGEON?

The answer of course is "neither." You're a human being. So why are you walking around with your feet ducked out or with inward-facing pigeon toes? "I was born that way" is not a valid answer because although genetics influence foot shape and size, we are all born with feet that we can keep neutral (i.e. pointing between straight and 10 degrees). Only over time do we start developing poor standing and movement patterns that create chronic stiffness and start to pull our foot angle hither and yon.

QUICK TEST: FOOT TORQUE

To better understand the positive effects of screwing a neutral foot into the ground, we're going to do a quick test. With our hands.

1) Crouch on all fours
2) Place your left palm on the ground with fingers splayed
3) Your hand should be flat on the ground, with your forearm vertical above it as if you were going to do a push-up

THE FEET AND ANKLES

4) Keeping your hand on the ground, externally rotate it counter-clockwise like you were undoing a screw

5) Watch what happens to your palm. It should lift off the ground a little.

6) The same principle of torque applies to your feet. When you have your feet in a neutral position and screw them into the ground (keeping your big toe down), your navicular and bone lifts up, enhancing the stabilizing potential of your arch. To see this in action, get up and stand with your feet straight and shoulder width apart.

7) Keeping your feet planted, externally rotate the left foot counter-clockwise and the right foot clockwise until you feel tension in the outside of your feet, hips and glutes. You should also see your foot arch noticeably rise up in both feet.

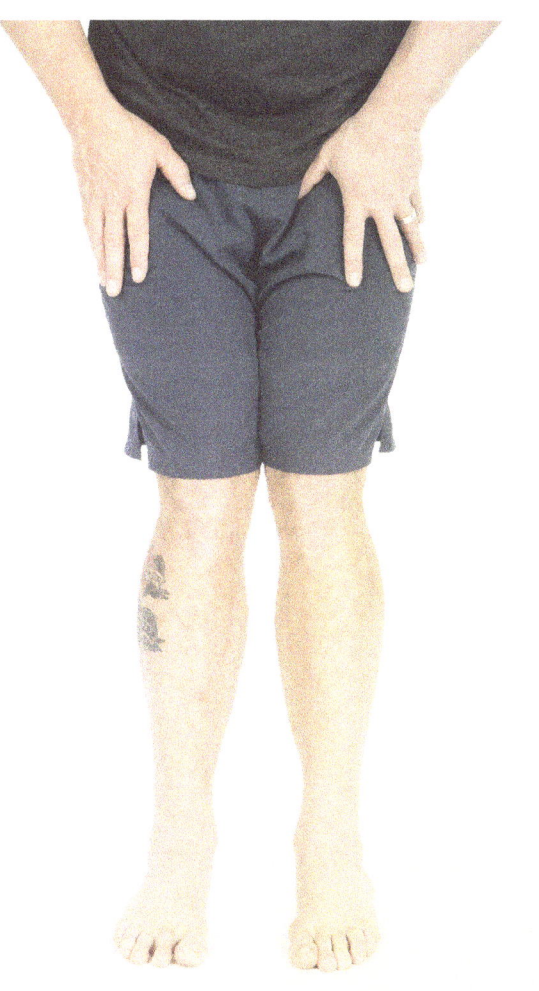
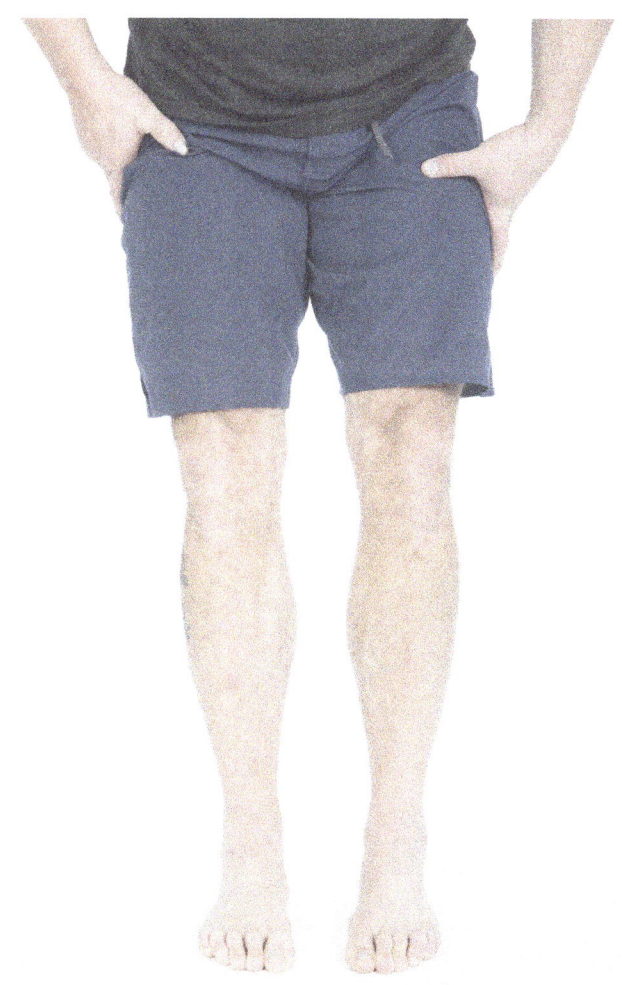

The most common questions we get about the feet are about the arch. It's no great surprise, as the sporting goods market is flooded with so-called "arch supporting" shoes and orthotics and yet people's arches are collapsing left and right and are frequently painful. But before we debunk the marketing myth of arch support or start addressing how to reclaim our foot's natural capabilities, we need to deal with an essential truth: calling it "the arch" is misleading and over-simplifies the complexity of this essential mechanism.

The arch is not one single entity. In fact, it's comprised of 3 structures, namely the medial longitudinal arch, the lateral longitudinal arch and the anterior transverse arch. These 3 combine to create what is commonly referred to as "the arch."

The footwear industry would like us to believe that our poor weak little arches can't hold themselves up without a huge hunk of carbon fiber or plastic glued into our shoes. Wrongo! If you look at an arched bridge (like the one trains pass over), how many supports do you see in the middle? None. Because arches don't need third party backup. The arch is its own support. So let's stop relying on shoe company advertising ploys and start restoring these amazing arches to their full capabilities.

Even if you've annihilated your arches through poor positioning and wearing the wrong shoes and orthotics that are a Band-Aid at best, all hope is not lost. Certainly, it's not ideal that you've stretched out the ligaments in your feet to the point that they can no longer sustain a normally aligned navicular bone. But the ligamentous structures are only one of the foot's primary support mechanisms. So let's try working on the other two.

While we can't do much about restoring your ligaments and tendons— other than me imploring you to go barefoot whenever possible and replace the flip flops and heeled shoes with flat footwear—you can re-program the muscles and fascia in your feet with just a few minutes of daily mobility exercises.

Another very simple way to improve the level of available foot support is to work on screwing your feet into the ground. In a webinar on mobilitywod.com that my friend and colleague Dr. Roop Sihota hosted, he prescribed a simple and remarkably effective piece of homework for attendees: while standing with your feet straight, accumulate 10 to 20 minutes a day of screwing your feet into the ground. To do so, stand with your feet straight and keep your big toes on the ground as you turn the left foot counter-clockwise and the right one clockwise until you feel tension in your hips and the outside of your butt. Make sure your feet stay planted as you do so, rather than ducking them out. Just try 1 minute at a time, so you don't fatigue too quickly. You will be amazed how activating your arches becomes an autonomous habit if you do this every day for a couple of weeks.

Of course, nobody maintains peak tension in their feet all day long. They'd feel like someone had beaten them with a bat. But just firing those arches up regularly can re-awaken natural foot behavior on land that you can then apply when you're out on your board or in your boat. This isn't just for flat footers. No matter how high your arches are, you need to try this drill.

If a car's wheels are wonky, trying to strengthen the sub-frame is hardly going to matter. That's why in the rest of this chapter we're going to further explore the importance of correct foot positioning, the ills of missing ankle capacity and foot tightness and strategies for restoring full range so you can paddle and boat faster and more safely.

We'll also look at what you're doing right and wrong on your board, in your craft and in your land-based training. Once again, we will try to break down mechanics to their most basic elements, re-tool your technique and reinforce it in the gym. I hardly think that when she was winning an Olympic gold medal, Erin Cafaro Mackenzie was worrying about her foot position, or that on mile 31 of the Molokai 2 Oahu race, Connor Baxter was checking to see if his arches were still in play.

By getting proper foot positions down on land—as *The Talent Code* author Daniel Coyle would say "myelinating your pathways"—we'll try to make sure that your feet are also optimally aligned on the water and that you're not defaulting to positions that get your whole body out of whack, reduce power and endurance and increase injury risk. Now let's put our best foot forward (yeah, I know that was horrible).

STANDARD #7
ARE YOU STANDING, WALKING, RUNNING, STEPPING AND JUMPING WITH NEUTRAL FEET?

MOTIVATION

If your feet are ducked out or pigeoned in, it's going to be incredibly difficult for you to align your legs, hips and spine correctly when you stand, let alone when you walk, run, surf, paddle, row, etc. What we should be aiming for in every situation where your feet are on the ground (or on your board), is for both of them to be in a neutral position, which is a fancy way of saying they should be straight. This will not only offset problems at the foot and ankle, but will also help prevent issues further up at the knee and hip.

BRIEFING

Sometimes I worry that when I'm walking down a street, I'm going to smack headfirst into a lamppost because I'm preoccupied with other people's feet. Nope, this isn't some weird fetish. Rather, I'm astonished by how many people are traipsing around with horrible foot mechanics.

The foot and ankle system is incredibly complex. There are 26 bones, 33 joints and more than 100 tendons, muscles and ligaments in each foot, without taking into account what's going on above it at the ankle. To put it into context, that means more than a quarter of the bones in your entire body reside in your feet. When we add in ligaments and fascia, we have 3 unbelievably strong support mechanisms that are capable of carrying us through more than a century of active years on and off the water. Unfortunately, the complexity of the system also means there's almost unlimited potential for disaster.

Can you recall the first time you went surfing or paddleboarding? Chances are your feet were fried afterwards. Maybe they even cramped while you were still on the board. Most people assume that's just because we're challenging ourselves with reactive balance on a profoundly unstable and fluid surface. There's some truth in that, but for the most part, the reason your feet are giving you grief is that they're weak.

You're not going to be your best as a paddler, rower or surfer unless you remove restrictions, strengthen underused structures and stop moving your feet through improper motor patterns. First up, let's help you reclaim the best foot position you're capable of.

We'll start with a quick test to see what we're looking at when it comes to your personal podiatry.

FOOT POSITION QUICK TEST #1: SITTING TO STANDING

Standing? Really? A bit basic, isn't it? Not really. We consider standing to be a complex skill that most of us do wrong. We covered how to stand during the bracing sequence, but indulge me while we go over it again in the context of foot positioning.

1) Sit down on a chair or box

2) Stand up

3) What position are your feet in? If they're ducked out or pigeoned in, you failed the test. If they're straight ahead, or at least only turned out to a maximum of 10 degrees, you passed. At least partially. Let's do it again.

4) Sit back down and stand up. Pay attention to your knees. If they caved in, you either reinforced that poor foot positioning from step 3, or you undermined the good work your feet did.

5) Repeat the sitting to standing steps, but this time try pulling your shoulder blades back and down, sitting straight up and squeezing your abs

6) Now, while you're still seated, plant your feet shoulder width apart pointing straight ahead and screw each foot into the ground. As you push yourself into a standing position, stay active and make sure your knees come out instead of collapsing inward. Also, make sure you maintain ab tension.

FOOT POSITION QUICK TEST #2: BOX/BENCH/STOOL STEP-UP

Ok, so now we've examined how you stand, we need to go further and look at how you step.

1) Stand in front of a box, bench or stool that will support your weight

2) Step onto the object with your left foot, keeping your torso as upright as possible and pushing yourself up into a standing position using just that leg

3) Look at the left foot. If it's straight or straight-ish and your arch isn't collapsed (even if you have "flat" feet you still have a slight arch), you aced it. If the duck or pigeon have come home to roost again, you didn't.

4) Repeat the test with your right foot. It's not unusual for one foot to behave itself while the other misbehaves. But to move efficiently and safely you must have 2 fully functioning pegs. Unless you're planning to become a flamingo.

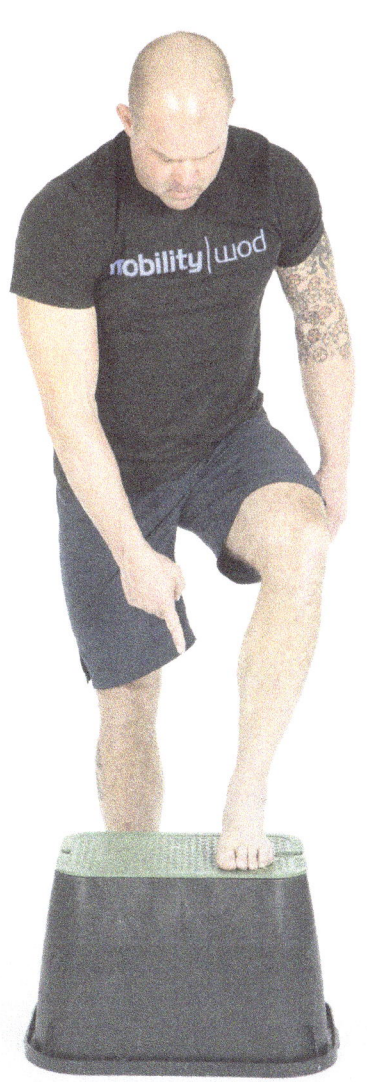 

FOOT POSITION QUICK TEST #3: JUMPING ROPE

1) If you have a jump rope, then use it for this test. If not, just jump lightly without it so your feet leave the floor a couple of inches.

2) Jump for 2 minutes and have a friend video you

3) Review the footage and see if your feet stay neutral throughout. Your arches should not collapse and you should land on the balls of your feet, lightly transitioning to a heel tap to unload your calves before springing back up again. One form tip: point your toes down with each jump. If your feet are turned in or out, your knees are caving in or you're landing on your heels, you need to try again.

MOBILITY MOMENT: FIXING YOUR FEET

If you had problems keeping neutral feet with engaged arches during any of the quick tests, don't give up hope. By dedicating just 10 minutes a day to foot, ankle and lower leg mobility, you can dramatically improve range of motion, restore slide and glide and de-gristle tissues matted down from years of neglect and abuse. Pick 2 of these exercises and spend 2 to 5 minutes per foot on each one. Yes, it's going to feel ugly, but you want to be a better waterman/woman, right? Then knuckle down and get it done. Find all of these exercises in The Feet and Ankles section of the mobilizations appendix.

- Foot smash
- Posterior tibialis tack and floss
- Banded ankle capsule mobilization with Voodoo Floss
- Toe plantar flexion
- Double ball ankle tack and strip
- Heel cord tack, twist and floss
- Shin anterior compartment smash

THE FEET AND ANKLES

People with high arches have a mechanical advantage over flat footers in some ways, as the natural shock absorbing function of their feet has remained intact. But while high arches are certainly not undesirable, they can cause some issues of their own.

One is that maintaining an active arch all day can feed a lot of neural tension into your foot, ankle and lower leg system. This tightness can run all the way up the inside of your leg, and can result in difficulty keeping the big toe down when screwing your feet into the ground, whether that's standing on a SUP/surfboard, squatting or jumping.

To address the issue, try these 2 mobilizations. First, sit on the ground and put the outside of your right foot on the floor. Grab a lacrosse or Yoga Tune Up Ball and press it into the inside of your heel. Do this for a few minutes and then repeat on the other side.

Next, we're going to move up a little higher and take on the posterior tibialis. If you have a significant arch in your foot, it's likely that this muscle, which runs up the inside of your shin bone (or tibia, if you want to get all technical) is brutally tight. To address this, again rest the outside of your right lower leg on the ground. Take your ball of choice or a kettlebell handle and carefully apply pressure to the area inside of the shin bone, being cautious to stay on the soft tissues. Slowly move up and down and back and forth to iron out the stiffness for a few minutes, then repeat on the other leg.

It's not just the inside of the lower leg that gets really annoyed by having to hold up your arches. On the outside, the peroneals can get fried as they continually work hard to keep the integrity of that nice high arch. To help alleviate this tension and feed some slack back into the system, you can try placing a lacrosse ball on the outside of your ankle and resting your lower leg on it.

Then push down with your hands on the inside of your ankle and rotate, flex and dorsiflex your foot for a couple of minutes. Move the ball up the outside of the calf. If you find a tight spot, hang out for a while. If you need a greater stimulus, place a second ball on the inside of the ankle/calf to add more pressure.

WATERMAN 2.0

QUICK TEST: POLLING YOUR PLANTAR FLEXION

Plantar flexion is a prerequisite for creating instant stiffness when quickly changing foot position on a surfboard, SUP, slackline or other such surface. It's also essential for kneeling on your SUP, sprint canoeing and when trying to emulate our good mate Jamie Mitchell on a prone paddleboard (good luck catching Mitcho, by the way). Let's see how capable your feet are with this simple test:

1) Kneel down on the ground, with your torso upright

2) Sit back onto your heels

3) Your hamstrings and calves should touch, and the instep of both feet should comfortably touch the ground

4) Camping out for a few minutes a day in this position will not only feed slack into the fascia and musculature of the feet and ankles, but will also feel great on your quads if they're all gnarly from a long rowing or squatting session. If you feel restricted in this position, do the quad smash and then repeat this mobilization. Also, check out the shin anterior compartment smash as tightness along the front of the shin is often a limiting factor, too.

THE FEET AND ANKLES

STANDARD #8
CAN YOU PERFORM A LUNGE AND MASTER WARRIOR POSE II?

MOTIVATION

Many people often throw poor hip extension into the mix, further inhibiting their ability to get into that lunge stance and preventing them from creating rigidity from the back leg. Then, in addition to placing bucket loads of neural tension on our ligaments and tendons and shearing forces through the musculature of the hips and lower back, we also start trying to make up for the mechanical malfeasance by trying to create an extra hinge in the knee. So now both the front and back knees are in jeopardy.

BRIEFING

Ok, don't be freaked out, but we're about to drop some yoga knowledge on you. If you've been surfing for a while and know your way around a yoga studio, you'll probably get the answer to the following question (hint: the answer might be in the standard name): what yoga pose does the surf stance closely resemble? Yep, you got it. Warrior Pose II.

The reason that this position is so transferable to surfing is that it requires you to create stabilizing torque in the back leg by screwing the foot into the ground – just as a boxer or fencer does. All too often we see surfers who have no idea about this concept, and as a result, put most of their weight on the front leg. This tilts them forward of their midline, not only messing up their balance on the wave, but also overtaxing the front leg. If they collapse the arch of the front foot, the forward knee caves in. That's why we see so many MCL (medial collateral ligament) strains and tears in our surfers. There's also a lot of tendonitis in the posterior tibialis (muscle that runs up the inside of the calf) going around.

Meanwhile, that errant back leg is also in disarray. If it's screwed into the ground correctly, then it's providing a stable platform that helps us maintain integrity to handle bumps on the wave face, changes in direction and all the other things the board likes to do as it skims across the water. But if we're lacking internal rotation in the back hip, the arch of the rear foot will collapse and we'll start looking to the ligaments of the foot and lower leg to provide artificial stability.

To make sure things never go that far, let's help you through a lunge and Warrior Pose II progression that's directly transferable to surfing. Not a surfer? Do it anyway to test and advance your understanding of how to create torque from the feet up.

LUNGE PROGRESSION #1: STANDARD LUNGE

Before we start adding weight, an overhead stability component and the motor control demands of the Warrior Pose II, we first need to be able to perform a basic lunge with correct form.

1) Perform the standing bracing sequence
2) Keeping your torso upright, take a large step forward with your right foot
3) As you plant your right foot, screw it into the ground
4) Lower your torso into a surfer's crouch without rounding your lower back
5) Maintain working tension in your abs and the arches of your feet

6) Your weight should be evenly distributed between your front and back legs

7) Switch sides

LUNGE PROGRESSION #2: WAITER'S LUNGE WITH DUMBBELL/KETTLEBELL

To test the integrity of your lunge archetype, we're now going to add a motor control load that elevates your center of gravity and forces your body to deal with an open torque system at the shoulder while performing the lunge.

1) Grip a dumbbell with your left hand

2) Perform the standing bracing sequence

3) With your left palm facing you and thumb forward, press the DB/KB overhead. Your thumb should now be facing backwards.

4) Do a lunge with your right foot forward

5) Return to the starting position

6) Perform 10 reps

7) Repeat with the opposite arm and leg

8) You might wobble a bit from side to side, which is normal as your body reacts to the added demands of the dumbbell or kettlebell. But keep at it until you can maintain full extension and external rotation in the weight-bearing shoulder while maintaining hip torque in your front and back legs.

LUNGE PROGRESSION #3: WARRIOR POSE II

The different orientation of your hips and shoulders in Warrior Pose II make it a valuable practice tool as we try to stop you hanging on your front leg and create a more evenly balanced, stable stance. Remember that it ALL starts with optimal foot positioning.

1) Stand next to a wall with your core braced. We're going to use the wall to emphasize activating abduction.

2) Lock the outer right heel against a wall (toes should NOT be against the wall) with the foot angled inward approximately 30 degrees away from the wall

3) Externally rotate your left hip to 90 degrees and step out to bend your hip and knee to 90 degrees

4) Push the right heel into the wall with the force generated from your hip abductors (in other words, try to push the wall away from you)

5) Abduct your shoulders to 90 degrees and use your right hand to assist with pushing the wall away in order to keep your spine as neutral as possible

6) The position should resemble the starting stance of a fencer. Once mastered, progress to not using a wall.

If you want to improve your footwork on your board, stop leaping one legged between Bosu balls and start re-training the abductor hallucis. Wait, the whatta? Yep, the abductor hallucis. This small but potentially mighty muscle group runs from your heel to your big toe, and is involved in many foot and leg functions—from inverting your heel to rotating your tibia when you screw your feet into the ground to flexing and abducting the big toe. When functioning properly, it also controls the inward rolling of your foot—the kind of motion that causes valgus knee, an internally rotated hip and all the resulting upstream issues.

If you sit most of the day and wear cushy shoes, your abductor hallucis is probably in the same shape as that old Christmas sweater grandma bought you 8 years ago—dusty and underused. Luckily, bringing the hallucis back to life doesn't require a rigorous training program. Rather, you just need to stand and walk more, go barefoot whenever possible and use a flexible shoe that allows your foot to function naturally at all other times.

WATERMAN 2.0

SORTING OUT SURFER'S TOE (= TURF TOE)

One of the foot issues we see a lot with our football players is turf toe. You probably know it as surfer's toe, but regardless of the terminology, it's the same issue on turf or in the surf. Basically, it's a sprain of one or more of the ligaments that attach to the big toe. And it hurts like hell.

With football players, turf toe often occurs when they cut and change direction rapidly. Though you're obviously not trying to feint and dodge around 300 pound linemen on your board, you are trying to move along and across it rapidly as you react to water conditions and adapt your position accordingly. Plus, you're gripping the deck with your toes and trying to prevent the rest of your body from going over the side of the rails as you respond to all the stimuli the water serves up.

Just as with football players, surfers can often prevent this painful condition. Freeing up the tacked down tissues along the inside of the foot using the exercises listed in this chapter and the mobilizations appendix is the first order of business. Then we need to make sure you're not hanging on the medial side (inside) of your legs while you surf. Once again, screwing your feet into the ground helps bolster this medial seam and prevents the arch and, soon enough, the knee from collapsing inward.

CHAPTER 7
THE HANDS, WRISTS, ELBOWS AND ARMS

"I could not help concluding this man had the most supreme pleasure while he was driven so fast and so smoothly by the sea."
—Captain James Cook

In the previous chapter, we examined the importance of the foot complex as a primary feedback mechanism for the waterman. But it's not the only extremity that we need to put under the microscope as we reach for full capacity and optimal mechanics. We must also take a long hard look at the hands and everything upstream, including the wrists, forearms, elbows, biceps and triceps.

When functioning correctly, your hands are powerful sensory organs. On the water, they can function as data gatherers by themselves, such as when you're swimming, prone paddling or body surfing, and can also provide invaluable balance—see Laird using his opposite hand to steady himself against the ferocity of the Teahupo'o "Millennium Wave," and in the process, redefining what's possible in big wave surfing.

When you add a paddle, the hands become even more potent motion sensors. Sure, you're using your eyes and proprioception to gauge your positioning, but the paddle also enables your hands to collect invaluable, real-time feedback about the thousands of micro changes that occur when you take to the water.

Just as with the feet, your hands are one of the most nerve-dense areas of the body. Every time you push the water away in the ocean or your paddle wiggles in a wave, those nerves send impulses through the nerve spindles that run up your arm, through your neck and shoulder and into the command center of the central nervous system.

This is not a one-way connection. Large areas of the brain are devoted to the sensory input delivered by your hands. Once the information is processed—again in fractions of a second—the brain accesses its stored motor patterns and sends data whizzing back down the neural pathways to your hand and the paddle, oar or whatever it's gripping. You make the necessary corrections while simultaneously collecting the next data set.

If there are no impingements, this two-way information flow happens seamlessly and at maximum speed. But as we've seen already throughout this book, soft tissue tightness clamps the canals responsible for carrying neural feedback to and from the hands, limiting your processing power like a garden hose with your foot stalling the water flow. So now you're working harder to go slower.

In this chapter we're going to examine the capacity of your lower arm joints—i.e. the wrists and elbows—and see how this impacts your water sports performance. We'll also take a crack at restoring slide and glide to the soft tissues located upstream and downstream of these joints, as well as looking at the importance of hand position and mobility.

STANDARD #9
DO YOU HAVE FULL WRIST FLEXION?

MOTIVATION

Are you able to paddle with junky wrists? Absolutely. In fact, I'm living proof (see the upcoming Me, My Wrist and I sidebar). And yet if our wrists are not coming close to end range flexion, we're severely limiting the capabilities of our hands as sensation absorbers and steering rudders. And I don't care how good your J-stroke is: you're not going to out-technique crappy positioning.

If the wrist is at an odd angle, then the elbow flares out. Suddenly, the shoulder is unable to sit back in the socket and so it compensates forward. Now you're working around your pec each stroke. As you're no longer generating power through rotation, you make another compromise and start hinging from the thoracic spine. Now the cervical spine is upset and overextended, and your head moves forward of your midline.

The lumbar spine also gets thrown off kilter by all the upstream drama, and now the relationship between the lower back and pelvis is messed up. You push your butt back to provide artificial stability, while the knees cave in and the arches follow suit. Yes, poor lower arm positioning can start a volcanic eruption of positional doom that's very difficult to stop (the opposite of the mechanical mudslide that happens when things go wrong further up the chain, like when the head, neck and shoulder are misaligned).

BRIEFING

If the wrists lack full flexion and extension, then the sensory organs of the hands are going to be compromised from both neuromuscular and mechanical perspectives. Similarly, if you can't get your wrists in the correct position to either move your hands through the water or manipulate your paddle or oar, then you're unlikely to get close to your speed and power potential.

In today's world, our fingers are constantly on the go—hammering away at our keyboards, swiping our tablet screens and picking away to send text messages. Putting the wrists, hands and fingers in these weird, unnatural positions feeds undue neural tension up through our arms thousands of times a day. Is it any wonder we're bedeviled by carpal tunnel syndrome, junky forearms and elbow tendonitis (aka tennis, golf and paddler's elbow)?

We're going to see how badly all of these behaviors have messed you up, and have a go at improving your wrist flexion capacity.

WRIST FLEXION QUICK TEST: PLANCHE PUSH-UP

Carl Paoli, friend, creator of freestyleconnection.com and author of the best-selling book *Free+Style*, can perform push-ups in just about any conceivable position. When he's feeling particularly sadistic, he likes to put me and our athletes into variations like the planche, which quickly raises mobility and motor control red flags.

WATERMAN 2.0

In this case, you simply cannot get into and maintain the top position of a planche push-up if you're lacking full wrist flexion, let alone complete a full rep with correct form (shoulders externally rotated, elbows tucked in, etc.).

1) Get on all fours on a flat surface

2) Assume the push-up starting position, but invert your hands so that they're behind your forearms

3) Keeping your hands flat on the ground with fingers splayed and your forearms vertical (so your shoulders are directly above your hands and elbows), assume the top starting position

4) With your elbows tucked in, your feet together and your abs and butt braced, lower into the bottom position of the push-up, then use your arms to force your body back to the starting stance

5) If you can't even get into the top position, don't bother with the motion component yet. If you can achieve the starting stance, but cave or feel pain during the planche push-up itself, then console yourself with the fact that you're part way there. Unfortunately, there are no participation prizes other than picking a couple of the following mobility exercises and performing them several times a week until you can master this entire progression.

MOBILITY MOMENT: WRIST FLEXION PRESCRIPTION

If you fell short on the previous quick test, you don't have enough play in your wrists. To change this, I've come up with these mobilizations to liberate your soft tissues above and below the joint. As with other range of motion limitations, a lack of wrist flexion typically can't be blamed on the joint itself, unless you have a history of breaking it. It's usually stiffness in the hands and forearms that's robbing the wrists of their natural capacity. So let's do something about it. Find all of these exercises in The Hands, Wrists, Elbows and Arms section of the mobilizations appendix.

- Forearm ball smash
- Forearm barbell rollout
- Leopard Claw forearm scrape

When we're addressing wrist issues, I'm not speaking to you in abstract generalities. I know all too well the lower arm destroying results of going hard in sub-optimal positions. In my case, "going hard" meant paddling several hours a day, often twice a day, 300+ days a year. Plus, I'd broken my right wrist a couple of times, broken my hand and dislocated my elbow. And I had no soft tissue practice. Not exactly a recipe for optimal function.

While a good builder doesn't blame his tools, indulge me for a moment while I partially blame my tools! Our kayak paddles had a massive offset, so I had to lift my front elbow really high on each stroke or my wrist would be jeopardized. The trouble is that when you're talking thousands of strokes per week, the ol' elbow doesn't want to go high. So I was slamming down on my right wrist over and over again. If you've seen a video of me performing the clean and jerk, that's why I have to use a mixed grip—because my right wrist is shot.

Luckily, today's paddles have far less of an offset. Plus, the double-bent shaft was an ergonomic blessing from the heavens and means that even with my wrist issues, I can paddle for hours without pain. But having better equipment doesn't let me off the mobility hook. I still regularly smash my forearms, perform banded wrist distractions and work on hand dexterity.

Neither is having a brilliant paddle an excuse for horrible form. The last stroke should look the same as the first, no matter how long you're on the water. And neither should you see the shoulder coming forward, elbow flaring or wrist cocking. If that's what you're doing all the time, even that feather light, ergonomically dreamy paddle won't save your soft tissues, wrists, elbows and shoulders.

QUICK TEST: BIRD DOG

One of the ways to see if you have normal wrist function is to have a training partner or coach watch you do the bird dog. Not only is this a great stability exercise, it can also serve as a diagnostic tool and window into potential wrist issues in the extensors which run all the way up your forearms and attach on the lateral (outside) part of the elbow and the flexors on the medial side (inside).

To do the bird dog:

1) Get down on all fours

2) Raise the left leg until it's straight behind you

3) At the same time, lift your right arm straight up with your hand open and palm facing down

4) Your wrist should be in a neutral position without any funky up-down and/or left-right compensations. If you can't achieve this, then try some of the exercises in this chapter or the mobilizations appendix.

STANDARD #10
CAN YOU FULLY ARTICULATE YOUR HANDS WHEN YOUR ELBOWS ARE EXTENDED?

MOTIVATION

If you spend most of your water time in a canoe, you're lucky that this discipline allows you to maintain a neutral grip with fairly low demands on the overhead shoulder. Plus, double torque paddles unload the wrist compared to those old self-torture implements my friends and I used to wield. And yet even canoeists wrap their wrists to help them deal with the extreme forces involved in paddling fast and hard, and are still subject to the wrist drifting toward the radial side (outside) when their grip is off.

SUPers have a different challenge. While the bottom hand is (or should be!) neutral, the exaggerated overhead element with the top hand places an unusual load on the shoulder. And as we've seen, as soon as one shoulder cheats its way forward to hunt for artificial stability, those poor elbows and wrists are in trouble. And don't get me started on the elbow, wrist and hand issues kayakers face, with all that twisting and turning of the paddle.

Rowers aren't off the hook either. Though the movement of the oar and the erg handle should be consistent, neural tension from over-gripping and fatigue start to kick in after a while. This causes the wrist to go into flexion—no wonder all the rowers we work with have such gristly forearms and sore hands.

Basically, if you're a paddler or rower, you have atypical mechanical challenges at the hand, wrist and elbow. Mobilizing will certainly help, but unless we also go after strength and positioning, all the forearm smashing in the world is just putting out fires.

BRIEFING

I often say that the hands are crafty. The old Russian coach who I "borrowed" this saying from meant that our hands and wrists are so dexterous that they can mask a lot of mechanical faults higher up the chain at the elbow and shoulder. However, poor shoulder positioning, typically expressed as forward translation and the resulting flared elbow, will eventually create more problems than those sneaky hands can handle.

For me, this meant waking up one day without being able to feel my right hand. Thousands of strokes with a high offset paddle and zero mobility work had destroyed my right wrist, and no amount of clever, sleight-of-hand tricks could deny this inevitable shutdown.

And yet to paddle or row effectively, you've got to be able to manipulate your hands in all directions at all stages of the stroke. This is usually most difficult at the catch, when your bottom elbow is fully extended—that is assuming you're not missing extension range at the elbow hinge that will prevent that bottom elbow from fully extending. If that's the case, then buy some Voodoo Floss and start doing bodyweight exercises to liberate the elbow and restore extension.

If you get tingling, numbness, soreness or other issues in your wrists and/or hands, I'm talking to you. And it's our responsibility to fix the problem now before you end up with wrists like mine, which have been slammed shut far too many times. Plus, hands that are unable to pronate and supinate like they're supposed to.

To assess where you're at on the wrist and hand function/dysfunction continuum, we've got to text the dexterity of your hands when your elbows are extended.

Who wants a nerve sandwich for lunch? No thanks. But, unfortunately, that's what we're creating every time we take a stroke in a bad position. Office workers struggle with carpal tunnel and wrist/forearm tendon issues because they spend all day typing with their hands pronated and shoulders internally rotated. Add water sports into the mix, and it's no wonder the paddling and rowing communities have trouble in this painful area.

Giant nerve bundles originate in your neck and run all the way down to your fingertips. That's one of the reasons you've got to look at your shoulder mechanics and head/jaw/neck positioning before traveling downstream. Not to mention removing the kink in the nervous system that occurs when we slouch at our desks and in our boats. If the soft tissues anywhere along the line are tacked down, you're putting pressure on the nerve tunnels. And often we have clamped-down tissues on both sides—hence the "nerve sandwich."

I'll go out on a limb (pun intended) here and say that most of the treatments for carpal tunnel, tingling and other nerve and tendon issues of the forearm, wrist and hands are bunk. Surgery for carpal tunnel? Really?! You can head the issue off at the pass by regularly de-gristling your brutally tight tissues before things ever get to that stage, or to the point where you simply can't row or paddle anymore.

If you're simultaneously enhancing your movement patterns, you'll go a long way to taking the pressure off those screaming nerves and will stop tugging on the tendons that are giving you so much grief. Good mechanics protect your nervous system and regular mobility work will restore slide and glide to those trouble spots. Unless of course you want to keep wearing that silly looking brace, stay off the water and book that surgery.

WATERMAN 2.0

HAND DEXTERITY PROGRESSION #1: EXTENDED ARM, SUPINATED PALM

This is an easy one, or so you would think. Let's see how well your hands and wrists can move when your elbow is extended, but without the demand of any load. To do so:

1) Extend both arms straight out in front of you, with your palms facing down

2) Keeping your elbows fully extended, turn your palms up toward the ceiling

3) While supinating your hand (turning it upward), you should be able to also keep your hand flat. Many paddlers, windsurfers, wakeboarders and rowers can't do this because their lower arms are extraordinarily tight. Now try holding your paddle in this position. Then switch sides.

THE HANDS, WRISTS, ELBOWS AND ARMS

HAND DEXTERITY PROGRESSION #2: CHIN-UP HANG (UNDERHAND GRIP)

You'd be surprised at how many of the paddlers we work with fall apart on the pull-up bar, particularly when we have them use a chin-up grip. This is because they've taken so many strokes in sub-optimal positions that their hands are junky, forearms are fried and elbows are like rusty old hinges. Let's see how you do hanging in the start position:

1) Stand underneath a pull-up bar and externally rotate your palms (left hand goes counter-clockwise, right hand goes clockwise)

2) Reach up and grab the bar

3) Fully extend your arms until they're straight

4) Remember to keep your core tight, legs together and scapula pulled back. Your feet should be a few inches in front of you, with toes pointed down to activate your glutes (which protects the lumbar spine).

HAND DEXTERITY PROGRESSION #3: CHIN-UP (UNDERHAND GRIP)

WATERMAN 2.0

If you aced the test on the hang, let's dial it up a notch and have you do a full chin-up.

1) Repeat steps 1 to 4 from the chin-up hang
2) Keeping your shoulder blades pulled back and abs engaged, pull yourself up until your chin is above the bar
3) Looking straight ahead and maintaining the hollow hold position, slowly lower yourself back down until your arms are straight
4) Repeat as many times as you can with good form

HAND DEXTERITY PROGRESSION #4: PLANCHE PUSH-UP

Now we're going to utilize the planche for a different diagnostic purpose—to see how much hand rotation you're capable of when your elbows are at end range.

1) Get on all fours on a flat surface

2) Set up to do a push-up, but invert your hands so that they're behind your forearms

3) Keeping your hands flat on the ground with fingers splayed and your forearms vertical (so your shoulders are directly above your hands and elbows), assume the top starting position

4) With your elbows tucked in, your feet together and your abs and butt braced, lower into the bottom position of the push-up, then use your arms to force your body back to the starting stance

If you have normal range of motion, you should have no trouble getting your hands backwards and performing multiple planche push-ups. And remember, normal is what we're aiming for—not some kind of weird over-dexterity you'd only see in a circus. If the planche hurts or you're forced to turn your hands out, then your wrist flexors are tight, you're missing wrist extension and you won't be able to create stabilizing torque at the shoulder.

Your elbows will follow your hands' bad example and also flare out. Similarly, if you do a regular push-up and can't go to the floor without flaring your elbows and turning your hands out, this is another diagnostic heads up that you've got elbow and wrist limitations.

Really this is reversing the mechanical ills caused by internally rotated shoulders on the water. It's also analogous to what happens when your lower leg tissues are tacked down and you duck your feet out. Neither is acceptable!

If you're a paddler, you should live on the pull-up bar. Well, not literally, unless you're also a bat. But pull-ups, both with the traditional overhand and underhand chin-up grips, should become a staple of your land-based training if you want to get the most out of each stroke and reinforce solid shoulder, elbow, wrist and hand sequencing.

The pull-up takes you to end range at the shoulder, elbow and wrist, and requires you to maintain grip and motor control through eccentric lengthening, while under load. If you have improved competency when you're at end range, you'll certainly have more capacity when it comes to the mid-range pulling that paddling and rowing require. Performing pull-ups with multiple grips also encourages more functional relationships between the scapula and spine and scapula and shoulders.

When I see paddlers, especially SUP athletes, hinging in the thoracic spine, I ask, "How many pull-ups can you do and how often do you do them?" Unfortunately, the answers are often somewhere close to "none" and "never." If the steering wheel of the scapula is better aligned and the surrounding musculature has better strength and endurance, those shoulder issues you've been having might just vanish.

We should be trying to liberate those inflamed soft tissues that are clamping down on nerves and feeding slack into the system to take the heat off inflamed tendons and ligaments and the joints they're tugging on. But instead we medicate the pain away, deal with the limited performance and just keep pushing until something breaks.

Or maybe your coach/trainer has tried to lengthen the tissues with static stretches. If these are so effective, then why do your range of motion and pain issues persist? Because this archaic approach doesn't work. Instead, you need to improve your on-water positioning, enhance motor control and strength endurance with multiple grip positions in the gym and follow a systems-based mobility approach to restore function.

MOBILITY MOMENT:
RESTORING YOUR FOREARMS, WRISTS AND ELBOWS

The good news is that even if the first or second progressions tripped you up, just a few minutes of mobility work each day can restore healthy tissue function. All the structures of the forearms are accessible, giving you massive opportunity to regain full capacity and stop pain in its tracks.

THE HANDS, WRISTS, ELBOWS AND ARMS

Pick a couple of these exercises and spend at least 2 minutes per side, at least 3 times a week. Remember, you're not making change unless you observe change, so if it takes 10 minutes or more for a mobilization to make a difference, then commit to that. Find these in The Hands, Wrists, Elbows and Arms section of the mobilizations appendix.

- Forearm ball smash
- Forearm barbell rollout
- Elbow Voodoo Floss
- Banded wrist distraction with Voodoo Floss

The pull-up is a must-have in your strength and conditioning program, but it's not a cure all. In working with paddlers and rowers for the past decade, I've also found that performing ring rows on gymnastics rings and the TRX Duo Trainer is beneficial for improving shoulder-to-elbow-to-wrist sequencing.

As with the pull-up, you'll want to play around with different hand positions so that you have a bigger movement window for various rotational shapes when you're on the water. Some variations include:

- Ring row with palms facing each other
- Ring row with palms turned up
- Ring row with palms turned down

Golfers have golfer's elbow, tennis players have tennis elbow, so we can claim paddler's elbow, I think. The issue is the same. The elbow gets hot because we're going through umpteen duty cycles with it in a crappy position—typically flared out to compensate for a slumped shoulder. This creates unnatural vector lines of force that put undue stress on surrounding muscles, ligaments, tendons and fascia. Systemic tightness in the surrounding muscle groups—including wrist flexors and extensors, biceps and triceps—then starts tugging the elbow hither and yon.

People often overlook the fact that the elbow isn't just a simple open-and-close hinge joint, it's a rotational hinge joint. While this allows us to manipulate our hands—a good thing—it also creates the opportunity for all manner of issues. Typically in water athletes suffering from elbow pain and/or loss of function we see the shoulder internally rotating and the hand going the other way to try and resist this (plus the forces created by the water itself). So you have a large pulling load plus a torsion force—i.e. how we tear duct tape. The poor elbow is caught in the mechanical crossfire. No wonder it gets so upset.

Our prescription to resolve elbow dysfunction is two-fold. First, we've got to sort out our mechanics so that we're creating and maintaining a stable shoulder that will encourage better elbow positioning. Second, we have to relieve systemic neural tension that's lighting the elbow on fire with regular mobility work.

In addition to smashing the forearms, biceps and triceps, we'd do well to get our Voodoo on. I'm not talking about black magic, but rather the Voodoo Floss mobility tool. Once upon a time we used old bicycle inner tubes to create compression around a joint. Thankfully, we're past that and now have a tailor-made version that serves the same purpose, but with more comfort and greater effect.

To wrap the floss around your elbow, overlap each strip by 50 percent and wrap at 50 percent tension. When you're almost out of floss, tuck the end in. Then perform bodyweight movements that will create a "tack and floss" effect, such as push-ups and TRX Duo Trainer rows, for several minutes.

Simply extending and flexing the arm you've wrapped will also have a positive impact. Regular Voodoo Flossing improves sliding surface movement and liberates the tacked down tissues surrounding the elbow hinge. Don't be alarmed if there are red lines on your skin once you unwrap the floss—they'll disappear soon enough.

Warning: I'm about to freak some people out! In recent years, isolation exercises have become persona non grata among many athlete communities as we've seen a transition to compound, functional movements. While I wholeheartedly support the end of the curls-bench press-crunches only workout that have dominated gyms for so long, there is a time and place for bicep curls. There, I said it!

Doing barbell bicep curls with a wide grip takes your elbows through a full range of motion with your hands supinated, which will reinforce what you're doing with the TRX Duo Trainer and on the pull-up bar. We're not going for strength or power here, but rather trying to enhance motor patterns. In this case, it's hand rotation with elbow flexion and extension.

I'm not alone here. Pavel Tsatsouline, the man who popularized kettlebell training in the US, and legendary coach Dan John also advocate wide-grip barbell curls. Do a couple of sets of 15 to 20 reps with a light to moderate weight twice a week.

CHAPTER 9
PREPARATION AND RECOVERY

"The three most important things in life: surf, surf and surf."
—Jack O'Neill

The athletes we work with have some of the most sophisticated and dialed-in training routines and racing strategies on the planet. And yet, without the correct preparation and recovery, their progress is going to be minimized, their competition performance blunted and their chances of chronic injuries and sickness increased.

Throughout the sporting world, everyone from pros to weekend warriors are trying to get ahead with incremental improvements from better equipment, performance apparel and a million and one other things. And yet when we're talking about optimizing your potential, the greatest gains can be made by removing major roadblocks. Typically, these include:

- Inadequate sleep
- Dehydration and improper rehydration
- Inadequate nutrition
- Constant stress state
- Inability to transition between sympathetic (fight/flight/freeze) and parasympathetic (relaxation and recovery) states
- Lack of a movement and mobility practice
- Insufficient warmup and cooldown routines

In this chapter, we're going to go beyond how your body moves and tackle some of the most common items on this list of performance potholes. By combining what you learn here with the movement and mobility strategies that come before and after, it's my hope that you will stop holding yourself back and start becoming the best possible waterman or woman that you can be.

STANDARD #11
DO YOU HAVE AN APPROPRIATE HYDRATION AND FUELING STRATEGY?

MOTIVATION

As you've seen, there are plenty of factors that can prevent you from reaching full potential. Other than sleep, it's arguable that none is more crucial than hydration. To function in any environment, your body water reservoir needs to be sufficiently full to support hundreds of processes. Drop below a certain baseline, and lots of bad things start to happen.

Suddenly, you can't get enough fuel to your muscles to continue the contractions needed to surf, row and paddle effectively. Your stomach, small intestines and liver aren't getting the goods they need to break down and distribute nutrients and assimilate fluids and inflammation increases. Your skin can't cool itself adequately while you're trying to regulate your core temperature. And changes start occurring in your brain that disrupt the hunger and thirst impulses, compounding all of the other issues. Basically, you become a dried out, low performing husk.

To help you hydrate better before, during and after your time on the water, we turned to my good friend Dr. Stacy Sims. If I could pick a sister, Stacy would be it (she's blushing, by the way). In addition, she's a consultant research exercise and nutrition physiologist at a little school called Stanford, as well as the founder of Osmo Nutrition. Stacy works with elite watermen and women of every description, as well as triathletes, swimmers and cyclists. So you can trust her to sort out your hydration strategy, whether you're a world champion like some of our featured athletes or an everyday Joe like the rest of us.

BRIEFING

When I took my C1 outrigger canoe across the 32-mile Channel of Bones for my first Molokai 2 Oahu crossing, I was lucky enough to have some wind at my back. A couple of months later, it was the turn of the SUP boys and girls and they weren't so lucky. There was barely a breeze and it was hot as Hades, which made for an extra miserable time. Sonni Hönscheid and one of our featured athletes, Travis Grant, toughed it out to take home top honors, but many seasoned pros fell by the watery wayside. More than a few of these had major hydration issues.

When we asked Stacy Sims about how athletes can survive a hot, grueling contest like Molokai or some of the crazy endurance feats we're seeing Shane Perrin and others complete, she quickly came up with a nutrition and hydration game plan. Even if you're not planning to enter such a contest any time soon, keep reading to get some valuable pointers on how to keep your energy and body water levels up during long races and training sessions (and yeah, maybe even those notorious family float trips!).

Two to Three Weeks Before the Race: A lot of Hawaii's top paddlers conk out during the Molokai 2 Oahu suffer fest (especially when the wind betrays them and stops blowing, like in the 2015 crossing), but it's the folks who live, race and train in cooler, less humid climates who really come a cropper. The key here is acclimatizing early enough so that your body can adapt to the added stress of atypically parching conditions.

The old school approach was putting on a ton of clothes and getting on a treadmill for as long as you could stand it. The trouble is that this places your body in unrealistic circumstances, sends cortisol and other stress hormones through the roof and, if you don't rehydrate properly, this can throw you into a chronic state of hypohydration and systemic dehydration.

A better approach is passive dehydration. The simplest way to implement this is to hydrate adequately before and during a hard training session, and then go sit in a sauna for up to 30 minutes. The first time you do this, your resting heartrate will be high, as in 140s-160s, but don't let that worry you. A hot tub won't work as well because the circulating water will dissipate the heat, minimizing your adaptation to it. No sauna available? Then attend a hot/Bikram yoga class. Actually doing the poses is optional—it's the heat we're after here.

At first you might only manage 5 or 10 minutes. That's just fine. Add a few minutes to each session and try to work up to no more than half an hour over the course of 7 days in a row. Here's what will happen from a physiology standpoint. Your body will not only become better accustomed to the heat so that you don't freak out when you start competing in hotter climates than you're used to, but will also regulate internal processes more efficiently and effectively.

The critical factor with this kind of heat training is that your total blood volume will expand. Why? Because the strong heat stress of the sauna with the dehydration causes significant strain on the body, signaling the need for more total blood. Not only will your body produce more blood, you will start to dilute sweat so that you're not excreting the sodium stores you need to pull fluid where it's required.

You'll also be able to better regulate your core and skin temperatures so that you can maintain adequate fluid levels in extreme heat with lower metabolic cost. And you'll react more quickly to the demands of a hot environment so that you're not wasting energy trying to ramp up heat dissipation on the fly.

The hot yoga/sauna approach places your body under stress and raises your heartrate, but does not create as great a demand as trying to acclimatize during strenuous paddling, rowing or surfing. While performing these activities, 80 percent or more of your blood flow is being channeled to the muscles, meaning your body is less able to adapt to the hotter environment than with the passive dehydration approach.

One Week Before Competition: Stop the heat acclimation with passive dehydration to allow your body to recover. As you taper your training for the race, ensure that you are putting a pinch of sea salt in your water to aid proper absorption. Eat plenty of watery fruits and vegetables such as watermelon and tomatoes and, assuming you have no history or genetic predisposition to hypertension or high blood pressure, sprinkle a little salt on these foods, too.

The mainstream media has been pushing "drink 8 glasses of water a day" for years. The trouble with this is that if you go to the restroom a lot and see clear urine, you might mistakenly think that you're well hydrated because you're pounding all this water. So why do you still feel thirsty all the time?

Because if you put water into your system without sufficient sodium it just lingers in your small intestines until your body can tap into its sodium stores and get the osmolality up to between 210 and 260. Depleting sodium stores sets us up for chronic dehydration. Add in the "salt is bad" falsehood and we've got a major sodium deficiency issue.

Conversely, if we take in way too much sodium and push the osmolality way above 260, the small intestine can't send fluid through our hydration pathways until we get more water and drop that number. Just a little pinch of salt in your water ensures that you're getting enough sodium to maintain body water levels between meals, while lightly salting food does the same thing. When it comes to the week before a race, particularly one like Molokai 2 Oahu that lasts several hours or even multi-day events such as the MR340 and Texas Water Safari, you simply cannot wait until the morning that the contest starts to top up your fluid levels.

Race Day: For endurance events, a big breakfast on race day is essential. You should aim to take in 800 to 1,200 calories, depending on your size. While the food you take in has to be personal preference, it should contain a good balance of macronutrients—i.e. protein, fat and carbs. Some of the athletes I work with soak oatmeal overnight and then add nuts and seeds, berries and protein powder on the morning of the race. If you're still hungry, then eat a couple of pieces of whole grain toast with butter and salt sprinkled on top.

The combination of pre-race jitters and the overwhelming stimuli of the water during the race can be mentally exhausting and predispose you to dehydration. Combat this up front with mindful meditation and strategies to reduce extra physical stress, such as blisters and sunburn.

Around 40 to 60 minutes before the race, aim to eat a small snack (a protein-based bar with around 200 calories will work here) or, if you're not gluten intolerant, a piece of bread with jam. This will top off your glucose level before you hit the water. I get asked a lot about caffeine and while I advise you to avoid the heavily caffeinated, synthetic pre-race/workout formulas because of their mega doses and artificial ingredients, if you're used to drinking coffee in the morning, then don't avoid it on race day.

During the Race: Even during an extended competition, you need to take in your calories on shore and focus on hydration on the water. While eating a small amount of real food on the water is OK, your main go-to should be a solution that combines sodium, sucrose and a little glucose.

Most mass market brands are too concentrated with carbohydrates/carbohydrate derivatives and will overload your stomach and small intestines, which will slow or reverse fluid absorption. So avoid them and go with a more precise formula. You can also pop glucose tablets as needed to keep your blood sugar up enough for consistent high output.

Another key consideration during the event is keeping your skin temperature down. Your body will already be fighting hard to manage your rising core temperature, which will significantly decrease power output and endurance if it rises above 103 degrees. If your skin is also very hot, you'll divert too much blood flow away from the gut, brain and muscles. This will be exaggerated with the inflammation response to sunburn.

My advice is to cover as much skin as possible, and to take advantage of the latest performance fabrics, many of which use silver, carbon and a cooling additive to keep skin temperature under control. This will allow you to work more effectively at higher internal temperatures. You can also wear a cap on your head to prevent it from overheating. Going back to the head, neck and jaw alignment concept, wearing a hat also allows you to maintain a neutral head position if you keep your eyes focused on the brim, particularly when you start to fatigue.

Don't overdo the skin cooling though. Ice against the skin is a no-no because it causes a constriction response, sending hot blood back into circulation and increasing the amount of heat your body stores.

This is the phase from the end of the race until 3 hours afterwards. It's essential that you pursue a two-pronged approach to rehydration and refueling. First, drink a solution that includes adequate sodium and potassium to spur rehydration. If you don't have any performance nutrition products on hand, go back to the reliable method of drinking 20 ounces of water with a pinch of sea salt and some lemon juice.

Second, you should take in 20 to 30 grams of high quality protein within half an hour of getting off the water. The protein boosts the muscle tissue level of leucine, which prompts muscle repair and recovery and stems the rising tide of cortisol and other catabolic stress hormones.

Remember that the higher your basal cortisol levels are, the more you risk having hormone problems (e.g. low testosterone and in women, low testosterone, estrogen and progesterone) as cortisol "steals" these hormones to create more cortisol, especially under times of stress. The other result of elevated cortisol is increased inflammation, which also impedes reparation and recovery.

WHY MASS MARKET SPORTS DON'T HELP HYDRATION

If you go into any grocery store, you'll see several cheap options for so-called hydration formulas. The same goes for the shelves of your local "nutrition" store—though these products will be higher in cost and have sillier names.

Unfortunately, despite the hyped up claims multi-million dollar ad campaigns would have you believe, many of these products are virtually worthless. One of the main issues is their high concentration of glucose. The body is channeling a large percentage of its blood flow to the muscles and cardiovascular system during exercise, and so can't be redirecting invaluable fluid to the gut to process a lot of carbs.

That's why NFL players know better than to down their "sports drinks"—because the full-force solution is just too much to handle during practices and in games. Many find that it causes stomach cramps, increases core temperature and contributes to greater fluid loss.

So wait a tick, you're saying that sports drinks that claim to hydrate can actually DEHYDRATE me? Sadly, yes. And don't trust the supposed science that creators of such products throw at you, either. Unfortunately, many of the studies that purport to show the efficacy of sports drinks were funded by the very companies who benefit from the findings. Such bias undermines the trustworthiness of the data, even though it and pictures of our favorite athletes quaffing these drinks are often enough to talk us into buying these companies' dubious wares.

A better approach is to avoid such brands and instead find formulations whose claims are backed up by independent scientific studies. Most of the smaller brands can't afford to funnel big money to nutritional scientists and so must rely on genuine results. As ever, positive impact on your performance is the ultimate goal, so experiment to find what works for you.

A BETTER FUEL AND REST STRATEGY

Another benefit to taking in whole protein or a high quality branched chain amino acid complex soon after exercise is that they extend insulin sensitivity by 2 to 3 hours. This means that when you eat your first full meal, which I recommend eating no longer than an hour and a half to 2 hours after the race (by all means, sooner if you are hungry!), you're primed to restore glycogen that has been decimated in the muscles during competition.

This meal should be a balance of more protein, carbs and healthy fats.

A couple of hours later drink another shake that contains 20 to 30 grams of complete protein to further enhance recovery.

Sleeping the night after a race can be tricky because your metabolism and core temperature remain elevated. Plus, in race venues like Hawaii, you may be in a hot environment with no air conditioning. You can help lower your core temperature by drinking tart cherry juice and other cold fluids, putting your hands and feet in cool water (a cold shower works wonders for resetting the nervous system) and performing some soft tissue mobility exercises.[8]

In the days immediately after a demanding race, your body often craves chips and other junk food. Really it's the sodium and fat you're after, so eat watery fruits and vegetables, good fats (avocados, walnuts, coconut) and salt your food. Also aim to consume 20 to 30 grams of protein every few hours to keep the levels of leucine and other amino acids high.

Unless you're involved in a stage race or multi-event competition, avoid heavy training as it will spike cortisol and other stress hormones that inhibit recovery. Light exercise is beneficial, as is mobility work (and no, Kelly didn't pay me to write that!). You need to get at least 8 to 9 hours of sleep, and don't be afraid of supplementing this rest with naps.

Over the past few years, there has been an almost continual back and forth in the sports performance community about whether you can get away with just drinking when you're thirsty, or if the very sensation of thirst means you're already dehydrated. Our take? If you've pre-hydrated adequately in the 2 to 3 weeks prior to the race and topped up your fluid and electrolyte levels in the 24 to 48 hours preceding your race or hard training session, then drinking to thirst is likely fine, particularly for a shorter event.

However, if your body water level is low because you've failed to prepare adequately, then you need to drink water with a pinch of sea salt in every 20

---

[8] Ann Liu et al, "Tart Cherry Juice Increases Sleep Time in Older Adults with Insomnia," *The FASEB Journal*, April 2014.

ounces periodically throughout the competition. If it's a longer, endurance contest, then follow Stacy Sims's advice about adding in a solution that combines sodium, glucose and sucrose. The key here is that your preparation should be the best you can manage so your body isn't reliant on last-minute hydration fixes.

SHORTER RACES: A MODIFIED HYDRATION/NUTRITIONAL STRATEGY

Let's be honest, most people aren't going to enter an elite distance race anytime soon. So what about hydrating and eating for shorter races? Let's ask Stacy Sims to write a little more about the different strategy needed for these.

The Week Before the Race: Just as with the preparation week before a world-class contest, you should pull back on your training in the days leading up to a shorter event so you're not flat on race day. You should also ensure that you're eating clean and drinking water with a pinch of salt so that you're not putting up any roadblocks in your hydration pathways or tapping into your body's sodium reserves unnecessarily.

Two Days Before the Race: My colleagues and I often say that it's the day before the day before that's critical to pre-race hydration and nutrition. You must get adequate sleep and eat plenty of watery foods so that you're not in a mad rush to top up body water levels right before the race. Cutting back your training will help prevent sending cortisol levels spiking and DHEA levels spiraling into oblivion, which would increase inflammation and reduce sex hormone levels.

It's also beneficial to eat nuts, seeds and other rich sources of essential minerals. This doesn't just mean sodium, but also potassium, magnesium and selenium, which are involved in hydration and hundreds of other bodily processes.

The Day Before the Race: You need to make sure that you're eating enough so that you're not getting too hungry and drinking sufficient water and salting your food to prevent extreme thirst from kicking in. Keep protein levels up and make sure you're also taking in a reasonable amount of carbohydrates and fat, too. The night before race day can be stressful as you're nervous and excited about the event, so try some of the strategies I suggested for the night after a race in the A Better Fuel and Rest Strategy section to bring your core temperature down and encourage restful sleep.

Race Day: You don't need the same massive breakfast as someone taking on a 4 or 5 hour endurance event. That said, eat a solid breakfast that isn't going to leave you famished right before the race. You should also take in a couple of glasses of fluid (water with a pinch of salt can work here). For a race under an hour, you won't need electrolyte-rich formulas in your hydration pack. Rather, just use salted water and, if you need it, pop a glucose tab toward the end of the race to keep you flying. If you've been hydrated adequately in the days leading up to the competition, you won't experience the ills of systemic dehydration in the course of a brief race.

Recovery Between Heats, Semifinals and Finals: In contests that involve heats, semifinals and finals or different disciplines on the same day, it's even more important that you rehydrate with sodium and potassium-laced fluid and get 20 to 30 grams of complete protein in a shake or bar (remember though, no soy unless you're allergic to whey! It takes 50g of soy to match the leucine content of 25g of whey) within 30 minutes of the first heat ending. This is also a sound strategy after a single race—the recovery aspect is just more pressing for multi-event competitions.

Rest of the Race Day/Next Day: Keep taking in electrolyte-enhanced fluids and getting regular protein-rich meals and snacks. As your race wasn't an ultra-marathon, you can train at a moderate intensity and not compromise recovery.

Just as our children should be using size-specific boards and paddles, we can't keep treating groms like mini-adults when it comes to hydration. Their physiology is just too different, particularly when it comes to pre-adolescent children.

Kids younger than 12 dilate before they sweat, and don't cool as effectively as adults because their thermoregulatory mechanisms aren't fully developed.

This means that during training and races, the "drink to thirst" strategy that some adults pursue often doesn't work for children. It's the job of coaches and parents to make sure kids are sipping water that has a wee bit of sodium, potassium and glucose throughout training sessions and competitions so that the children aren't relying on their still-developing thirst responses to guide hydration. This liquid should be as cool as possible.

After training or racing, kids need protein just as adults do to stimulate recovery. They must also hydrate and at some point, replenish glycogen with carbs. While some people push chocolate milk on young water athletes, I'm not a big fan of it due to the sky-high sugar content. If you do give groms a dairy drink once they get back on dry land, low-fat milk with a touch of maple syrup is a better bet, along with a banana.

Just as we can't continue applying adult hydration principles to our kids, neither should we assume that women are just slightly smaller men. Female physiology is—surprise, surprise!—significantly different, and is affected by the hormone rise and fall during, before and after ovulation and menstruation.

Elevated levels of estrogen and progesterone complicate hydration. Increased estrogen shifts fluid from the bloodstream, reducing plasma volume by up to 8 percent. Estrogen also encourages women's bodies to retain glycogen, limiting the amount of glucose needed to fuel muscular contraction and gut function. This means that women's muscles use more fatty acids, which spares carbohydrates and caps anaerobic capacity. Progesterone increases total body sodium losses, which elevates the risk of developing hyponatremia.

These hormonal factors mean that women must work extra hard to hydrate adequately before, during and after training and competition. To avoid further hydration issues, women should also be careful to avoid chronic overtraining, which lowers the DHEA levels that help regulate estrogen and progesterone.

PREPARATION AND RECOVERY

Failing to get adequate fluid into your body at the optimal osmolality can doom anyone's performance to failure. And yet too many water athletes have gone too far the other way. In their concern about becoming dehydrated, some have taken to consuming an unholy quantity of water. When taken to extremes, doing so can cause you to drown internally because your body can't absorb or excrete the extra fluid and blood sodium levels get too low. This is exactly what happened to an unfortunate competitor in the Texas Water Safari some years back.

So how do you avoid such a fate? Well first, as we've repeated umpteen times already, you simply must be responsible for dialing in your nutrition and hydration well before you hit the water. That way you're not risking the systemic dehydration that prevents adequate water distribution to the brain, gut and muscles.

Second, the fluid you take in should be electrolyte enhanced, either in a formula like those offered by Osmo Nutrition or, if you want to go back to basics, go with the trusty ol' pinch of sea salt in water. You should also use common sense. Slugging 10 pints of beer isn't going to do you much good and neither is consuming a similar amount of water over the course of a few hours.

STANDARD #12
ARE YOU PHYSICALLY PREPARED TO GET ON THE WATER?

MOTIVATION

It's an indisputable fact that you simply cannot paddle, surf or row your best without an adequate warmup. We've studied athletes of all skill levels across all sports for tens of thousands of hours and those with effective warmup routines go faster, are more efficient and last longer than those who jump right into training or competing. To say nothing of lower injury rates.

So what are we trying to do when we warm up? Well first, you want to raise your core temperature and promote the flow of oxygenated blood to your muscles. When we're at rest, a significant portion of our blood flow goes to and from our gut so that we can digest food and assimilate fluids. While we need to keep sending some blood in and out of the digestive system (and to the brain) during exercise, most needs to be channeled to our muscles. The trouble is that without a warmup, it's harder for our bodies to make this transition.

Another thing we want to achieve before we ramp up to high intensity exercise is to take the soft tissues and joints we'll be using through a full range of motion. We can also do some skill reinforcement work without the stimulus of the water so that we're readying our neural pathways to send the appropriate motor pattern information to our bodies.

BRIEFING

When you watch a NASCAR race, you'll notice that the drivers don't just plonk down in their seats, buckle up and go. No, they spend a long time on warmup laps. Or think about Olympic 100-meter sprinters. We see them at the warmup track, bounding up and down, practicing their start and doing drills like high knees and butt kicks. They can put in over an hour of prep time for less than 10 seconds of all-out effort. So why do we water athletes, who will be exerting ourselves for a lot longer, just grab our boards/boats/whatever craft and charge headlong into the ocean, river or lake without priming the pump?

PREPARATION AND RECOVERY

To get you ready for the water, we're now going to take your shoulders through the various archetypes and also fire up your hips.

The sequence is:

1) Forward shoulder wheels
2) Back shoulder wheels
3) Horizontal swing
4) Bent over swing
5) Extension flick
6) Back scratchers
7) Blocked hip rotation
8) Side opener

Perform 10 repetitions of each movement before moving onto the next. You can do this warmup before you lift and prior to water-based training.

FORWARD SHOULDER WHEELS

1) Stand with your feet shoulder width apart

2) Extend your right arm overhead and then in front of you and down, as if doing the swimming front crawl, with your palm moving toward the floor

3) Twist your torso as you would in a swimming stroke and end with your right palm behind you

4) Alternate arms

BACK SHOULDER WHEELS

1) Stand with your feet shoulder width apart

2) Extend your right arm overhead and reach behind you as if you were doing the swimming backstroke

3) As your arm goes up and back, twist your torso just like you would while swimming

4) Alternate arms

HORIZONTAL SWING

1) Stand with your feet shoulder width apart and your abs braced

2) Swing your arms across your chest (think Michael Phelps before an Olympic final)

3) Uncross your arms and after you return them to their natural sides with your hands and elbows at shoulder height, swing them behind you

BENT OVER SWING

1) Stand upright and hinge at the hips

2) Once your torso is parallel to the ground, swing your arms across your chest

3) Keeping your core braced and torso in the hinge position, swing your arms back the other way and up behind you

PREPARATION AND RECOVERY

1) Standing with your feet shoulder width apart, raise your arms until they're straight out in front of you with your fingers extended and palms facing down

2) Swing your arms behind you, scooping the air with your hands as you turn your wrists up

WATERMAN 2.0

BACK SCRATCHERS

1) Stand with your feet shoulder width apart
2) Extend and raise both arms out to your sides until they're parallel to the floor
3) Reach your left arm behind you as if trying to scratch an itch on your lower back
4) Alternate arms

BLOCKED HIP ROTATION

1) Stand with your feet shoulder width apart
2) Lift your left heel off the ground while keeping your right foot planted
3) Keeping your torso upright, twist it to the right and swing your left arm across your body
4) As you do so, swing the right arm behind you
5) Switch sides

PREPARATION AND RECOVERY

1) Stand with your feet shoulder width apart
2) Lift your left heel off the ground while keeping your right foot planted
3) Maintaining an upright torso, swing your right arm above you and reach as if you're trying to pull something off a high shelf
4) As you do so, swing your left arm across your body at waist height
5) Swing your right arm down and across your torso as you move your left arm back to its natural side and then up into the reaching position
6) Your right heel should come off the ground while your left foot remains planted

Now we're going to reinforce 3 of the fundamental shoulder shapes—overhead, the front rack and the hang—with a little load. The 3-position carry—waiter, front rack and suitcase—does exactly that, using a kettlebell, sand bag or dry bag. We got this great sequence from our friend Gray Cook, co-creator of the Functional Movement Screen (FMS), Functional Capacity Screen (FCS) and Selective Functional Movement Assessment (SFMA) and a keen paddler.

While the kettlebell has the advantage of being a consistent weight and shape, the sand bag and dry bag are more portable and can be filled with sand or water to vary the load. Of the 3, the dry bag is the cheapest and compresses down to the size of a softball so you can easily take it with you to the beach, lake or river.

The drill is simple. You're going to carry your object of choice above your head in the waiter carry position until you start to fatigue. You'll then slowly lower the kettlebell or bag into the front rack position. When this starts to burn, you drop down again into the suitcase carry. When one arm is smoked, simply switch your burden to the other hand and repeat the waiter-front rack-suitcase sequence. The goal is to go for 10 minutes. While this may seem like a long time, moving the load between the 3 positions and switching hands should keep you feeling fairly fresh.

You need to only use a load that you can handle with correct posture—upright, abs braced, arm positioned properly—for the allotted time. A good starting point for an active male is 35 pounds (16 kilograms) and 22 pounds (10 kilograms) for women. But see what works for you.

Here are a few pointers on each carry variation:

PREPARATION AND RECOVERY

During each of the carries, your shoulder blade on the active side should be retracted—i.e. pulled back—and down, with your shoulders squared. You should also look straight ahead. Remember that this is not an all-out metabolic drill like a heavy farmer's walk. You should be able to diaphragm breathe throughout. Holding a conversation with a training partner/coach during the carry is another good tip for breathing regulation.

For the waiter carry, make sure your wrist is not bent. You should be able to balance a mug of coffee on your fist (though don't try this at home, kids). Push the kettlebell or bag to the sky to maintain an active shoulder and make sure your arm forms a straight line with your ear and hip to ensure stability. When you get fatigued, slowly lower the load down into the front rack position.

WATERMAN 2.0

FRONT RACK CARRY

In the front rack carry, your knuckles should face outward and the palm side touching your collarbone. It's important to ensure that the scapula remains pulled back and down and that the shoulder isn't translated forward. For each of the carries, keep your steps short and toes pointed straight ahead, and walk in a narrower line than if you weren't carrying anything. This will reduce the stability demands and encourage you to maintain good positioning.

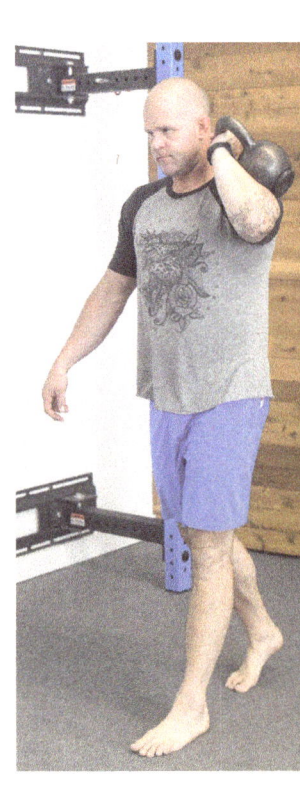

SUITCASE CARRY

A lot of people make a key mistake in the suitcase carry or farmer's walk by hunching their traps up like they're impersonating the Incredible Hulk. This just fatigues you quicker. Instead, push the weight down as you pull your shoulder blade back. This preserves the scapula-to-spine and scapula-to-shoulder relationships and can give you 20 or more extra steps.

The carries can be used as a warmup and as part of your workouts on non-paddling days to improve motor control, strength and the robustness of your shoulders.

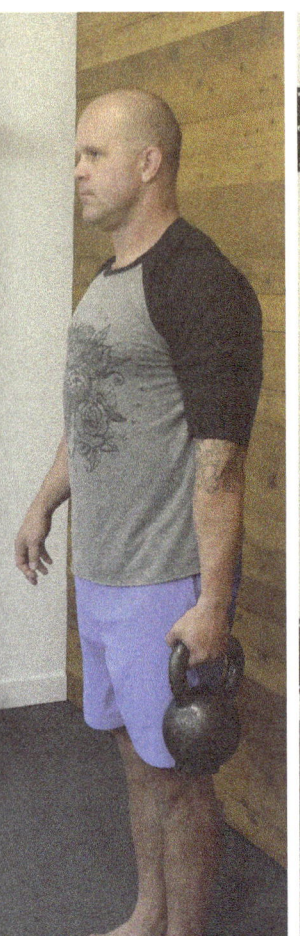
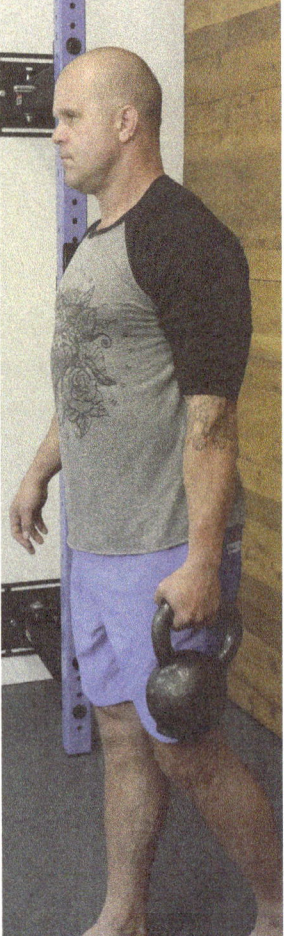

STANDARD #13
ARE YOU RECOVERING EFFECTIVELY?

MOTIVATION

We're not going to get too deep into neurobiology (and there was much rejoicing!), but it's fair to say that the brain has far more circuits dedicated to going 0 to 60 than taking you back down to 0. This is a function of evolutionary survival. Back in the day, you needed to outrun predators and escape from other threats in your environment at a moment's notice and to pursue and kill your prey so you didn't starve. Now, this is hardly the reality for most of us in today's world, but our survival instincts remain unchanged.

In the previous standard we explored how to take advantage of our Tesla-like acceleration with a thorough, movement quality-focused warmup. Now let's look at some ways to come back down again so we can tap into better rest and recovery.

As with Stacy Sims's refueling and rehydration strategy, our prescription begins the moment we're done training or racing at high intensity. You want to now reverse what you did in the warmup and bring your heartrate down, lower your sensory arousal and trigger the lymphatic system to push garbage (lactic acid and all of his inflammatory friends) out and pull groceries (nutrients, electrolytes and oxygenated blood) in.

The first thing to do is either paddle slowly for 5 to 10 minutes or, if you're on land, walk, row or perform bodyweight exercises such as lunges and air squats for the same duration. Your brain will get the message that you're no longer needing to hurtle through water, time and space, and will signal to your body to start acting accordingly.

While I was in PT school at Samuel Merritt, a professor had a terrific maxim about recovery: "You don't put away a wet horse after galloping in the rain. That's a quick way to kill the horse." I recognize that, in all likelihood, you are not a horse. But the analogy still holds for you. Going out and paddling, surfing or rowing hard for 2 hours is your equivalent of galloping in the rain. Now, you're not going to die from not cooling down because if that was the case, we'd all be dead already. But if you don't do some intentional work immediately following exercise, you're certainly going to kill recovery, limit progress and performance gains and increase your risk of injury.

Once you've completed your cooldown, spend 10 to 15 minutes on mobility drills before you slam your protein shake or post-workout meal. Your mobilization strategy could include working on some of your known issues (like that wonky shoulder or chronically tight lower back) and/or targeting the areas most highly taxed during your water- or land-based workout. Or try mobilizing upstream and downstream (below and above) a painful area. I also find it useful to regularly move from the top of my body (neck and shoulders) to the bottom (calves, ankles and feet) over the course of a week to make sure I'm finding and dealing with all possible tight spots. If you know you're struggling with a particular archetype, such as with your paddle overhead, you can also mobilize in this position of restriction to improve capacity.

BRIEFING

You'd think that pro athletes would be better at recovering and in some cases, you'd be right. But the "performance high" that many world-beaters get is so intense that many of them can't sleep after training or competition without drinking alcohol, smoking weed or taking a handful of pills. I'm not making accusations or trying to be a sensationalist here—we work with dozens of these individuals on a daily basis and know that transitioning from the fight or flight response of the sympathetic state to parasympathetic recovery is no easy task.

Cooling down, mobilizing and rehydrating/refueling is an effective three-pronged approach to starting your recovery from surfing, paddling and rowing yourself into the ground (or, should I say, the water). But just as it can take hours to replenish your body's water and glycogen levels, it can also take a long time to get your body back into a resting state after exercise. Here are 6 ways to trick your body and brain into chilling the heck out, courtesy of Jill Miller and Stacy Sims:

1) COLD WATER IMMERSION/THERMIC CYCLING

Immersing yourself in cold water should become one of your daily strategies for getting more and better quality sleep. Top athletes used to take ice baths simply because they reduce inflammation, but have now realized that exposure to cold water also resets the nervous system. This helps you move from the state of sympathetic arousal and into what Jill Miller calls "drousal"—when your body downshifts into "rest, digest and recovery" mode. Even immersing your palms and/or soles of your feet in cold water for a few minutes will lower your core temperature to encourage better quality sleep.

Another benefit of enduring the initial horrors of the cold shower is that it forces the lymphatic system into high gear. As we explored earlier, one of the reasons that it's a bad idea to sit for a prolonged period after exercise is because it stops your body from efficiently flushing out waste products and bringing in restorative nutrients. A cold shower gets things moving again, and cycling a hot bath with a burst of chilly water or a sauna with a plunge pool or ice bath may even enhance the circulation-boosting effects.

Scientists at Virginia Commonwealth University School of Medicine also found that cold showers trigger noradrenaline from the brain's "blue spot" (locus coeruleus), helping to counteract the effects of depression.[9] Chilly showers may also increase testosterone production, which is key for muscle growth and repair.

2) STOP LOOKING AT SCREENS AND CHANGE YOUR LIGHTBULBS

Your pineal gland may be small, but it has a mighty impact on sleep. That's because this pinball-sized part of your brain is responsible for releasing melatonin a couple of hours before you slip into sleep. Back in the good ol' days before TV, it's fair to assume that most people had fully functional pineal

---

9   Nikolai Shevchuk, "Adapted Cold Shower as a Potential Treatment for Depression," *PubMed*, 2007.

glands. But now that we look at our computers and phones all day and follow that up with—guess what?—more screen time in the evening, this natural function is under assault.

The blue light emitted by smartphones, tablets, TVs, laptops and the rest of our gadgets stimulate our brains in all the wrong ways. They turn off or at least compromise the effectiveness of the pineal gland, preventing it from releasing enough melatonin to ensure a restful slumber.[10] If you're a reader, you're better off either using a passively backlit screen like a Kindle, or going back to paperbacks and hardbacks. And if books or magazines aren't your thing, try digging out those classic board games that your parents used to force you to play or just free associating with your friends and family in the art we used to call conversation.

It's not just technology that's messing with our melatonin. One endocrine-focused study found that exposure to LED lightbulbs before bedtime suppressed melatonin production in 99 percent of subjects, and reduced the duration of peak melatonin by an hour and a half. John Marshall, a professor at The Institute of Ophthalmology in London, told *Digital Trends,* "Until recently, we lit our homes with incandescent bulbs and they were relatively biologically friendly, in that there was very little blue. More commonly now they're LEDs and these light sources have a lot of the potentially damaging blue, to the extent that I don't use them." Non-LED bulbs with warmer orange or yellow light will limit such effects.[11]

3) MOBILIZE SOME MORE

Gut smashing sounds like some kind of medieval torture, but while it can feel weird the first time, it's actually a great way to trigger the parasympathetic response and improve your breathing. In addition to rolling an MWOD Supernova Ball slowly across the lower sections of your abdomen, you can

---

10 Meeri Kim, "Blue Light from Electronics Disturbs Sleep, Especially for Teenagers," *Washington Post*, September 1, 2014.

11 Joshua J. Gooley et al, "Exposure to Room Light Before Bedtime Suppresses Melatonin Onset and Shortens Melatonin Duration in Humans," *Journal of Clinical Endocrinol Metabolism*, December 30, 2010; Simon Hill, "Is Blue Light Keeping You Up At Night?" *Digital Trends*, July 26, 2015.

utilize a softer implement like the Yoga Tune Up Coregeous Ball higher up to free your diaphragm. This not only enhances down-regulation, but is also highly beneficial if, like me, you suffer from asthma.

Your gut is one of the body's primary lymph sites. The lymphatic system doesn't just get rid of exercise-induced byproducts, but is also responsible for sending disease-fighting cells into your bloodstream. Rolling around on and breathing into a ball for 5 to 10 minutes stimulates this crucial lymphatic response. Applying a shearing force to the abdomen can also stimulate the vagus nerve, which relays sensory information to your brain and is a key component of the parasympathetic nervous system.

Another reason to gut smash is that it feeds slack into the region I like to call the "high quads," where stiffness can impede hip range of motion and limit the rotation that's so vital to effective paddling. The psoas, one of the primary contributors to lower back pain, attaches to the front of the pelvis, so giving it a good smashing can help you loosen that pesky lumbar spine. I also believe that abdominal massage and mobility work can prevent sports hernias by liberating that gristly, tacked down tissue that very few watermen or women ever deal with.

To increase the immune-boosting, relaxation-inducing, diaphragm-liberating impact of gut smashing, you might want to think about using a smaller Yoga Tune Up Ball to trigger the sub-clavicle off switch for your sympathetic nervous system, which is located just under your collarbone. To do so, roll the ball slowly across the soft tissues in your upper pecs.

If you've got some time left, then flip over and spend another few minutes on freeing up the thoracodorsal fascia of the lower back. Heading upstream and going after our old nemesis the thoracic spine is also a beneficial complement to mobilizing the abdominal area.

4) EAT YOURSELF RELAXED

While I've never been a fan of popping pills, I do take a few things before bed to help me recover better. These include high quality fish oil, which reduces inflammation, stabilizes mood and improves cognitive function. I've also found success taking the neurotransmitter 5-HTP. This is a derivative of the amino acid tryptophan, which the body then converts into the sleep regulating chemical serotonin.

Another go-to for me is ZMA, which combines zinc, magnesium and vitamin B-6. Magnesium is utilized in over 300 bodily processes and when you're stressed and/or exercising hard, your system just vacuums it up. You could eat a lot of nuts and seeds, which are rich sources, but if you take in too many omega 6 fatty acids from these foods you might send your inflammation levels soaring.

Zinc has been proven to help prevent and shorten the duration of colds and respiratory infections, and also plays a part in tissue growth and repair, hormonal function and cell metabolism. Working out hard on the water diminishes zinc levels, so it's important to top them up. Vitamin B-6 is also a key contributor to repairing the tissue damage caused by exercise, as well as assisting in cell regeneration and preventing that nasty next-day soreness.

You should also eat a high protein and/or fat meal within 3 hours of going to bed. Yes, I know this flies in the face of everything mass media has advised, but your body needs slow-burning fuel that will enable replenishment while you're asleep. Forget what you think you know about weight loss and trust me on this one.

5) SLEEP IN A MONASTERY

OK, you don't actually need to go visit your local monks to get better sleep. But going to bed in similar conditions to those you'd find in a monastery—cool, dark, quiet, with no electronic devices nearby—can do wonders for your recovery.

Lying down in a room that's between 60 and 67 degrees is proven to send you to sleep faster and to enhance the quality of your zzzs by reducing cortisol, the stress hormone that promotes fat retention and limits the production of muscle building testosterone (men) and estrogen (women) like some kind of hormone gobbling Pacman.

Sleeping in a cool room improves metabolic function, leading to better fat utilization and increased calorie burning at rest and the next day. Cold slumber may also reduce the risk of diabetes, according to researchers at the National Institutes of Health.[12] If you're in a hot environment, particularly one without air conditioning, you could use cooling pads to keep your mattress and pillow in the ideal temperature range all night.

Just dialing down the thermostat isn't going to give you maximum benefits, however. You should also limit the intrusion of honking cars, barking dogs and other noises that can wake you up or at least disrupt sleep. The fix? Spend a couple of bucks on some soft foam earplugs with a high decibel rating.

The third component of the better sleep bedroom is darkness. To fall asleep quickly, we need our bodies to produce enough melatonin. The trouble is that those thin curtains or blinds leak light, which also seeps under the door to the hallway and bathroom, and emanates from eternally blinking electronic devices (more on this in a moment). So the melatonin producing sites in the brain are getting mixed messages: it's dark, but yet it's still light.

And when we do overcome our compromised melatonin response and fall asleep, our eyes are still being exposed to light because our eyelids are partially translucent. To quote Harvard's Charles Czeisler, as Kat Duff does in her brilliant book *The Secret Life of Sleep,* "Light affects our circadian rhythms more powerfully than any drug."

The solution is simple. Get a sleep mask. Replace those inadequate blinds or curtains with blackout curtains. Turn off all lights inside and outside your bedroom. And give your light-emitting phone, tablet and laptop the heave ho.

Another reason to ditch the technology is that the wireless signals might interfere with brain function and further disrupt circadian rhythms. In our tech-obsessed society, we all check our mobile devices far too often, which increases anxiety and keeps cortisol running at high tide. So putting your phone, tablet and all of your other gadgets out of reach at both before bed and during the night is a wise plan. If you need your phone because you're a medical professional, firefighter, soldier, etc., or use it as an alarm clock, then at least turn off its Wi-Fi while you're sleeping.

---

12 P Lee et al, "Temperature-Acclimated Brown Adipose Tissue Modulates Insulin Sensitivity in Humans," *Diabetes*, November 2014.

WATERMAN 2.0

6) CUT OUT EVENING CAFFEINE (AND THINK TWICE ABOUT THAT NIGHTCAP)

When I was struggling with asthma in my teens and twenties, I used to supplement all-too-frequent puffs on my inhaler with enough caffeine to kill an adult gorilla. But once I'd got my condition under control with the help of Jill Miller's diaphragm, soft tissue and first rib mobilizations, I recognized that being caffeinated to the eyeballs 24 hours a day was hardly ideal for rest and recovery. According to the National Sleep Foundation, it can take up to 6 hours to process half the caffeine in an 8 ounce cup of Joe, so if you're drinking a latte with dinner and are tossing and turning at midnight, that might well be the reason.[13] But a nightcap's OK because it helps you sleep, right? Well, not exactly. While I'm not against an evening tipple now and then, drinking beer, wine or your drink of choice every night might not be such a good idea. A study conducted on behalf of the National Institute on Alcohol Abuse and Alcoholism found that while having a nightcap within an hour of hitting the hay can help you fall asleep quicker, it also disrupts the second half of your sleep cycle.[14] So if you're shooting for maximal recovery, avoid alcohol altogether or at least have a drink or two earlier in the evening.

---

13 "Caffeine and Sleep," The National Sleep Foundation website, available online at https://sleepfoundation.org/sleep-topics/caffeine-and-sleep.

14 "Alcohol and Sleep," *Alcohol Alert*, 1998.

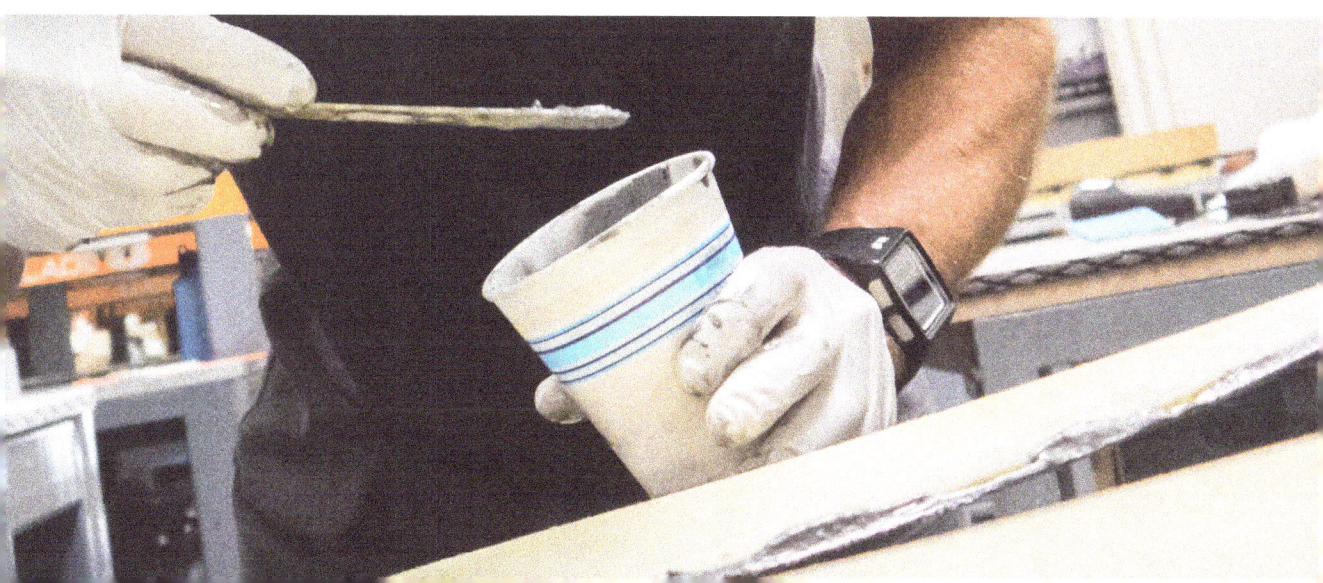

CONCLUSION

"Out of the water, I am nothing."
—Duke Kahanamoku

I wrote this book with one simple goal: to help you become a lifetime waterman or woman without the pain, injuries and missed training time that bedevil so many of us. As I stated in the introduction, your body was designed to not only last for 110 years, but also to thrive throughout the length of this lifespan. All too often poor mobility and motor control, incorrect movement patterns and environmental factors—too much sitting, inadequate nutrition and hydration, poor sleep habits, etc.—conspire to damage us and keep us off the water.

By following the blueprint in this book, I hope you've become more aware of your body's capabilities and are on the road to realizing your potential. You may not win an Olympic gold, push the boundaries of your sport or match the other achievements of our featured athletes. But that's not the point. I just want you to be the best YOU can be, whether you're a newbie, junior athlete, seasoned veteran or anyone in between.

The concepts we've explored have been field tested on the top performing water athletes in the world. Through thousands of hours of observation and trial and error, we've eliminated the gimmicks and fads that don't work and given you what does. The good news is that, aesthetics and a few minor anatomical differences aside, your spine is the same as Laird Hamilton's spine, your shoulders are the same as Emily Jackson-Troutman's shoulders and your hips are the same as Danny Ching's hips. Translation: what works for them will work for you.

It's unrealistic to expect massive change in a day or two, but by achieving the standards, doing the drills and performing the motor control and mobility exercises daily, you will see early and lasting progress. Then add in the tips from the athletes and experts who've shared their knowledge and you'll advance even further. We're all busy, but dedicating just a few minutes a day, every day can make all the difference. You're on the road to becoming Waterman 2.0!

MOBILIZATIONS APPENDIX

Now that we've taken you through each of the standards, it's time to move on to the mobilizations appendix. In this section, you'll find a complete list of exercises that will help you move better and more sustainably and express more power and speed.

Try to accumulate at least 2 minutes per side for each mobilization. But keep going until you start to see a positive change - the 2 minute recommendation is just a minimum effective dose. If something feels painful or wrong, you need to back off a bit or stop altogether - if it feels sketchy, it is sketchy. Try testing and re-testing your positioning before and after a mobilization. So for example, if you want to assess your wrist capacity, see what it's like before you do the forearm ball smash and again afterward.

You can also try pairing 2 exercises for the same area, such as the quad smash and couch stretch—to amplify the positive effects of both. In addition to following the mobilizations here, don't be afraid to self-experiment a little bit as you "freestyle" in your own variations of the exercises. A small daily investment in your mobility will yield big results, so commit to consistency.

For bonus mobilizations, visit our website (www.mobilitywod.com) and keep an eye on our social media channels.

BANDED LONG SIT

1) Loop a thin resistance band around an upright anchor like a squat rack post or beach sign
2) Sit in front of the anchor facing it
3) Loop the band around your back so it's positioned just under your armpits

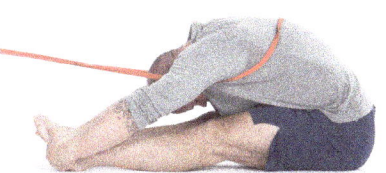

4) With your legs flat on the floor and straight out in front of you, point your toes
5) Get your belly tight and then let the band fold your torso forward, sliding your hands down your shins as you exhale and move into the pike position
6) Take a big nasal inhale and straighten back up to the starting position, with your torso upright

HIP CAPSULE MOBILIZATION

1) Kneel on the ground and move most of your weight onto your left knee, positioning it directly under your hip
2) Lower your hips toward your left side, keeping your weight over your left knee. Picture attempting to pop the head of your femur out the side of your butt.
3) Keeping your weight over your left leg and pushing your hips to the left side, crawl forward a little and emphasize the tissues at the front of your hip capsule
4) Switch sides

SIDE HIP SMASH

1) Lie on the ground and place a lacrosse ball, mini Supernova or other small ball by your left hip
2) Turn onto your left side and prop yourself up on your left elbow as you move the soft tissues just behind your left hip onto the ball

3) Slowly roll back and forth across the ball
4) Switch sides

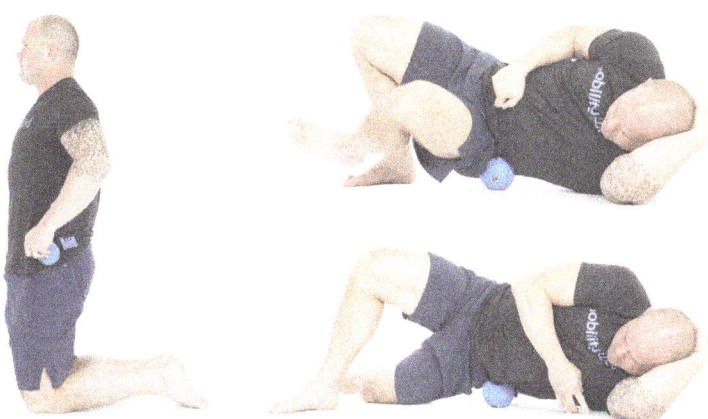

COUCH STRETCH

1) Kneel in front of a wall, a plyo box or, as the name suggests, your couch
2) Place your left shin flat against the wall, box or couch and turn your foot slightly inward
3) Your right foot should be straight and flat on the floor in front of you
4) Push your left hip toward the ground, squeezing your butt as you do so
5) Try moving into the corners by tilting your torso slightly to the outside or inside of your back leg
6) After a minute or 2, put your left hand into a "sprinter's start" position (making a bridge with your thumb and forefinger on the floor) and push your torso halfway upright
7) Repeat step #4
8) After another minute or 2, push through your right foot, remove your left hand from the floor and move your torso into an upright position. Try to squeeze your glutes. If you find yourself losing your balance, place a box, weight bench or something else to the side of you to hold on to.
9) Switch sides

GLUTE TACK AND FLOSS

1) Sit on a lacrosse ball, mini Supernova or other small ball
2) With your hand flat on the ground behind you for support, slowly roll back and forth across the ball
3) You can also move your knee toward and away from the midline to get into the tissues from a different direction
4) If you discover a sore spot, camp out there for a while until you feel relief
5) Switch sides

HIGH GLUTE SMASH AND FLOSS

1) Lie flat on your back with your feet up on a couch, bench or plyo box
2) Position a lacrosse ball on the left side of your upper glute
3) Slowly drop your left knee down and outward to move the ball to the outside edge of your glute
4) Move your knee back toward the middle, rolling your glute back across the ball
5) Repeat 30 to 40 times and then switch sides

WATERMAN 2.0

HAMSTRING SMASH

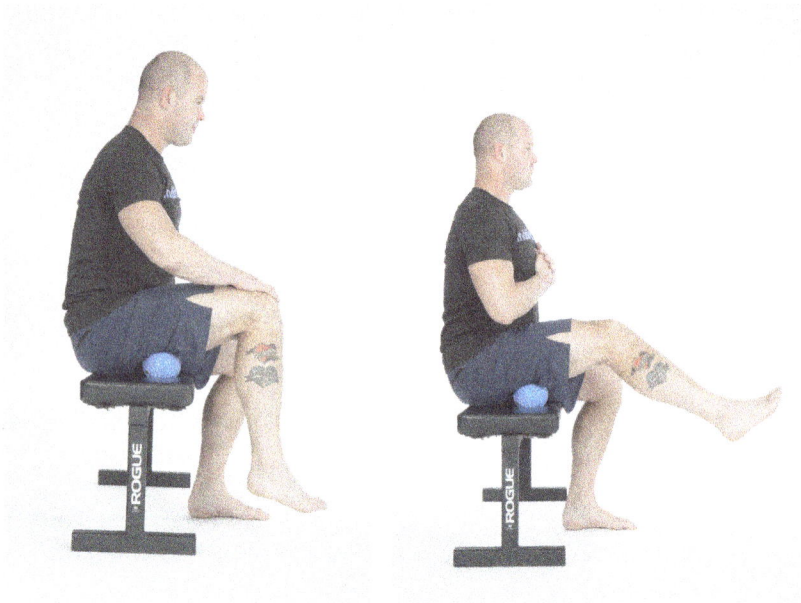

1) Sit on a bench, plyo box or hard chair
2) Place a lacrosse ball or small Supernova under your right hamstring, just below where it meets your butt
3) Slowly roll from side to side across the ball
4) You can also try extending and flexing your knee for a different stimulus
5) Keep moving the ball down until you finish with it just above the back of the knee
6) Switch sides

BANDED POSTERIOR CHAIN MOBILIZATION

1) Loop a medium mobility band around a squat rack post or other anchor at about hip height
2) Put the other end of your band around the top of your right thigh as you face away from the anchor
3) Take a step forward with your right foot to take up the band's tension
4) Hinge forward at the hips and place both palms flat on the floor
5) Bend your right knee a little and then straighten your right leg again
6) You can bias the lateral side of the left hamstring by placing both hands on the ground on the outside of it, and emphasize the medial side by moving your hands to the inside
7) Repeat 40 to 50 times and then switch sides

EXTERNAL ROTATION HIP OPENER

1) Stand in front of a counter or bench, and place your right foot on it
2) Turn your right foot onto its outer edge
3) With your left foot on the floor behind you, lean forward with an upright torso until you feel tension in your right hip
4) After a few seconds, relax and repeat. You can bias different aspects of the hip by leaning more to the inside or outside, and by twisting your torso toward and away from your midline.
5) Switch sides

WATERMAN 2.0

SINGLE LEG FLEXION WITH EXTERNAL ROTATION

1) Get into a lunge position with your right leg behind you and your left foot straight and plated on the floor
2) Next, push your left knee outward and toward the floor as you flatten your back
3) You can keep progressing until the outside of your left knee is almost touching the ground. To bias the lateral hip, lean your torso more to the outside and vice versa to emphasize the medial side.
4) Switch sides

HIP CAPSULE INTERNAL ROTATION

1) Kneel on the floor and move your weight onto your left knee, ensuring your knee is under your hip.
2) Drop your hips back and toward your left side
3) Keeping most of your weight over the left knee and lowering your left hip toward the ground, crawl forward a little to emphasize the front of the hip capsule
4) Switch sides. To increase the effect, try looping a band around the top of the forward leg

QUAD SMASH

1) Lie face down on the floor
2) Place a roller or ball under your left quad just above the knee
3) Slowly move side to side across the roller or ball. You can also pull your heel toward and away from your butt.
4) Move the roller or ball down your quad until you're just below the pelvis
5) Switch sides
6) You can also use a kettlebell to smash your quads while seated

GUT SMASH

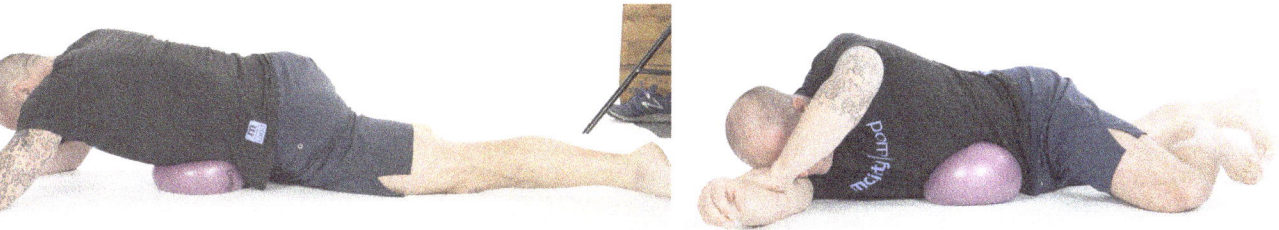

1) Lie face down on the floor
2) Place a ball of your choice at the bottom of your gut, just above your pelvis
3) Slowly roll across the ball
4) Move the ball up your abs and across them, camping out in any sore spots. You can also take deep nasal diaphragm breaths into the ball while it's stationary.

WATERMAN 2.0

OBLIQUE SIDE SMASH

1) Lie on your side on the ground
2) Place an MWOD Supernova just above your left hip
3) Slowly roll across the ball
4) You can also turn slightly more onto your front to capture the inside of the obliques

QL SMASH

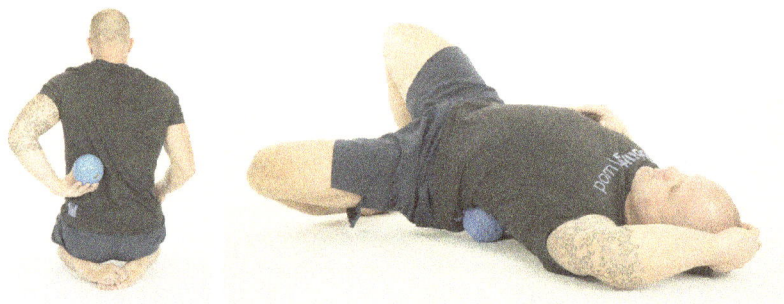

1) Lie on the floor on your back
2) Place an MWOD Supernova on one side of your lower back, just above your pelvis
3) Slowly drop your left knee toward the floor
4) Come back to the middle position, repeat 20 to 25 times and then switch the Supernova to the other side

5) Move the Supernova up your back and perform 20 to 25 reps on each side. Repeatedly move the ball up and end just below the base of your ribcage.

LATERAL HIP OPENER

1) Sit cross-legged
2) Move your right foot over your left knee
3) With your right leg keeping your left hip down, bring your left arm up over your head and lean to your right side
4) Lean over toward your right hip
5) Switch sides

WATERMAN 2.0

KNEE VOODOO FLOSS

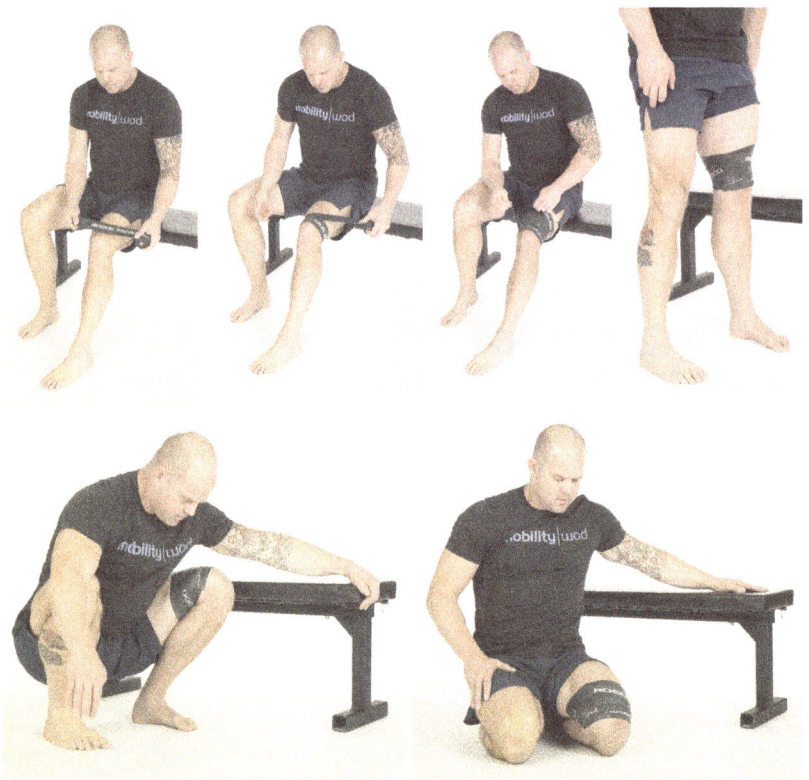

1) Wrap a Voodoo Floss band around each knee, using 50 percent tension and a 50 percent overlay and then tuck in the end of the band
2) Perform 10 to 15 squats, spending a few seconds in the bottom position of each rep
3) To get your knees into end range flexion, you can place your elbows inside them and then push out
4) You can also improve knee flexion by getting into a high kneel and then sitting back on your heels

MOBILIZATIONS APPENDIX

ADDUCTOR SMASH

1) Lie face down on the ground
2) Position the inside of your right leg on a roller
3) Drive your right hip toward the ground to create pressure against the roller. You can also straighten your leg and turn your knee outward.
4) If you hit a tight spot, camp out for a little while and try also moving your right heel toward your butt, before extending your knee again
5) Switch sides

CALF SMASH

WATERMAN 2.0

1) Sit on the floor
2) Place a roller or ball on your left calf just below the back of your knee
3) Slowly move side to side across the roller or ball
4) Keep moving the roller or ball down the back of your calf until it's just below the heel bone. You can also cross the right leg over the top of the left to increase the pressure and vary the stimulus by circling your left foot.
5) Switch sides. To alter the stimulus you can wrap a mobility band around the active foot.

BONE SAW

1) Kneel down with both legs extended behind you and your palms flat on the floor
2) Place the front of your right shin on top of your left calf
3) Pushing your hands into the ground and keeping your palms flat on the floor, rock back to push the front of your right shin into your left calf
4) You can also change up the stimulus by see-sawing the shin back and forth across your calf
5) Repeat the motion as you move your shin down your calf. After a minimum of 2 minutes, switch legs.

KNEE GAPPING

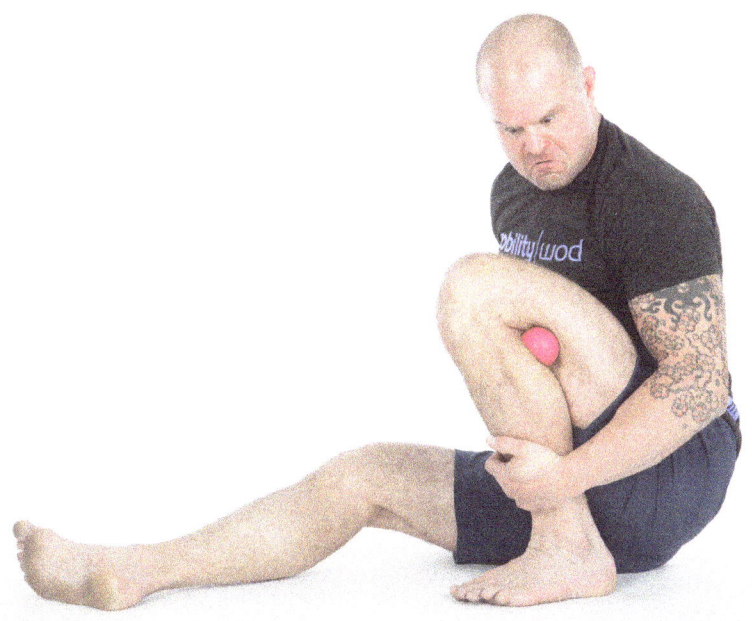

1) Sit on the floor and place a lacrosse ball or MWOD Gemini at the back of your left knee
2) Slide your left heel back toward you to pin the ball or Gemini between the bottom of your hamstring and the top of your calf
3) Rock forward on your left foot a little, creating a pinching motion at the back of the left knee
4) Repeat 40 to 50 times and then switch sides

OLYMPIC WALL SQUAT

1) Lie on your back in front of a wall or plyo box, with your butt close to it
2) Place your feet shoulder width apart or slightly wider on the wall or plyo box

3) Force your knees outward. Your legs should be parallel to the flat surface, mimicking the bottom position of a squat.
4) To increase the stimulus, repeat steps 1-3 with the ends of a medium resistance band looped below your knees, with most of the band behind your back. You can change the emphasis of the exercise by making your foot position narrower and wider.

TRAILING LEG HIP EXTENSION

1) Take a big step forward with your right foot and move your left leg back so you're in an exaggerated lunge
2) Clench your left glute and drive your left hip toward the ground
3) Switch sides

MEDIAL AND ANTERIOR SMASH

1) Lie on the ground and roll onto your left side
2) Place an MWOD Gemini on the outside of your left quad just below the hip and an MWOD Supernova opposite it and between your legs
3) Slowly kick your feet back and forth
4) Move both balls down your leg, repeating step #3 until you're just above the left knee
5) Switch sides

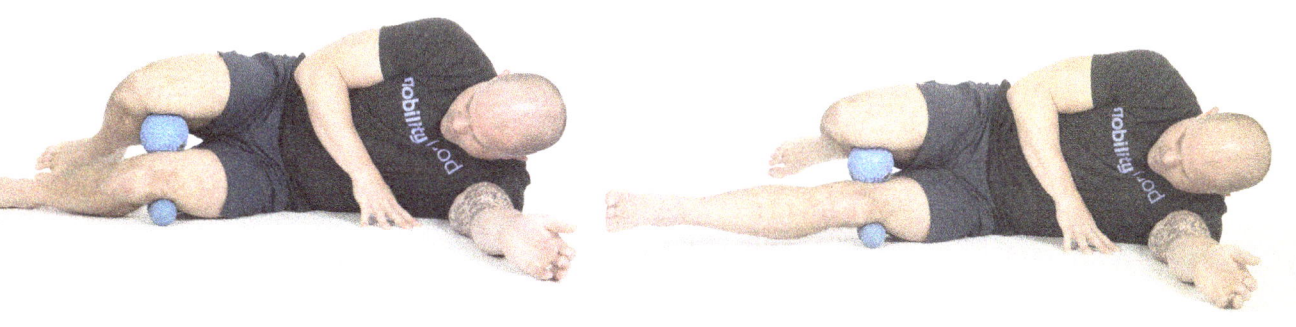

WATERMAN 2.0

T-SPINE OVERHEAD EXTENSION ON GEMINI

1) Lie on your back on the ground
2) Position an MWOD Gemini horizontally inside your shoulder blades and at the base of them
3) Extend your arm overhead
4) Bridge your hips up a few inches and then slowly lower them back down
5) After 15 to 25 reps, move the Gemini slightly higher. Eventually end with it on your traps at the base of your neck.

LAT SMASH

1) Lie on your right side on the ground
2) Extend your right arm above your head
3) Place an MWOD Supernova or roller below your left armpit
4) Slowly roll side to side across the ball or roller
5) Move the ball or roller down and continue rolling side to side across it. Stop where the lat muscle inserts into the ribcage.
6) Switch sides

T-SPINE FLEXION ON GEMINI

1) Repeat steps #1 and #2 from the t-spine overhead extension
2) Curl your torso into a half sit-up and then slowly lower yourself back down, sinking into the Gemini
3) Repeat 40 to 50 times

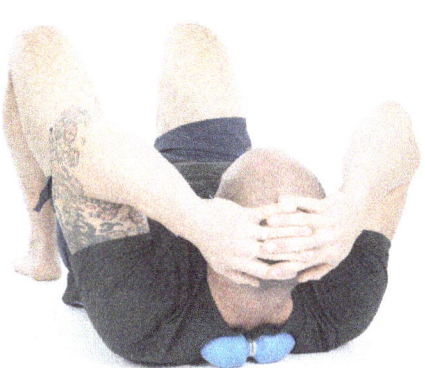

WATERMAN 2.0

THE SHOULDERS

FIRST RIB PIN AND SPIN

1) Standing in front of a squat rack pole or sign post, hinge at the hips and use your left hand to place a small ball between the right base of your neck and the pole
2) Drive into the ball as if you were trying to tackle someone
3) Extend your right arm and move it up and down
4) Complete 40 to 50 reps and then switch sides

TRAP BARBELL MOBILIZATION

1) Place a barbell in a squat rack at about shoulder height
2) Stand in front of a barbell, turn 90 degrees to the left
3) Take a small side step to move under the bar and align the top of your right trap with it
4) Drive upward into the bar
5) Extend your right arm and slowly swing it up into the overhead position
6) Do 40 to 50 reps and then switch sides

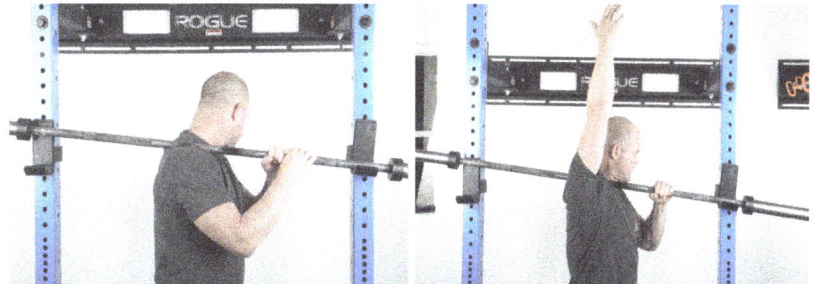

WATERMAN 2.0

SCALENES PIN AND SPIN

1) Sit on the floor and place a small ball at the base of your neck on the left side with your right hand
2) Gently twist the ball into your skin and turn your head up and to the right
3) Complete 20 to 30 reps and then switch sides

SUBSCAP TACK AND FLOSS

1) Put a barbell in a squat rack
2) Use your left hand to put a ball on top of the bar and hold it in place
3) Get your right arm up over the top of the bar and then drive your underarm down into the ball
4) Maintaining downward pressure on the ball, extend and flex your right arm
5) Complete 40 to 50 reps and then switch sides

SUPER FRONT RACK

1) Loop one end of a medium resistance mobility band around the pole of a squat rack or similar anchor
2) Facing the anchor, hook the other end of the band around your left wrist
3) Turn your palm upward and wind your shoulder into external rotation
4) Rotate your body underneath the band and get your shoulder under it as you turn to face away from the anchor
5) Squeeze your abs and left glute to keep your back flat
6) Grab the outside of your left elbow with your right hand and move your weight forward
7) Collect at least 2 minutes and then switch sides

WATERMAN 2.0

BANDED BULLY WITH EXTENSION BIAS

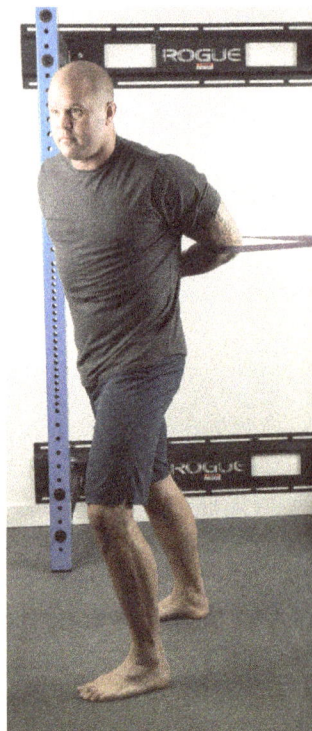

1) Loop one end of a medium resistance mobility band around a squat rack pole or similar anchor
2) Hook the other end of the band around your left elbow
3) Facing away from the anchor, place your left hand behind your back, using your right hand to keep it there
4) Take a big step forward with your left foot and turn your torso to the right
5) As you do so, pull your left elbow forward
6) Shift your foot position to the right several times to emphasize the soft tissue in your t-spine
7) Switch sides

BANDED LATERAL OPENER

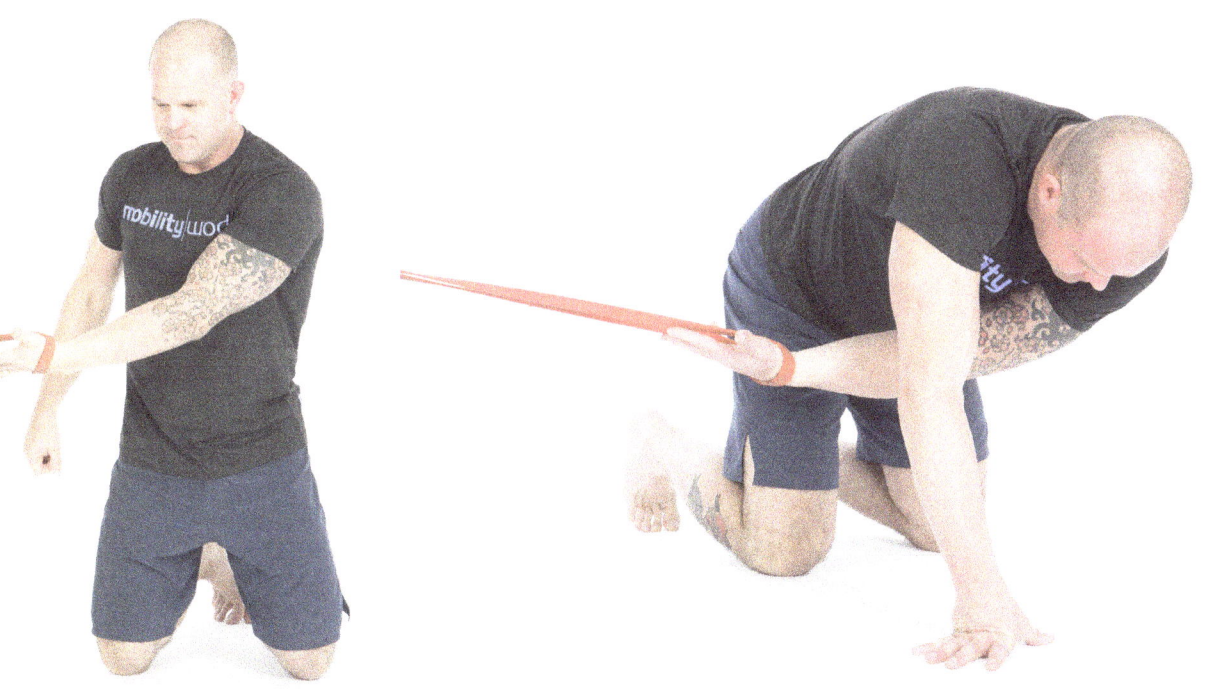

1) Hook one end of a light resistance mobility band around a squat rack pole or similar anchor just above hip height
2) Kneel down perpendicular to the anchor and loop your left wrist through the other end of the band
3) Keeping your knees on the ground, bend over and place your right palm on the floor
4) Sweep your left arm across your chest and take up resistance against the band
5) Hold for 10 seconds, relax and repeat for at least 2 minutes. Then switch sides.

TRICEPS SMASH

1) Lie on your back and place a roller next to your right armpit
2) Extend your right arm overhead with the top of your right triceps on the roller
3) Roll your arm back and forth slowly across the roller and after 2 minutes, switch sides
4) Flip over onto your belly with the roller on the floor just in front of your head
5) Extend your left arm in front of you so your left triceps is resting on the roller
6) Extend and flex your left arm on the roller for 2 minutes and then switch sides

MOBILIZATIONS APPENDIX

SHOULDER INTERNAL ROTATION ON LACROSSE BALL

1) Lie on your back on the ground
2) Place a lacrosse ball behind your left shoulder, where your arm meets the back of your armpit
3) With your left arm in a scarecrow position, and while pushing your shoulder into the floor, rotate your arm backwards until the back of your hand touches the floor (or as far as your range of motion will take you)
4) Rotate your arm downward until your left palm touches the floor. If you find it hard to keep your shoulder down, have someone place their foot on the front of your shoulder.
5) Do 40 to 50 reps and then switch sides

SINK MOBILIZATION

1) Stand facing away from a sink or squat rack with a bar placed at shoulder height
2) Reach back and grab the bar with your hands just wider than shoulder width apart
3) Keeping your abs braced, lean forward until you feel tightness in your shoulders
4) Hold for 10 seconds, relax and repeat for at least 2 minutes

WATERMAN 2.0

BICEPS BARBELL SMASH

1) Lie on your left side on the floor
2) Place one end of a barbell at the top of your left biceps
3) Put your right foot on the other end to keep it in place. You can also roll onto your left side and use the outside of your left quad to pin the barbell down.
4) With your left arm straight out to the side, curl your left biceps up and into the barbell
5) Keep moving the end of the barbell up your biceps until it almost reaches the shoulder. If a barbell is too great of a stimulus, have a friend lightly push their foot into your biceps instead.
6) Switch sides

PEC WALL SMASH

1) Stand in front of a corner edge of a wall or the upright pole of a squat rack and place an MWOD Supernova between your chest and the wall or rack
2) Lean into the ball
3) Keeping your abs tight, raise and lower your arm
4) You can start with the ball just under your collarbone and then move it down to the bottom of your chest, as well as moving inward and outward across the pecs
5) Spend at least 2 minutes and then switch sides

NECK TACK AND FLOSS

1) Lie on your back and place a small MWOD Supernova just below the base of the back of your skull
2) With your forearms crossed on your forehead, slowly rotate your head from left to right
3) Repeat for at least 2 minutes

SUPRACLAVICLE SCRUB

1) Use your right hand to place a small MWOD Supernova just above your left clavicle (collarbone)
2) Starting above the inside of the bone, use your right hand to twist the ball into the soft tissues
3) Slowly work your way along the collarbone to the outside of it
4) Switch sides

LOWER RIB SMASH WITH INTERNAL ROTATION

1) Lie on your back on the floor
2) Place a lacrosse ball on your lower ribs between the base of your left scapula (shoulder blade) and spine
3) Roll toward your left side
4) With the ball still in position, slide your left hand behind your back and lower your left hip toward the ground
5) Rotate to your left side with your hand pinned behind your back. Try to force the ball into the edge of your shoulder blade. You can also move the ball up and down.

SHOULDER CAPSULE RESET

1) Lie on your back on the ground with a kettlebell by your left shoulder

MOBILIZATIONS APPENDIX

2) Roll to your left and grab the kettlebell with both hands, using the right one to help move it above your left shoulder
3) Extend your left arm
4) Let the weight of the kettlebell reset your left shoulder in the back of the capsule
5) Switch sides

THE FEET AND ANKLES

FOOT SMASH

1) Stand up and place a small MWOD Supernova or MWOD Foot Roller under your right foot
2) Slowly roll your foot over the ball or roller
3) Work backwards from your forefoot to heel
4) Switch sides

 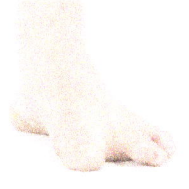  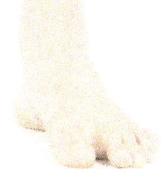

WATERMAN 2.0

POSTERIOR TIBIALIS TACK AND FLOSS

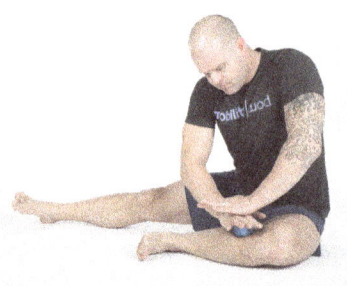 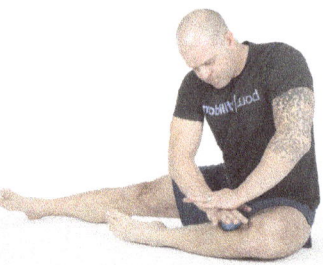

1) Sit on the ground
2) Place a lacrosse ball on the inside of your left heel
3) Slowly roll the ball back and forth with your hand
4) Work up the inside of the calf until you're just below the knee
5) Switch sides

BANDED ANKLE CAPSULE MOBILIZATION WITH VOODOO FLOSS

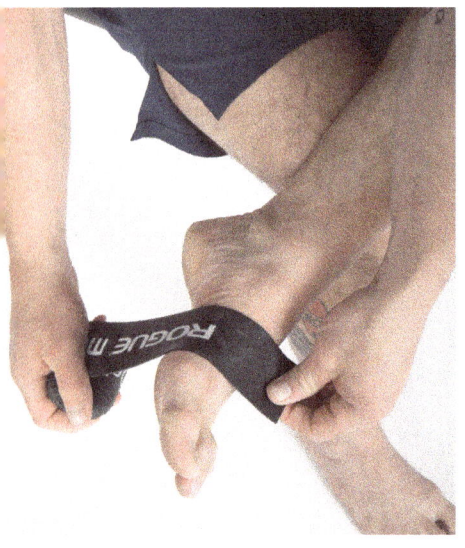 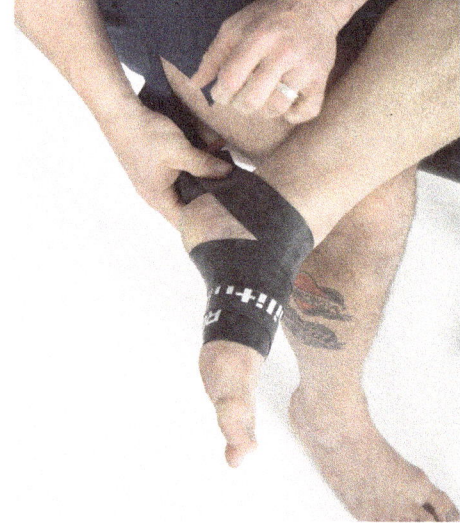 

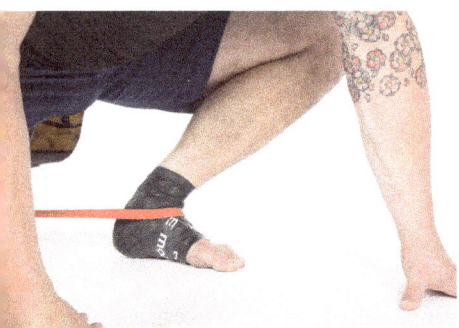 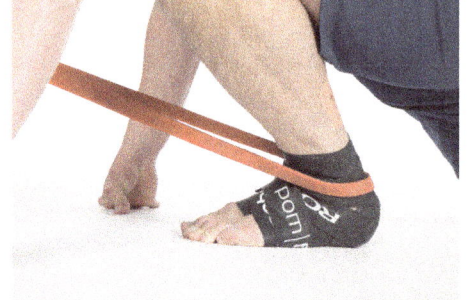

1) Wrap your left ankle in a Voodoo Floss band, using 50 percent tension and a 50 percent overlay and then tuck in the end of the band
2) Move your ankle through its full range of motion using some of the other ankle mobilizations in this section. You can also do some bodyweight exercises such as squats and lunges.
3) Switch sides

TOE PLANTAR FLEXION

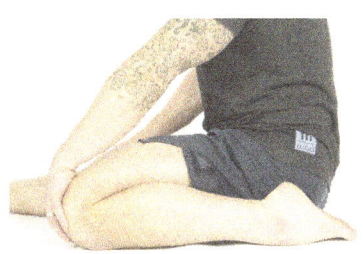 

1) Sit on the floor with your right leg out in front of you and your left leg folded behind you
2) Lean back and lift your left knee off the ground

DOUBLE BALL ANKLE TACK AND STRIP

1) Sit on the ground and put a lacrosse ball or Yoga Tune Up Ball between the outside of your left ankle and the floor
2) Place another ball on the inside of your left ankle

3) Pull up on your forefoot with one hand while pushing down on the heel with the other
4) Repeat 20 to 30 times and then switch sides

HEEL CORD TACK, TWIST AND FLOSS

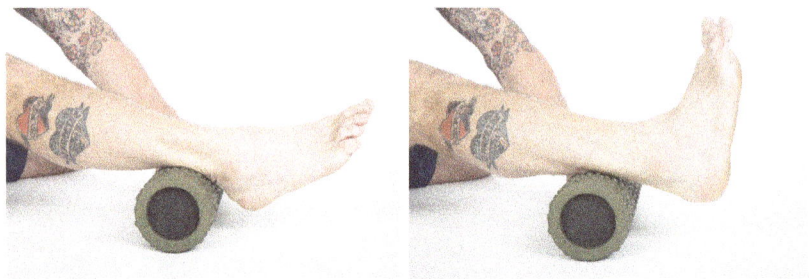

1) Sit on the ground and place a roller behind your right calf, just above the heel bone
2) Pull your foot up toward you and then push it away from you. You can also circle your foot and increase the pressure by placing your left leg over the right.
3) Switch sides

SHIN ANTERIOR COMPARTMENT SMASH

1) Get down on all fours
2) Place a roller below your right knee on the outside seam of your lower leg
3) Slowly move your right hip to the outside to move the ball or Gemini across the outer wall of the front of your shin

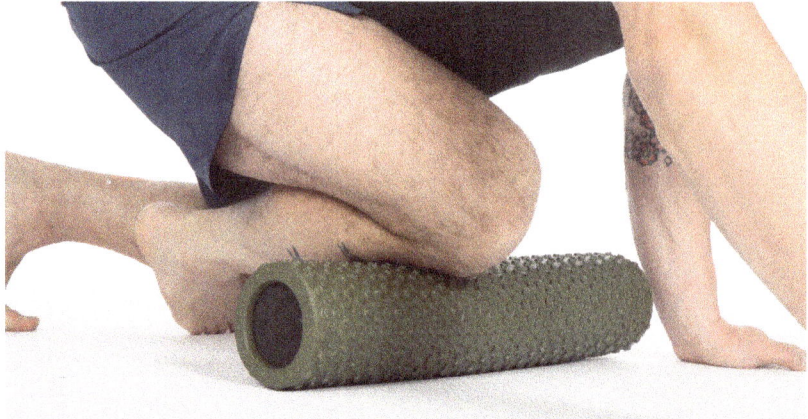

4) Move the roller down the outside edge of the front of your shin until you're just above the ankle joint
5) Switch sides

THE HANDS, WRISTS, ELBOWS AND ARMS

FOREARM BALL SMASH

1) Place your right arm on a counter or plyo box
2) Turn the palm up and place an MWOD Gemini ball between the underside of your forearm and the surface below. Then place a small MWOD Supernova on top of your forearm and hold it down with your palm.
3) Push down on your forearm with your left hand
4) Alternate between slowly circling your hand and moving it up and down
5) Move the lacrosse ball up the forearm until it's just below the elbow
6) Switch sides

WATERMAN 2.0

FOREARM BARBELL ROLLOUT

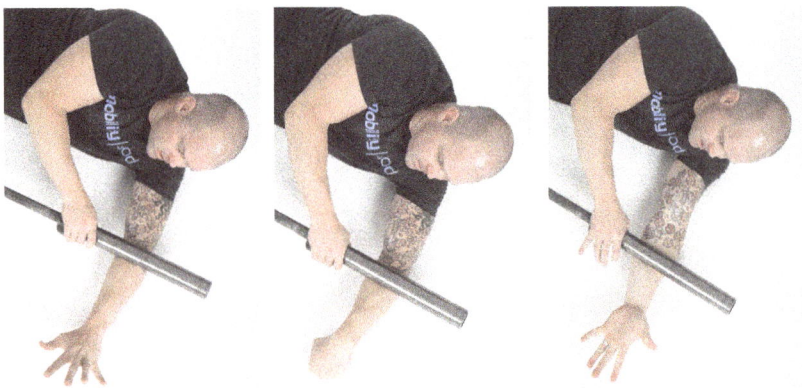

1) Lie on your back on the floor
2) Place one end of a barbell at the top of your left forearm, just below the crease of your elbow
3) Put your right foot on the other end to keep it in place. You can also roll onto your left side and use the outside of your left quad to pin the barbell down.
4) With your left arm straight out to the side, roll the barbell slowly down it. You can also curl your left wrist up and down.
5) Keep moving the end of the barbell down your forearm until it almost reaches the wrist
6) Switch sides

LEOPARD CLAW FOREARM SCRAPE

1) Apply some lotion or aloe gel to your right forearm
2) Grip the MWOD Leopard Claw with your left hand
3) Slowly scrape the tool down and across your forearm
4) If you start to get red bumps in an area, move the Leopard Claw further down your forearm
5) Switch sides

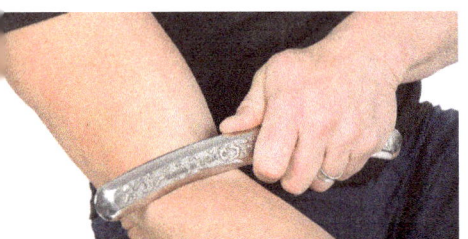
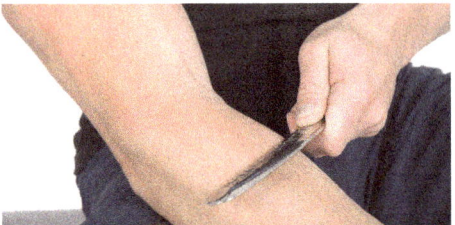
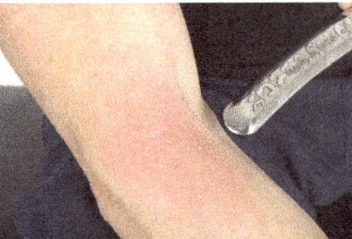

MOBILIZATIONS APPENDIX

ELBOW VOODOO FLOSS

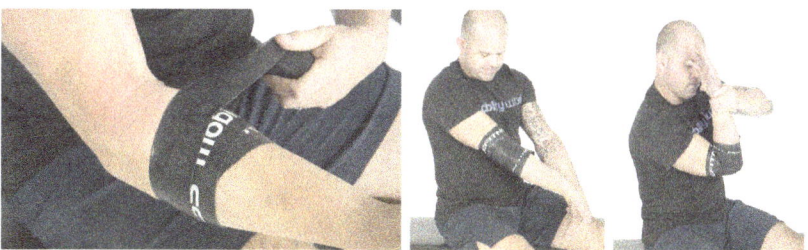

1) Wrap your elbow with a Voodoo Floss band, with 50 percent tension and a 50 percent overlay and then tuck in the end of the band
2) Move your elbow through a full range of motion
3) Switch sides

BANDED WRIST DISTRACTION WITH VOODOO FLOSS

1) Wrap your left wrist with a Voodoo Floss band, with 50 percent tension and a 50 percent overlay and then tuck in the end of the band
2) Loop one end of a medium resistance mobility band around a squat rack post or similar anchor
3) Put the other end of the band around your left wrist, with your left palm on the ground and facing away from the anchor
4) Pin your left hand to the ground using the right one
5) Flex and extend your elbow
6) You can also change the stimulus by turning your palm to face the anchor point
7) Switch sides

WATERMAN
WISDOM
THE PROS

ATHLETE PROFILE
KAI LENNY

AGE: 25
BASED IN: Spreckelsville, Maui
SPORTS: SUP, kiteboarding, surfing, windsurfing

CAREER HIGHLIGHTS: Won 7 SUP world titles and the World Kiteboarding Championships, set a new course record for Molokai 2 Oahu while winning the 2016 title, won the first ever SUP surfing event at Pipeline, won the Top Male Paddler and Best Performance awards at the 2016 SUP Awards, surfed Peahi at age 16

LIFE ON THE WATER: I'm in the water almost every day from dawn until dusk. Then my family and I often go back out to surf together after dinner. While it's important to continue the waterman legacy of people like Laird Hamilton, Dave Kalama, Buzzy Kerbox and Robby Naish, I'm also living this lifestyle because it's fun and I can't think of anything I'd rather do. It's really hard for me to take a rest day, and usually I'll still sneak a quick surf in. I start to feel sluggish if I'm not in the ocean—it's like my body demands it.

SHARING THE LOVE: I set up the Positively Kai Foundation to award grants to organizations that are educating kids about the ocean and water safety. I've always enjoyed working with kids and am eager to share my love of the water with as many people as possible. I'm blessed to have the opportunities I've been given, and want to pass this on in a positive way.

TRAINING TO WIN: SUP is still my focus because I'm passionate about it, but I also spend a lot of time kiting, shortboarding and windsurfing. I adapt each day's plan based on what the wind and waves give me. My goal is to be competent enough to compete at the highest level in all of these disciplines and to just follow wherever my interest leads me. I'm also getting into producing movies and it's another exciting new challenge.

PREPARING FOR THE UNEXPECTED: My land-based training is geared toward working on my weaknesses and making sure my body can handle anything that can happen on the water. This includes developing single-leg balance and strength so I feel stable on my board, and being limber enough to deal with the worst wipeouts. Mobility is a constantly moving target because of how varied my schedule is and all the things I like to do on the water, so I have to adapt what I'm doing daily.

KAI LENNY'S TOP 3 TIPS FOR SUP SURFING

1) It's important to be aware and acknowledge others in the lineup especially if they are on a craft that doesn't have the ability to catch the waves with as much ease as you on a SUP. I typically let a set of waves go through before I catch my wave. Just because I can catch every one doesn't mean I should. Even if I hang back a bit, by the end of my session I have still caught so many waves.
2) The beauty of paddle surfing is there are waves to be ridden that nobody cares to look at. Because the sport allows you to perform at a high level in poor conditions, you're guaranteed to "score" by yourself or with a few friends versus hustling toward a better wave with a ton of people. I always seek out a wave that's not quite as good and still end up enjoying it.
3) When riding the wave, my biggest improvement has come from being more patient, breathing through my turns and relaxing rather than tensing up. That doesn't mean don't push your turn hard. But you can move your board aggressively by just doing the move like a yoga pose, which uses your entire body's flow and leverage. A step-up involves holding your turns slightly longer. I try to never ride flat, but instead am always thinking of snowboarding so I'm riding heel to toe.

ATHLETE PROFILE
DAVE KALAMA

AGE: 53
BASED IN: Kula, Maui
SPORTS: SUP, surfing, windsurfing

CAREER HIGHLIGHTS: Perfected tow surfing with Laird Hamilton and the Strapped crew, was an early SUP pioneer, finished 2nd in Molokai 2 Oahu, trains elite paddle athletes

LIFE LESSONS: Heavy water puts you in a wide range of situations that are beyond your control. When you're getting held down, what you can decide is whether you stay calm or panic. It's habit forming because everyone is forced to deal with problems in life and the way you learn to handle adversity on the water carries over. You also get those times when you're a couple of miles offshore and you're just awestruck by your surroundings. That's when I realize how thankful I am to have these experiences, and to live this life. If you can't acknowledge the beauty of nature in those moments, then I'm not sure you're fully alive.

THE MEANING OF PEAHI: Now that it's been more than a decade since I first towed in with Laird and the rest of the guys, it has given me an even greater perspective on what a special time it was and how fortunate I was to share it with them. In the 50s and 60s, Greg Noll, Pat Curren and Mickey Munoz were figuring things out as they went along and just surfing for the sheer joy of it. I'm reluctant to compare us to them, but we had the same spirit a generation later. We were in just the right place, in the right frame of mind and with the right people to discover how majestic Jaws really was and what was possible out there. A lot of people might say they have your back, but you

find out who will really come through for you in situations that are literally life or death. That created a bond that will last for the rest of our lives.

LIFE AFTER JAWS: Nothing will ever replicate what we experienced at Peahi, but I've found other things on the water that bring me joy. I've really come to value working on boards and equipment, which I think adds another dimension to the waterman experience. I've also been passionate about teaching since a ski coach in high school told me to attack the next run like a race car. It was a simple explanation, but it showed me how important a few well-chosen words can be in a teaching situation. Now that's what I try to do when I'm coaching: find a way to help people with what I say as much as by what I do. You see something change in their eyes when it clicks and they get better, and that's very rewarding.

DAVE KALAMA'S TOP 5 TIPS FOR IMPROVING YOUR STROKE

1) You need to maximize your functional reach—i.e. how far you can reach while still retaining a solid stroke. It's not the absolute furthest you could go, but most people still aren't going far enough. Even if you're hinging at the hips, stacking your shoulders and rotating well, you're still leaving a lot of torque on the table if you're not reaching out and engaging all your major muscle groups at the start of the stroke.

2) Don't be afraid of sticking your blade too far into the water. The blade must be completely submerged to get a powerful catch and you can even go a couple of inches deeper and still be OK. Most people leave some of the blade above the surface, which is short circuiting their entire stroke.

3) Pull the paddle out just enough to clear the surface of the water. One of the biggest rookie mistakes is yanking the blade 2 feet out of the water each time, which is 1 foot and 11 inches too much. You're going to slow your stroke and put a lot of stress on your top shoulder if you're doing that.

4) If you see a big slurp and swirl after each stroke, you're trying to pull the paddle too much. Instead, you should be knifing the blade into the water and using the paddle as a lever to launch the board forward. The more you disturb the water, the less efficient you're being.

5) Be smooth. You see a lot of people lunging at the water or jerking the paddle violently. That's a massive waste of energy, as is putting the shaft in a Kung Fu grip. You should hook your fingers of your bottom hand and let your palm relax, as you try to maintain smooth power application from the catch to the exit.

ATHLETE PROFILE
BRODY WELTE

AGE: 42
BASED IN: Hampstead, North Carolina
SPORTS: SUP, surfing

CAREER HIGHLIGHTS: Team USA Head Coach for ISA World Paddleboard Championships, founded PaddleFit and created the PaddleFit Games

A SYSTEMIC APPROACH TO SUP TRAINING: Part of SUP's appeal is that almost anyone can jump on a board and go. While that's great, for any sport to progress, people need to learn how to move effectively, efficiently and safely. That's why I go outside the SUP world to gather the best ideas from people who improve the best athletes in the world—like Kelly Starrett, Gray Cook and Mark Verstegen—and incorporate their know-how into a comprehensive on-water and on-land program. Then we add in expertise from experienced watermen and women and tailor each athlete's programming to their unique goals and needs. We've got to include technique, skill and conditioning within a formalized practice that gets proven results.

GOING GLOBAL: Outside the US, a lot of the people who attend our clinics have no idea who any of the biggest names in SUP are. They just view the sport as another fitness modality like the ones that are big in their countries, such as soccer, cycling and skiing. That's good in a way because it means we're starting fresh without having to re-train people who've watched the pros on YouTube and tried to copy their strokes. We can coach mechanics, program conditioning and help them rapidly improve without the movement mistakes we often see in countries where SUP is already pervasive.

WATERMAN 2.0

THE FUTURE OF SUP RACING: As a coach for Team USA, I've been lucky enough to see firsthand how the standard of SUP racing has vastly improved. One of the most promising things is that we see teams from countries like Ireland and Costa Rica that aren't considered traditional water sports powerhouses. This validates that SUP can thrive anywhere. While getting the sport into the Olympics is still a work in progress, having it in the next Pan Am Games is a big step.

BRODY WELTE'S TOP 5 TIPS FOR PADDLING PROGRAMMING

1) Work with a qualified coach. If you look at any professional athlete or successful business person, they will have a coach/mentor in their life to guide them. Water sports are highly technical and require extensive knowledge and expertise to do well.

2) Have a comprehensive program to help achieve your goals. Paddling is an essential component of training, but so are nutrition, recovery, strength and conditioning and preventative mobility exercises to keep you healthy.

3) Learn how to paddle correctly. There is a biomechanically sound way to paddle that is efficient and will minimize injuries. Building a foundation of sound paddling technique opens the door for you to pursue your goals.

4) Sustainability should be one of your main aims. Yes, you will have times when you need to ramp up your training to prepare for a competition, but your overall program should be something that you can keep doing the rest of your life.

5) Enjoy your time on the water. There are enough things that you need to be 100 percent serious about and paddling is not one of them. The more enjoyment you get out of being on the water, the more motivation you will have for accomplishing your goals. Keeping your passion for paddling will help you make it through the times when you have to grind it out.

ATHLETE PROFILE
CONNOR BAXTER

AGE: 23
BASED IN: Pukalani, Maui
SPORT: SUP

CAREER HIGHLIGHTS: Won Molokai 2 Oahu 3 times, won 7 world titles, won the overall champion title at the 2015, 2016 and 2017 Pacific Paddle Games, won the Male Paddler of the Year award at the 2014, 2016 and 2017 SUP Awards, won 8 straight Maui 2 Molokai titles

THE MEANING OF MOLOKAI: Growing up in Hawaii there are a lot of historic races, but nothing comes close to M2O. So many of the legendary watermen crossed the channel before it was a race, and now that it's a contest, it attracts the world's best paddlers. It's a spiritual experience as much as it is a competition. I was 14 when I took my first crack at Molokai and it was a big achievement just to finish. Then I became determined to win it. To have done so 3 times racing against so many of my friends is an honor. I look at what Jamie Mitchell did in winning the prone category for a decade, and it motivates me to keep coming back and improving.

NEVER STOP: I've still got so much to learn. I look at how powerful and efficient Danny Ching and Travis Grant are and realize that I'm not at their level yet. There are so many talented young paddlers right now—Mo Freitas, Kai Lenny, Casper Steinfath—and we're pushing each other to live up to guys like Danny Ching, Travis Grant and Dave Kalama. My friend Zane Schweitzer and I train together all the time and he inspires me to be my best. I also look at Mo Freitas ripping so hard on the North Shore and it makes me want to get better at shortboard and SUP surfing. Competitions like The Ultimate Waterman force you to mix things up, which is how you stay passionate.

WATERMAN 2.0

TAKING CARE OF YOURSELF: Back in 2013 I was getting sick a lot and was just worn thin. I realized that I was over-committing and needed to cut back on the number of races and traveling. There are still a lot of premier events, but I'm spending more time at each venue—whether it's in Mexico, SoCal, Japan or wherever—so I can get accustomed to the conditions and get some training in. I've traveled to a lot of European countries and am prioritizing going on more surf trips with my friends. It's too easy to burn out and that's when it's not fun anymore.

CONNOR BAXTER'S TOP 5 TIPS FOR CHANNEL CROSSINGS

1) You've got to have a knowledgeable support crew. My Dad did a lot of sailing races and knows the M2O and Maui 2 Molokai channels very well, so he's able to give me great advice. A month before the race he's looking at charts and tides and trying to figure out the best lines for me to take. It's a huge advantage.

2) Be physically prepared. You can't stick to flatwater or just surf and expect to endure a 5 or 6 hour crossing. Instead, you've got to train in many disciplines and at different intensity levels, make sure you've got enough endurance and ensure you're proficient upwind, downwind and sideways. The channels can throw all these conditions at you, so you must be ready for whatever happens.

3) Learn how to hop bumps. When Molokai is windy and bumpy, I feel so comfortable. If you can time hopping between each bump, you'll only use half the energy you'd burn if it was flatter. Then when I have 5 or 6 miles to go and Travis, Kai or whoever is making their move, I have something left to kick into high gear.

4) Get your mind right. The first time out, your body will start hurting and your brain's going to start screaming at you to get in the support boat. You've got to resist that impulse and will yourself to keep going. When I start feeling like I want to stop, I combat it by just paddling harder.

5) Become comfortable with your equipment. Some guys switch out

WATERMAN WISDOM: TIPS FROM THE PROS

their board each year to try and get an edge, but I've used the same board for several years because I know I'll be alright on it for all 32 miles. It's the same with your paddle, fin set up and hydration pack. When I know my gear is just right, it makes me feel more prepared and relaxed before the race.

ATHLETE PROFILE
PAIGE ALMS

AGE: 30
BASED IN: Haiku, Maui
SPORT: Big wave surfing

CAREER HIGHLIGHTS: Won 2014/15 Big Wave Awards Women's Performance of the Year, first woman to get barreled at Jaws, nominated for Best Female Action Sports Athlete at the 2015 ESPY Awards, Won 2006 Explorer Women's Championship

REDEFINING WHAT'S POSSIBLE FOR WATERWOMEN AT JAWS: The world of female big wave surfing deserves more recognition. It's a magical thing, these 15 to 20 strong women doing this crazy sport in the biggest waves on the planet, and very few people know about it. We just need the chance to show what we can do. All of my favorite big wave guys—Kai [Lenny], Jamie [Mitchell], Greg [Long]—are so supportive. Maybe it's because they're out with us in the lineup and know we face the same challenges on big days. People talk all this crap on social media when I post a photo or another girl shares a video clip because they don't know what we really do. Most of them probably couldn't even handle an overhead wave. Then Shane Dorian or one of the other guys will get on and write, "That's the most amazing thing I've ever seen."

THE POWER OF BREATH CONTROL: I do a lot of breath holding and control work in the summer and fall. It's one of the things on my list before the big winter swells roll in. A couple of years ago I was lucky enough to take a freediving course with Kirk Krack at Performance Freediving. I had no idea of what the human body was capable of before then. Kirk showed me that anyone—not just surfers—can learn to hold their breath for several minutes and control their oxygen levels. Then I started putting those lessons into action when freediving and spearfishing with friends. It has also made me feel more assured that I can handle getting held down and avoid panicking when things get rough.

LET'S GET PHYSICAL: When I'm right physically, everything else seems to fall into place. It helped that my Mom was a massage therapist, but I've also learned a lot from trainers in the past couple of years. Rehabbing my injured shoulder has made me much more aware of my body and what I need to do to be ready for the biggest waves. I do a lot of resistance and agility work and plenty of endurance stuff. My trainer and I meet at the start of each week and see what the surf's going to do, what's going on with my work schedule and how I'm feeling. We then create a varied plan for the week, which helps me know what's coming. I feel mentally tougher when my body is resilient.

DON'T SLEEP ON RECOVERY: Rest has always been huge for me, and even if I'm flying halfway around the world I have to get a minimum of 8 hours a night. I'm amazed that someone like Kai Lenny can be out in the water all day every day. For me to recover from multi-day sessions at somewhere like Jaws—where I'm in the water, on a jet ski, on the boat, then back in the water—I need 9, 10 or even 11 hours of sleep to be able to go back out again. The same goes if I've had a bad wipeout and am sore all over. I'm certainly no stranger to 10 hour sleeps!

PAIGE ALMS'S TOP 3 TIPS FOR BEING MENTALLY STRONG IN THE SURF

1) What you do on land profoundly impacts your mindset on the water. When I'm physically ready, all my gear is fine-tuned and I'm feeling prepared, I have confidence when I hit the lineup. You can't just suddenly get into something without knowing what you're doing or going through the process. People who randomly huck themselves into big waves are the ones who get badly hurt.

2) Experiment with your equipment and get it dialed in on smaller days. Growing up, my mentors had me work my way through different board sizes—from 6 foot to 6 foot 6, then to 7, 8 and eventually 9. In surfing you're always going to different places and even if you just stay at one break, the waves give you something different every day. If you have some go-to boards, they become a constant that makes you think you can take on anything. It sounds weird, but it's almost like you form a relationship with your boards.

3) Work your way up to bigger waves. It's no good for a rookie to think they're going to charge into Peahi or Mavericks and come out OK. Instead you need to master small waves, then go overhead, then double overhead and so on. The more time you spend in the water, the better you'll get at reading the tides and conditions, knowing what your safe zones are and getting used to different situations. I think that's one of the reasons I've always felt calm out there. Even my first time at Jaws, when I should've been terrified, I just felt this sense of peace. That's something to do with growing up in the ocean.

ATHLETE PROFILE
DANE JACKSON

AGE: 24
BASED IN: Rock Island, Tennessee
SPORTS: Whitewater kayaking and canoeing

CAREER HIGHLIGHTS: 3-time Freestyle World Championships K-1 gold medalist, achieved the first descent of Encanto Falls, 2014 World Cup champion, 2011 C1/Squirt world champion, 3-time Whitewater Grand Prix champion, 10 World Championships medals

TRAINING VARIABILITY: Generally if I am pretty far from an event, training is just going out and having some fun messing around with tricks, lines and techniques. Then as I get closer to a major competition, I'll work on paddling faster for races and nailing my routine for freestyle. Personally, I like to paddle as long as I can in a day and keep going until I'm tired. Then do it all over again the next day. I try to really push my endurance as much as I can.

RECOVERY AND NUTRITION WHILE TRAVELING: Even without a great night's sleep I can usually just go ahead and do what I was going to do anyway. But sometimes getting over jet lag or a big international time change is pretty important before I go out on the water. I find that I run best on a lot of protein and quite a lot of fat. Breakfast is usually some form of egg sandwich with lots of bacon. Lunch is a turkey or ham sandwich, maybe a burger if I can get it. Dinner is often a burger if I didn't have one for lunch or maybe pizza.

A FAMILY FOUNDATION: Without my Dad dropping everything to commit to being a full-time kayaker, I don't know what my upbringing would have been like. My sister pushed me to learn kayaking and continues to challenge me.

She's also great fun to hang out with while I'm traveling. I'm not just an ambassador for Jackson Kayak, but also help Nick [Troutman] with video edits, photoshoots of new boats and all kinds of other media stuff.

DANE JACKSON'S TOP 5 TIPS FOR STAYING CALM DURING COMPETITION

1) Many people's natural reaction is to tense up, but you're only going to perform well if you can overcome this and make yourself relax. I want to be as loose as possible during each run and just let my training take over.
2) Try to have fun. At the end of the day, you're out on the river doing tricks with some of your best friends and, in my case, family members. If you approach it like it's a grind, you're going to miss out on the full experience.
3) While you should be relaxed out on the water, you also need to focus on what you're about to do and mentally rehearse your moves. The run is over so quickly that there's no room for error and you've got to dial in.
4) If you're thinking too much about making the podium or beating a certain competitor, you're going to put too much pressure on yourself and your performance will suffer. Just do the best you can. It's all you can do!
5) Even if you don't have the best result ever or fall short of your goal, you've still got to enjoy yourself no matter what. No career lasts forever, so you have to value each day and be thankful every time you go out on the water.

ATHLETE PROFILE
OSCAR CHALUPSKY

AGE: 55
BASED IN: Vila do Conde, Portugal
SPORTS: Surfski, kayaking

CAREER ACHIEVEMENTS: 12-time Molokai 2 Oahu Ocean Ski champion, captained the South Africa team at the 1992 Barcelona Olympics, won the Sella Descent, Lucky Strike Challenge and Umkomaas River Marathon multiple times, claimed 8 South Africa Ironman titles, became the first person to win junior and senior Ironman titles in the same year, co-founded Epic Kayaks, CEO of Nelo Kayaks

LESSONS FROM MY FATHER: My Dad never pressured my brother Herman and me into doing any sport. He'd just say, "I'm going swimming at 6 o'clock tomorrow morning and you can come with me if you want to." I soon took to swimming with him and training at a local club, and ended up ranked number 3 in the world in the 50 meter butterfly. Soon enough I got into paddling and Ironman competitions through the surf lifesaving movement. To motivate me, my Dad told me that if I won a Nipper [junior surf lifesavers] Ironman he'd buy me a racing bike. So I did and after he bought it, I got really serious about doing triathlons. One of my Dad's sayings is, "If you're going to do something, do it properly." This has stuck with me my entire life, on and off the water. Dad continues to live out his principles. He's 80 now, but still paddles most days and won his age group at the World Marathon Canoeing Championships.

FINDING FRIENDSHIP AND RIVALRY AT MOLOKAI: Because of the apartheid regime, I was banned from competing internationally during my peak. This

meant I had to wait 5 years to race against Grant Kenny. In my teens, I'd become the first person in the world to win junior and senior national Ironmans in South Africa. Grant did it a month later and became the poster boy for water sports in Australia. He had won Molokai for 4 straight years when I had the opportunity to race him in 1983. And he'd already won a bronze medal in the Olympics, while I wasn't allowed to compete until 1992. Grant's a great competitor, but I beat him to win the first of 7 straight titles at Molokai. We've remained good friends over the years. Molokai is the longest running elite race and everyone in our sport wants to win it. Every time you show up you're guaranteed to get a strong field. I claimed my twelfth title there 29 years after my first one and now my ultimate goal is to win number 13. I've won Molokai in my 20s, 30s and 40s and now I'm trying to do it in my 50s.

ACHIEVING BALANCE: For a lot of athletes, training and competing are everything. I've learned that if you're not having fun and enjoying life, then the fun is going to quickly go out of it. The only way I've stayed in the top 10 in the world for 43 years is by maintaining my love of paddling and by prioritizing friends and family. My wife and I have been married for 35 years, have children and still love each other's company. When a lot of athletes have kids their performance suffers or, if they make competing the only thing, maybe their marriage falls apart. For me it's never been an either/or thing. I'm lucky to have an understanding wife, but when I'm with my family, they come first. It's also important to not be too hard on yourself. If I want to eat a big steak dinner or have a beer, then I will.

A DIFFERENT WAY TO COACH: Clint Robinson beat me at the '92 Olympics. After the Games I realized that I hadn't done my best because I had bought into a training program that didn't work for me. So I wrote my own training plan and beat Clint a few months later at Molokai. This showed the importance of questioning everything, challenging accepted wisdom and not just doing what you're told. I try to apply the same approach of constantly

evolving in coaching. When I'm doing a downwinder, I think about how I can extrapolate what I'm learning. Next I look at what's working for my athletes. Then I put the two together. For me, coaching is a continual exchange—it's not just me telling people what to do. I want to see what they can teach me as well. You can learn from anyone, no matter what their level of experience is. Once I was paddling in the Sea of Galilee and this lady, who was a recreational paddler in her 60s, told me that she sat in her boat a certain way because it was more elegant. I tried her way, found it was more comfortable and so adopted it. You're never too old or too good to stop learning.

ATHLETE PROFILE
DANNY CHING

AGE: 35
BASED IN: Hermosa Beach, California
SPORTS: SUP, outrigger canoeing

CAREER HIGHLIGHTS: Gold medalist at the 2007 Outrigger World Championships and 2015 ISA World Paddleboard Championships, 8-time winner of The Battle of the Paddle, winner of the 2013 Carolina Cup

MENTORING: Growing up I was always surrounded by adults who shared their love and knowledge of the water. They taught me that life is not about how high you rise, but rather what you can do to help people at the bottom come up. My achievements give me the responsibility to help young people get out on the water and do their best, regardless of their ability level. And it's not this big, serious thing—it brings me joy to coach and encourage kids and adults.

MULTI-DISCIPLINE BACKGROUND: I grew up swimming, playing water polo, soccer and baseball, surfing, outrigger canoeing—everything. Doing all these different things helped me discover how my body moves in all kinds of different situations on land and in the water, and what I respond best to. Coaches can tell you what they observe, but it's your job to learn how you work. On the water, it doesn't matter if you're prone, kneeling, sitting or standing—paddling is paddling and everything carries over. You should never limit yourself to one discipline and never stop trying new things.

CANOE CLUB HERITAGE: My Dad and his friends got fed up with driving a long way to an outrigger canoe club, so they founded their own: Lanakila. He and my uncle were coaches, and he met my Mom there. And it's where I met my wife. Now it's up to me, Cliff Meidl and other younger guys to keep the club going. As a paddler, I'm not interested in what you can't do. I want to know what you can do. Now I know where your passion is and can start helping you build your skills. It's exciting that we have men, women and children of all ages coming to Lanakila and I hope we can keep growing our program.

FALL BACK ON TECHNIQUE: If you keep honing your technique, it will give you more top end potential. There are a lot of paddlers with huge engines who can just crank away, but that isn't sustainable over the long term. If you're dealing with an injury, are sick or are having a bad day, that raw power isn't going to be available, so technique is what you fall back on. If I can pass you going at 70 percent with good technique, I can certainly hammer you going all out. You've got to keep doing skill work, keep refining your stroke and turns, no matter who you are or what you've achieved.

DANNY CHING'S TOP 5 TIPS FOR RACE STRATEGY

1) To be your best on race day, you need to train to your weaknesses and then race to your strengths. So maybe you're fast but you have poor endurance. You can only use that speed if you can stay with your competitors over the long haul, so you've got to build up your stamina.

2) You have to know other racers' strengths and weaknesses and understand how these match or differ from your own. I know a lot of the younger guys will be fast off the line but can't close, so I hang back and bide my time. Someone like Travis Grant will never, ever quit, so if I'm to have any chance in a distance race, I've got to hit him with a couple of speed bursts in the last 2 miles and then try to get close enough to make it a sprint finish. You have to study the whole field like this as the water can present enough surprises.

3) You can't win a race on the first turn, but you can lose it. Once you come around that first buoy, start thinking about your approach to

the next one so it doesn't surprise you. If you can see a clear line, even if it means going wide, you can get through without being caught in the carnage. Also factor in when you're going to make your move to challenge the leaders, so you're ready to strike at just the right time.

4) When I used to train with kayakers, we'd talk about getting in "the pit" in training. This means getting to a point where the pain is so bad that all you want to do is stop. I've applied this to all levels of racing. One time at a local outrigger race, I pushed so hard at the finish that I couldn't stand up. My teammates literally carried me out of the boat. You've got to get comfortable with that kind of commitment when things get tough or you'll regret not giving your all later on.

5) I avoid training as if a race will give me perfect conditions because it rarely does. You can't control wind and waves, but you can battle test yourself in difficult circumstances. We used to take out old, leaky boats with wobbly seats once a week and go as hard as we could. At that point, it's just about who the best paddler is, how good your form is. If you can condition yourself to handle adversity, you'll be ready for anything come race time.

ATHLETE PROFILE
EMILY JACKSON-TROUTMAN

AGE: 28
BASED IN: Rock Island, Tennessee
SPORT: Freestyle kayak

CAREER HIGHLIGHTS: Won gold at the 2009 and 2015 World Freestyle Kayak Championships, 2007 Junior World champion, 2012 World Cup winner, 9-time GoPro Mountain Games winner, 4-time Payette River Games champion (won the 1x just 3 weeks before having her son)

WINNING THE PAYETTE RIVER GAMES 3 WEEKS BEFORE GIVING BIRTH: I had bigger things going on than performing, so for me it was like kayaking with a clean slate. Whatever happens doesn't really matter, just do what is best for me and my son and have fun! That mental approach set me up for success because I didn't care at all what the other competitors were doing or trying. I only focused on the things I could control.

CALLING ERIC JACKSON "DAD": My life, work and everything I do is based around the water. The lifestyle became a reality for me when I did it as a kid with my father, but now I have made it my reality, too. So it's had an impact on everything. He also exposed me to the fun and dangers of water at a young age, so I feel like I have a better understanding and respect for water than a lot of people who find the water later in life.

FINDING AND MAINTAINING BALANCE: I gave a TED talk called "Uncompromising"

WATERMAN WISDOM: TIPS FROM THE PROS

and it's about knowing what 5 things make you feel successful and happy and working toward them every day. My 5 are kayaking, being a wife and mother, exercising, working for my family's business [Jackson Kayak] and spending time with my family. I try to focus on these priorities every day and when I do so, I feel balanced. I take my son down to the river and put a lifejacket on him and my husband [world champ Nick Troutman] and I will run together if we've been away from each other for a while. We always sit down and eat all our meals as a family around the table. It's the little things that make it all work.

EMILY JACKSON-TROUTMAN'S TOP 5 TIPS FOR WATERWOMEN

1) Trust yourself as you know what's best for you. And remember that water sports are fun and should always stay fun. Many women forget this when they decide to compete.
2) You can do whatever you put your mind to. Don't let people convince you that you have a MUCH harder road because you're a girl.
3) Try and paddle with as many different groups as possible. This opens up different ways to enjoy the same sport.
4) Always set yourself up to feel good on the water. Before a big event, I brush my teeth! It gives me the illusion that I feel fresh and ready to go. The same goes for making sure my bathing suit is dry.
5) Remember that rivers are always changing. Just because you can do something in one place does not mean you'll be able to repeat it on the next river. So focus on being adaptable.

ATHLETE PROFILE
ERIN CAFARO MACKENZIE

AGE: 34
BASED IN: San Mateo, California
SPORT: Rowing

CAREER HIGHLIGHTS: Gold medalist in the women's 8 at the 2008 and 2012 Olympics, won the women's 4 at the 2007 World Championships and 2005 World Junior Championships, won the 8 and pairs at the 2009 World Championships

HANDLING PRESSURE AT THE HIGHEST LEVEL: When I was a junior athlete, getting nervous before a race or trial used to bother me and make me feel uncomfortable. But as I progressed I found that I actually performed my best when I had butterflies and pre-race jitters, so I learned how to embrace it. It got to the point where I felt nervous if I wasn't nervous. In the heats in Beijing, that's what happened and I came out feeling flat and slow. So in the final, I worked myself into a nervous state, knowing it would help me perform at my best. And that's exactly what happened.

TRAINING TO FIT YOUR BODY: In rowing it's always more—more volume, more time on the water, more reps in the gym. But when I did genetic testing I found out that I'm not wired for endurance and respond better to strength and power work. In 2007, my brother started training with Kelly Starrett at San Francisco CrossFit and told me that I was too thin and weak to make it to the top. I have some disadvantages compared to my rowing peers, such as

being 3 or 4 inches shorter than the top girls. It wasn't until I started training with my brother, my husband [Brian Mackenzie] and Kelly that I learned how to overcome this by becoming more powerful and developing speed endurance rather than just putting in more miles.

OVERCOMING ASTRONAUT SYNDROME: You hear that when astronauts came back from the moon they struggled to find anything that would match that experience. I haven't been into space, but it's a similar thing when you've had success on the water. When I made a brief comeback to help a teammate compete in the pairs in early 2015, it was a pretty easy transition from doing CrossFit 5 days a week to getting back into rowing shape.

This showed me that I had greased the pathways enough to come back, but I quickly found there was nothing new I could learn about myself through rowing. So now I'm looking for new challenges on the water and in life that can inspire me. I often say that if something doesn't get you up in the morning and keep you up at night when needed, then you're only doing it because you have to. You need to find that thing you love to do if you're going to stick with it and not get mentally and physically burned out.

ERIN CAFARO MACKENZIE'S TOP 4 TIPS FOR HANDLING RACE DAY PRESSURE

1) Use adrenaline in your favor. The only time to be nervous at the starting line is if you aren't nervous!
2) Breathe before you start. Taking some quick nasal breaths will help super-oxygenate your body as well as narrow your focus so you can concentrate on what truly matters.
3) Get comfortable with the idea of being uncomfortable. Before the race begins, visualize and embrace the pain you will be pushing through. Most nerves are really just fear of pain. Recognize that everyone around you will be hurting. It's the person who deals with it the best that wins.
4) Learn something about yourself in every race that you can use to do better the next time.

WATERMAN WISDOM: TIPS FROM THE PROS

ATHLETE PROFILE
GREG BARTON

AGE: 58
SPORT: Sprint kayak
BASED IN: Seattle, Washington

CAREER HIGHLIGHTS: Won 2 Olympic gold medals in 1988 and 2 Olympic bronze medals in 1984 and 1992, claimed 4 golds, a silver and a bronze at the ICF Canoe Sprint World Championships, co-founded Epic Kayaks

PURSUING OLYMPIC DREAMS: I first dreamt of paddling in the Olympics when I was 12. Fortunately, my first coach, Marcia Jones Smoke, was one of the best and had won a medal in the 1964 Olympics. She also coached my brother, Bruce, and he was a big inspiration to me. I watched Bruce compete in the 1976 Montreal Olympics, which made me believe I could emulate him. The process was fascinating, too—watching the heats and finals, the way the athletes prepared themselves for racing and their tactics. At that time, the rest of the world was so far ahead of us with long established club programs, but when Bruce finished 6th in the World Championships I started to believe we could become perennial challengers. Unlike Bruce, who excelled at the junior level, I was a late bloomer and didn't start winning medals until I was in my 20s. It was my love of the sport that kept me going and sticking with it that eventually paid off.

IT'S ALL IN YOUR MIND: As I rose higher in the sport, I soon realized that the mental aspect of performance was key. There were plenty of paddlers who were more physically gifted than me, but when it came to racing they just fell apart. In any race, you have to realize that there will always be something that's unexpected. Maybe it's someone who has a faster start than you

expected or keeps pace with you when you thought you could pull away. You just have to expect adversity and then deal with it. For me, breathing was an important way to keep steady in any situation. When I was 13 or 14, I found that the best pattern was to inhale on the left side of my stroke and exhale on my right. I also tried to keep the same routine before the start, from what I ate to my warmup to visualizing the race. That way I was experiencing something familiar no matter where I was competing.

PADDLER'S PASSION + ENGINEER'S EYE = BOAT BUILDER: When I competed, I would constantly try to find ways to go faster on the water, and I'd look at existing designs and think of improvements I could make. I was always fiddling with the position of my seat and tinkering with my foot braces, and also shaped some of my own paddles. People saw what I was doing and asked if I could help them, too. That's when I started thinking that maybe I could build my own boats. I got a degree in mechanical engineering and had done some practical work in the field by the time I made it to the Olympics. To me, designing paddles and boats was a way to combine my passion for paddling, my desire to move faster and an engineer's curiosity. Now I apply that to flatwater disciplines and surfski.

ATHLETE PROFILE
FIONA WYLDE

AGE: 21
BASED IN: Hood River, Oregon
SPORTS: SUP, windsurfing, kitesurfing

CAREER HIGHLIGHTS: 2016 Stand Up World Series and 2017 APP World Tour champion, 2014 Standup World Series Finals distance winner, won the 2017 Naish Columbia Gorge Paddle Challenge, became first woman to reach the final of a men's world tour SUP event

STANDING UP TO DIABETES: When I found out I had diabetes, it took my doctor a few weeks to sort out my insulin levels and it was so frustrating. But once we dialed the insulin in, there was no way I was going to let my condition stop me. I've always taken care of my body and now I have to pay even closer attention to my energy level and what I'm eating. But I'm determined to prove that people with diabetes can compete at the top level and can enjoy being outside on the water as much as anyone else.

REPRESENTING ON THE RIVER: With the Payette River Games, the Naish Columbia Gorge Paddle Challenge and the GoPro Mountain Games, it's evident that competing on whitewater is a huge growth segment for SUP. Some of the most competitive races in the past couple of years have been on rivers and now that the biggest names from Hawaii and Australia are competing too, the standard is just going to keep improving. As I train so much in fast flowing water, I think I have an edge.

A GLOBAL EDUCATION: From the time I was 3, my parents took me with them to Mexico every winter so they could windsurf. I didn't speak a word

photo by Laurie Black

WATERMAN 2.0

of Spanish when I started pre-school, but soon became fluent. The time we spent in Mexico taught me to appreciate other cultures and showed me that you can find good waves and the water sports lifestyle anywhere in the world. It definitely set me up well for traveling the globe as a SUP athlete.

FIONA WYLDE'S TOP 4 TIPS FOR WHITEWATER SUP

1) Go with someone who is experienced in rivers. The conditions are a lot different from the ocean or lakes and even if you're an avid canoer or kayaker, being with someone who knows what they're doing is a big plus. People who work at local outfitters often have up-to-date information about obstacles or storm debris in the river and can guide you to the best rental equipment for the conditions.

2) Get your equipment right. Inflatable boards are best as they can bounce off of rocks and are easy for transport. When picking your board, you want a wide deck that is designed specifically for whitewater, so you can have as much balance as possible. You also want a strong paddle that is just a couple of inches over your head. Get a proper Coast Guard-approved lifejacket and a helmet, and it's not a bad idea to wear protective knee, elbow and shin guards. I highly recommend wearing water shoes as river rocks can easily cut your feet. If you decide to wear a leash, make sure it's a quick release version and attach one end to your lifejacket and the other end to your board. You do NOT want to attach one end to your ankle as it could get caught on debris and create a very dangerous situation.

3) Before you start going through rapids, make sure you practice paddling back and forth across the river. This is called ferrying. Spend a lot of time paddling quickly on one side while angling your board upriver. An eddy is normally on the edge of the river and, surprisingly, the water goes the opposite way of the big flow of the river. In whitewater, you always want to make sure that you weight your downriver side of the board, because if you weight your upriver rail, your board will flip and you'll be swimming!

WATERMAN WISDOM: TIPS FROM THE PROS

4) Once you feel confident with those couple of skills, you're ready to hit your first small rapid. Check out the bottom of the whitewater feature before going over it to make sure there are no rocks or logs sticking out. Once it's all clear and you're paddling toward the rapid, keep your speed by paddling strong during your approach. When you're about to drop over the rapid, bend your knees and keep your paddle in the water as a brace. Think of your paddle as a third arm that you can rely on for balance. If you fall off, no worries! Stay calm and float on your back with your feet downstream so your feet and butt hit rocks if there are some, instead of other body parts. It's important to hold onto your paddle as you swim to your board. Once you're back on, paddle to the edge of the river next to the eddy and wait for your friends.

photo by Laurie Black

ATHLETE PROFILE
JAMIE MITCHELL

AGE: 41
BASED IN: Los Angeles, California and Gold Coast, Australia
SPORTS: Surfing, prone paddleboarding, SUP

CAREER HIGHLIGHTS: Won Molokai 2 Oahu prone division 10 years in a row, the first ever WSL Big Wave Tour event at Nazaré in Portugal and won the 2009 Battle of the Paddle

THE AUSTRALIAN WATERMAN FACTORY: I think Australia keeps producing some of the world's best water athletes because many of us grew up in the water. 80 percent of Aussies live on the coast so the ocean is a constant. The surf lifesaving movement is huge. I started in the Nippers program when I was 5 years old. Once I learned how to swim, I was training on a foam board until I was 10, and then a fiberglass board until I was 13. Next, my coach taught me how to paddle on my knees. From ages 15 to 16 I spent most of my water time on a surfski, and then a friend got me to join the local outrigger club with him. Add in surfing, and you can see just how many disciplines I was exposed to at a young age.

FROM PRONE TO SUP TO BIG WAVE SURFING: Preparing for Molokai for a decade was a significant mental and physical challenge. Each year I had to sacrifice a lot to stay on top and it got to the point where I thought, "What more do I have to prove?" SUP was just starting to blow up in 2008 and 2009 and I managed to take the 2009 BOP title in my first big race. But while it was a lot of fun, I never felt I did all that I could in standup because my eye was on big waves. Getting into the Eddie [Aikau Big Wave Invitational] and chasing swells was something fresh and became my way to

stay motivated. I always go all out and the power of big waves presented that new challenge I'd been looking for.

GETTING YOUR MIND RIGHT: Molokai molded me as a person and made me into a man. It taught me how to be dedicated and focused and to overcome adversity to reach my goals. This mindset carries over to big wave surfing. It's all too easy to burn nervous energy in the days leading up to a heavy session and then you have nothing left when the swell comes. I'm a pretty relaxed bloke—even before the start in Molokai I'd kid around with the other guys. So I try to be the same with surfing. I get plenty of sleep, eat clean and prepare all my gear well, while trying to just chill. But when it's go time and I'm heading out to the swell, I dial in because you have to make good split-second decisions or you're done.

JAMIE MITCHELL'S TOP 5 TIPS FOR REACHING YOUR POTENTIAL

1) You need to work hard to be the best. It sounds like a cliché, but there is no shortcut to success at the highest level. You've got to show up every day, put in your best effort and be consistent because there are plenty of good athletes in any sport who are doing everything they can to beat you.
2) You've got to truly love what you're doing because when it becomes a job or chore, you're done. That goes for training, too. Coaches like Brian Mackenzie push me really hard, but it works because we're also having a blast and changing things up. I'd never do the same session twice if I had my way. You're never too good to have a coach.
3) Find a training group in which people will encourage and challenge you. It's nice to go out on the water and just be alone with your thoughts, but when it comes to elite competition you've got to have people to chase and to help motivate you.
4) I've come to appreciate the waterman lifestyle even more since I started designing my own boards and equipment. You learn things about what works best on the water, and if you get involved with

creating gear you can share these lessons in a new way.

5) Building in breaks from my main activity has always been huge for me. Even when I was dedicated to prone paddling, I only spent 4 or 5 months a year doing it. The rest of the time I was off surfing, swimming or doing other things I enjoy. Mental burnout is in some ways worse than getting physically drained and cross training is a good way to avoid it.

ATHLETE PROFILE
JAY AND ANIK WILD

AGE: 38 (Jay), 46 (Anik)
BASED IN: Truckee, California
SPORTS: SUP, outrigger canoeing, surfski, prone paddleboarding

CAREER HIGHLIGHTS: *Anik*: Winter X gold medalist in freestyle skiing, competed on the FIS World Cup tour; *Jay*: Won the Tahoe Fall Classic and Jam from the Dam, 6th at ISA World Championships

A POTENT TEAM: Anik and I are about 10 years apart and that means we bring different things to our relationship. She taught me a lot about what it means to live, train and prepare like a true professional athlete, while I bring some youthful exuberance into the mix. We both paddle and coach together at Waterman's Landing, as well as both being CrossFit coaches. While we have our tense moments training, it's great to share the experience of being out on the water, whether that's on surfskis or SUP boards or in outrigger canoes.

FUNCTIONAL MOVEMENT AND MOBILITY: CrossFit has taught me and Anik the value of functional movement and making each training session intentional. You don't have to go long to do high quality work that's going to make you stronger and help you move better on the water. I'll be honest and say that we both need to do more mobility work, but we recognize that it can help us perform better. I know there are rest days when I should tackle all my trouble spots so I'm not restricted the next time I pick up my paddle. Plus, if you take a few minutes each day for preventative work, you hopefully won't need the hospitals, doctors and cortisone shots!

LAKE TAHOE LIFESTYLE: Living on the lake we're isolated from a lot of the politics and negative stuff that often impacts people involved in water sports. I love Southern California, but any time we're down there we look at each other and say something like, "I can't wait to get back to the mountains." We're lucky to work with so many great SUP athletes right where we live, and to have a great community through our CrossFit box.

OFFSEASON TRAINING: We can't be out on the water year round because of weather, but that's not an excuse to goof off. In addition to doing CrossFit, we use the Concept2 erg and Ski Erg to stay in shape and I've helped Paddlesport Training Systems develop their SUP and outrigger attachments for the rowing machine. It's important to mix up your workouts so that when the weather clears and you can go back out on the water, you feel strong and ready to go.

JAY AND ANIK WILD'S TOP 5 LAND-BASED WORKOUTS FOR PADDLERS

WORKOUT 1

Warm up for 5 to 10 minutes and then perform:
- 10 air squats
- 5 burpees
- 5 candlesticks
- 5 reps of single kettlebell front squats

1 minute rest

Repeat 6 times and then do:
- 10 x 50 percent bodyweight bench presses
- 20 sit-ups
- 10 x Russian kettlebell swings

WORKOUT 2

Warm up and then perform 5 rounds of:
- 15 dumbbell shoulder presses (find a weight that is making your shoulders burn by rep 12)

- 25 air squats
- 5 push-ups
- 5 sit-ups

Rest 1 minute between sets

WORKOUT 3

3 rounds of:
- 15 alternating froggers
- 5 burpees
- 30 second squat hold
- 10 squat jumps

1 minute rest
- 20 alternating froggers
- 10 burpees
- 30 second squat hold

1 minute rest
- 10 alternating froggers
- 5 burpees
- 15 second squat hold

1 minute rest
- 5 push-ups
- 10 sit-ups

WORKOUT 4

Warm up and then perform 3 rounds of:
- 15 walking lunges
- 10 sit-ups
- 5 push-ups
- 20 jumping jacks

1 minute rest
- 20 walking lunges
- 10 sit-ups

WATERMAN 2.0

- 5 push-ups
- 25 jumping jacks

1 minute rest

- 25 walking lunges
- 5 sit-ups
- 5 push-ups
- 30 jumping jacks

WORKOUT 5

- 100 sit-ups for time
- 100 air squats for time
- Max pull-ups in 1 minute
- Max push-ups in 1 minute

ATHLETE PROFILE
ZANE KEKOA SCHWEITZER

AGE: 24

BASED IN: Kahana, Hawaii

SPORTS: SUP, outrigger canoeing, longboard surfing, windsurfing, prone paddleboarding

CAREER HIGHLIGHTS: 2-time Ultimate Waterman champion, gold medal in SUP surfing at the 2016 ISA World Championships, winner of the 2016 Red Bull Heavy Water event, back-to-back winner of the Master of the Ocean contest, 2nd place in the 2015 World SUP Surfing Championships, author of the book *Beneath the Surface*

WHAT BEING A WATERMAN MEANS: To me, a true waterman or woman is someone who adapts in the moment as the ocean does. We should strive to better understand what it's giving us and then choose the right vessel based on those conditions. Or sometimes you just use your body to enjoy the waves. I'm blessed to have grown up in Hawaii and it has given me a deep appreciation of the power of the sea. Every time I'm out in it I feel more humble, grounded and connected. I get into the water with full respect, knowing that I can be pummeled. I say a little prayer to acknowledge the power of the ocean and to recognize that I'm tapping into a creation that's much bigger than me. Being out there in silence focuses me on every single moment so I can be totally immersed in the present.

THE HEALING POWER OF WATER: I volunteer for camps and have seen firsthand

how healing the ocean is for kids with cystic fibrosis and other conditions. It's the same for the kids who attend my InZane SUPer Groms events. If you pay attention you can see the children changing before your eyes—they're more playful, joyous and carefree when they're in the water. There's something about the ocean that recharges us. It's a giant filter and the life support for our planet, which is why the Hawaiian concept of kuleana—the value of responsibility—means so much to me. We owe it to ourselves and future generations to take better care of our natural world.

EVERYDAY READINESS: If you're going to be in the water a lot, you've got to feel confident in your body and know that it can get you into whatever position you need to be in. And if not, Kelly's mobility work can help you improve that readiness. Great technique takes time to develop, but is important for longevity, particularly for longer distances. I do most of my training in the ocean, but when I'm back on land I do 100 push-ups a day and some meditation each morning so I'm mentally clearer when I enter the water and can experience it to the fullest. Your computer or phone slows down if you have too many apps running and you'll need to restart it. The body and mind are similar, and the ocean is what gives me that physical, mental and spiritual reset.

GO FOR YOUR GOALS: I've been journaling first thing in the morning and last thing at night for many years. It allows me to better process what I've done, where I've been and what I'm feeling. I also use it to create action plans and to record my progress toward whatever goals I've established. My journal provides me with a time capsule that helps me go back to places I've visited and people I've met. I'm also a big believer in personal affirmations. Before each race I'll spend a couple of minutes affirming what I've learned, what the conditions are and what I'm going to do. It helps me execute in competition and focus all my preparation on that one event.

ZANE KEKOA SCHWEITZER'S TOP 4 TIPS FOR EMBRACING WATERMAN CULTURE

1) Learn to better understand water conditions, wind, tides and currents. There is no way for you to overcome the ocean—you have to go with whatever it will allow on any given day. If you can more accurately assess that, then you'll be safer, enjoy yourself more and have richer experiences.

2) Don't stick to a single craft or discipline. There are seasons in which I'm mainly SUP racing, but I'll still go out and surf on a shortboard or longboard with my friends, or hop in a team's 6-man canoe. It's important to be versatile so you can maintain your excitement and joy. Plus, each craft or board gives you a different perspective, depending on whether you're prone, sitting or standing.

3) Don't just view SUP, surfing or whatever as a workout. It might keep you fit, but it transcends the physical. Try to focus on noticing subtle things, like how the light reflects on the water or the smell of the sea air. Also pay attention to the rhythm of the waves. Being out in the ocean should be a rich, sensory experience every time.

4) I've learned a lot about the ocean, myself and other people from traveling around the world. It's amazing to see how people in Tahiti are truly at one with the water and what a central part of the culture it is there. It's also fun to learn a little bit of other languages and see what names they have for the water or certain breaks, like Teahupo'o. I've also seen how the ocean can bring people of different backgrounds together. You need to embrace these cultural traditions and be willing to learn from them because they'll make you a better waterman or woman and a more complete person.

ATHLETE PROFILE
TANVI JAGADISH

AGE: 18
BASED IN: Mangalore, India
SPORTS: Surfing, SUP

CAREER HIGHLIGHTS: Won 3 straight national SUP titles in 2014, 2015 and 2016, claimed back-to-back national surfing titles in 2014 and 2015, became the first woman to represent India in an international SUP or surfing competition at the 2016 ISA World Championships

SURFING IS FOR GIRLS: When I was growing up, my brother and his friends all surfed and though I wanted so badly to join them, my parents told me that "surfing isn't for girls." It wasn't until I met an American paddler, April Zilg, that I realized what women were capable of in the water. It took me 6 years to overcome other people's objections and my worries and start surfing. My grandfather first took me to the Mantra Surf Club and my brother became my coach and mentor. I improved rapidly, but had to battle through the disapproval of some family members and others in our community. Even after winning my first national title, it was hard to overcome the prejudice because girls in our society don't get support for being adventurous. I hope that by representing my country I can change some people's minds about female athletes, and show girls like me what they're capable of if they believe in themselves, work hard and push through boundaries.

MINDFULNESS OVER MATTER: I'm trying to balance training, racing, school and family time, which can be difficult sometimes. To fit everything in I usually get up around 3:30 AM. Before I get into the classroom or out into the waves I spend time meditating and doing Ashtanga yoga. It helps teach me

how to be fully present and calm in any situation, which is particularly useful during races and in heavy conditions.

SPREADING THE STOKE: Surfing and SUP are both growing fast in India, but one problem is that a lot of people cannot afford expensive lessons. That's why I plan to teach for free—to get as many people as possible out onto the water. I am also inspired by how tight the international paddling community is. At the 2016 world championships, I met people from 26 other nations and our flags flew alongside each other, which made me feel a deep sense of togetherness. I was very nervous going into my first international contest, but everyone was so welcoming and helped me a lot with advice on paddles, boards, technique and anything else I asked them about. It really felt like being part of a big global family.

ATHLETE PROFILE
JIM TERRELL

AGE: 53
BASED IN: COSTA MESA, CALIFORNIA
SPORTS: SPRINT CANOEING, SUP, OUTRIGGER CANOEING

CAREER HIGHLIGHTS: 2-time gold medalist at the Pam Am Games, 4-time Olympian, won multiple national championships in sprint canoeing, competed at the World Championships, founded Quickblade

EQUIPMENT, MEET ERGONOMICS: For the longest time kids were just using their parents' hand-me-down paddles. The trouble is that the blade face is far too big, so we began making a smaller one. But then we saw that it wasn't just about that—the shaft and handle needed to be tailored to smaller hands, too. The same goes for women's paddles. So we started scaling down the shafts as well, and then adding different tapers. The next advance was when we realized that while some of the powerhouses could handle a stiff carbon shaft, that wasn't going to work for smaller paddlers. So we devised the shaft stiffness index and gave people a few different choices. We don't want to overload our dealers with too many options, but the goal is to give everyone a paddle that's as close to perfect for them individually as possible.

THE ART OF THE PADDLE MAKER: The second we ship a new paddle, I'm thinking of ways to make it better. We have gone backwards sometimes—I tell people that I've got a big pile of throwaway paddles, but like Thomas Edison said when someone asked if he'd failed, "I have not failed. I've just found 10,000 ways that won't work." New technology allows you to create paddles more quickly, but you're still visualizing what you want to create and then making it happen: whether that's me and Dave Kalama working with foam

prototypes or creating 2D drawings and then sending them on for 3D rendering. One day soon I'll be able to create a design in my office and produce it right there with a 3D printer. No matter how you craft the paddle, it all starts with a passion for enjoying the water and helping other people get the most out of that, too.

FUNCTION FIRST: We're never putting out a paddle that's just a marketing ploy or a copycat design. Some people, including a good friend, thought the V-Drive was gimmicky, but after Mo Freitas won the 2015 Pacific Paddle Games distance race with it and Candice Appleby used it in claiming the overall title, I asked him, "Do you still think it's a gimmick?" I was giving him a hard time, but I was only half kidding: all these new designs are meant to perform.

The idea of putting dimples on a blade came from a friend who tests boats for the US Navy. I didn't have any hard data, but we did substantial testing and it showed that the dimples create little vortices that make the blade go in and out of the water more easily. We've also created an adjustable paddle that is better weighted and easier to change up on the go than previous versions. The elite paddlers still aren't using adjustables because they're usually clunky and unbalanced, but we might see that change soon because they're moving between flatwater and coming in and out of surf in competitions. The reality is that you can never craft the perfect paddle. That's why thinking about new designs keeps me up at night and motivates me to keep creating.

JIM TERRELL'S TOP 5 TIPS FOR MAXIMIZING PADDLING POTENTIAL

1) Danny Ching has been showing how much power can be generated from a staggered stance that almost looks like a sprint canoe posture. He's changing sides every 5 strokes or so, and shifting his feet each time. This way he can create more torque from the hips and really get over the top of the paddle. Travis Grant is the same way—he's able to go really fast without upping his stroke rate.

2) Your board will track better if you can make the water you displace go on the inside of your paddle rather than the outside. We investigated this by attaching 2 D-rings to a board loaded with 170 pounds and dragging it behind a motor boat. Then we took what we'd learned and applied it to the board-to-paddle relationship. If you angle your blade face to about 10 degrees, you'll stop fishtailing. That's how my friend Larry Cain can paddle 50 strokes on one side without his board going off track.

3) Don't over feather the blade in the exit phase of the stroke. We see a lot of paddlers, especially kids, whose coaches have over-emphasized feathering. This leads to over gripping the paddle as you twist the wrist. Then they wonder why they're getting carpal tunnel syndrome or tendonitis.

4) You should practice your side-to-side transitions. You can prevent losing valuable inches in your glide every time you change your paddle to the other side if you're transitioning hand placement effectively. Toss the paddle and quickly slide your bottom hand up to become the top hand. The top hand should drop down into the pulling position as it becomes the bottom hand again so you don't miss a stroke. You can stand on a bench to practice this on dry land.

5) Slow down! Kids and adult beginners are so eager to go fast on the first day when their skills aren't developed. That's why when I was coaching at Newport we spent most of our time on drills—making sure the kids had rotation, reach and the 4 phases of the stroke down at low speed before they dialed up the tempo. And if you're training kids, you should do less intervals with more recovery time.

ATHLETE PROFILE
NIC VAUGHAN

AGE: 26
BASED IN: Rancho Palos Verdes, California
SPORT: Big wave surfing

CAREER HIGHLIGHTS: 2015/2016 Big Wave World Tour competitor, 2015 Surfer Poll Awards "Heavy Water" nominee, 2014/2015 Los Angeles Surfer of the Year, 2014/2015 Big Wave Awards nominee for the largest wave paddled globally, 2014/2015 World Surf League "Prove It" video qualifier winner, multiple Big Wave Awards "Ride of the Year" entries

STAYING PREPARED AND READY: In the big wave surfing world we only get a dozen heavy days a year, maybe 15 if we're lucky. So that means that I spend most of the year making sure I'm ready once those opportunities arise. Maintaining homeostasis emotionally, physically and mentally is an important part of my life, and to do that I have to be active. I try to do something different each day to keep myself engaged. So one day it might be a long bike ride, the next could be a gym workout or yoga session and the next I'll take one of my longboards out for a prone paddle. All of these have different benefits: the cycling gives me strong legs, the paddling is one of the most crucial parts of surfing and the interval training on the rowing machine helps me go from 0 to 60 instantly to catch that perfect wave 4 or 5 hours into a big day.

DAILY BREATHING PRACTICE: I started using the Wim Hof Method a couple of years ago so that I could still function without oxygen and not push the panic button—like when I've got thrown off a wave. A while back I was surfing at Puerto Escondido when I got caught in an 18 wave set and was just getting

hammered on the head over and over. It was the closest I've come to drowning. I wish I'd had all that breathing practice behind me so I could've been more in control. Now that I've become more mindful of how important each breath is, I can also come down more easily after a long day in the water.

You're so engaged mentally and physically in every moment and in such a heightened state that returning to your baseline is difficult. The breathing work makes it easier. I've also added in a drill on the stationary bike that simulates what I experience while surfing. Once I'm up to a steady pace, I'll hold an inhale breath for 20 or 25 seconds while maintaining that cadence. Then I'll breathe normally for the remainder of the minute. I repeat this cycle for 20 or 30 minutes and it improves my surfing performance. I've also found that I can get back to 80 or 85 percent capacity now with just 1 or 2 deep, oxygenating breaths, which is huge when you're in the impact zone and getting pounded.

MO' MOBILITY, LESS PROBLEMS: When a big storm rolls in, I might have the opportunity to take advantage of it for 3 straight days. But on day 2 there are half as many people in the lineup as day one, and half as many again on the third day because it's so taxing. I used to wake up feeling sore and exhausted on that second day and it was a struggle to go back out. But now that I've started doing some mobility work—especially on my traps and lats—as soon as I get off the water I can recover a lot more quickly between sessions. When I'm not on a surf trip, I'm thinking about whether I'm moving well. If not, then I try to adjust my positioning. If my lower back or another area is sore, then I do soft tissue work and that usually takes care of the issue. It's a moving target, but mobility is a huge part of my physical practice.

RUNNING ON PREMIUM GAS: I'm not fanatical about my diet, but I try to eat as few processed foods as possible and usually choose the cleanest stuff I can get my hands on. That means a lot of lean meats and organic veggies. I'm into butter coffee, particularly before I go out for a big session. It gives me sustained energy. I'm also a big water guy—I have to be hydrated or my feet and calves cramp after a couple of hours.

NIC VAUGHAN'S TOP 3 TIPS FOR BIG WAVE SAFETY

1) When taking part in potentially dangerous ocean activities, focus on being aware of your surroundings at all times and avoid carelessly putting yourself in harm's way. Constantly be assessing your situation and take inventory of where danger might present itself. Note where your safety zones are and how you can quickly and effectively get there if necessary.

2) In the event of a bad situation, whether you find yourself in the impact zone of a 50 foot wave at Mavericks or stuck in a rip current at your local beach, you must focus on staying calm. It is imperative that you conserve your energy so you can efficiently apply it toward getting out of any such situation. Avoid panic by taking slow deep breaths, which will help to lower your heartrate, reduce energy burn and put you in a sharper mental state to make rational decisions. Relax and start taking tactful action toward your safety zone.

3) Once you've gotten to safety, take a moment to reflect and applaud yourself for successfully navigating through the dangerous situation. Think about what you did right, what you did wrong and how you can prevent that from occurring again. Each situation is a learning experience that will help you to be smarter, calmer and better prepared for a similar scenario in the future.

ATHLETE PROFILE
JOE BARK

AGE: 58
BASED IN: Rancho Palos Verdes, California
SPORTS: Prone paddleboarding, surfing, spearfishing, SUP

CAREER HIGHLIGHTS: Founded Bark Paddleboards, completed the Catalina Classic for 30 years and won it in 1988 and 1989, finished Molokai 2 Oahu many times

A CRAFTSMAN'S PASSION: I sometimes wake up at midnight with an idea for a new board design. When that picture comes into my head I run down to my truck, drive to my shop and work all night and all the next day. My enthusiasm is still the same as when I started shaping full-time in 1981—I can't wait to start tweaking and refining a board and will just keep going and going until it's ready to test. Then we get it out on the water and see how it performs and come back and make refinements. I'm constantly thinking about speed and stability. Often, the first concept that popped into my head is the best one.

PASSING ON THE FAMILY BUSINESS: My kids have been working with me in the shop since they could walk—it's all they know. When they were small they'd work for Slurpees—sweeping up, taping boards off. Now that he's older, my son Jack and I shape for a few hours every morning. I won't just teach someone halfway, but if they're willing to work as hard as I am I'll do everything I can to share what I've learned. The technology has changed, but the hands-on approach to making an idea become a reality is still the same. We're a working class company and that's the way we're going to remain.

SPENDING HIS 20S IN HAWAII: In those days the beaches weren't crowded, and I'd surf the inside, take the leftovers, just have fun with it. At night I'd make t-shirts in the garage of whatever house I was staying at. Guys would go surf at Puerto Escondido for a few months and then go to Hawaii for a couple of weeks. We all drifted between houses, working odd jobs and surfing as much as we could. In the summer I'd go back to California and shape boards, work construction and bartend so I could save up enough money to return to Hawaii for the winter swells.

LESSONS FROM THE CATALINA CLASSIC: One night when I was tending bar, 6 guys came in and were talking about how they just got the Catalina race going again. I'd already paddled Molokai on my prone board and completed the Catalina run with friends when I was in high school. Since I first did the race in 1983, it has become a brotherhood and these friendships will last for the rest of our lives. Nobody takes pictures or leaves until everyone has finished. SUP race organizers should learn from that.

You need the elite contests, but weekend races shouldn't be charging $150 entry fees. And the prizes shouldn't just be for the winners. They should do raffles, with everyone getting an equal chance to win boards and paddles. We've got to take better care of the people at the back of the pack if SUP is going to stick around. Chattajack has the perfect model: 300 people show up, there's no money and everyone just does it for the love of paddling.

JOE BARK'S TOP 3 TIPS FOR GETTING INTO SUP

1) When looking for a board, it's essential that you choose one that fits you. It's important to know what you want to do with the board, such as adventure or recreational paddling, touring or racing. Many boards are made specifically for certain ocean or flatwater conditions, and you want to make sure the one you pick is right for the paddling experience you want to have. You should also match the board to fit your size and ability level. Many people go for the same

designs that the top racers are using, not realizing that their experience level, body type and paddling style can be very different.

2) There are paddle groups all over the world that meet for their team workouts and this creates a fun way to put in the miles. I have found that everybody improves when you push and encourage each other. In a short time, the bond between paddlers grows strong and it's no surprise that these paddle groups are thriving. The global paddling community has a mentality of "the more, the merrier," and this can only grow the stoke and the sport of SUP.

3) Choose the right races. Some are hometown events that bring the local paddle community together for a great day of competition and others draw paddlers from all over to compete, like Molokai, the Catalina Classic and Chattajack. It's good for paddlers to choose races that they are comfortable participating in. Along with racing, the adventure side of paddling is also becoming very popular. Whether it be a trip down the local river for a camping trip or crossing big open ocean channels, adventure paddling is a fun way to get on the water and explore.

photo by Donald Miralle

ATHLETE PROFILE
LINA AUGAITIS

AGE: 37
BASED IN: Vernon, British Columbia
SPORTS: SUP, adventure racing, triathlon

CAREER HIGHLIGHTS: 2014 Standup World Series champion, 2014 Battle of the Paddle distance race winner and overall champion, became the first woman to complete the Yukon River Quest on a SUP board, won a gold medal at the 2014 and 2016 ISA World Championships

WATERWOMAN VERSATILITY: Before I started competing in SUP I competed at the World Triathlon Championships [placing third in her age group], ran marathons and ultras and was on the rowing, rugby and wrestling teams in college. I enjoy testing myself with new sports and am always up for a new challenge. My first expedition was paddling 750 kilometers from Whitehorse to Dawson on the Yukon River. Then I got into SUP, got hooked and found I was quite good at the racing side.

TRAINING INTENSITY: I'm always looking for new ways to dial up my training—like carrying a rock overhead while I'm running, doing pull-ups from a bridge overhang or stopping to do burpees. CrossFit has also pushed me to get more powerful and explosive. I've always had a pretty good engine, but I definitely needed to get stronger.

ACTIVE LIFESTYLE: A relaxing weekend for me and my husband Andrew and our children Tav and Aiste usually means hiking, camping and mountain biking with friends. In the winter we go backcountry skiing a lot, pulling the kids on sleds. My focus has been on SUP for the past few years, but I still enjoy really long runs and rides and would love to get back into adventure racing at some point. I love testing the boundaries of what I think my body can do.

PASSING ON A LOVE OF ADVENTURE: When I'm not competing, training or hanging out with family or friends, I teach outdoor education. We do some theory stuff in the classroom, but the best part is taking the kids camping and teaching them life skills like how to build a fire. Just about everything I enjoy is outdoors, and I want to share this passion with young people so that they're inspired to live an active life.

LINA AUGAITIS'S TOP 5 TIPS FOR KEEPING TRAINING FRESH

1) I seem to push even harder and feel more accountable when I am part of an organized group. Training with others helps with motivation, level of exertion and race strategy. It is so different to practice intervals and buoy turns with people who can offer pointers. Also, paddling in a group is a great way to socialize, get outside, enjoy a workout or go exploring.

2) It's important to have efficient technique in order to gain and maintain speed. Once you've established good technique, you then need the base endurance and strength to further develop it. You will see better results in a stroke clinic once you are comfortable on your board and in the conditions you find yourself in. Learning from a variety of sources and people is also important as you can take little bits and pieces from each one.

3) I've met a ton of people that paddle every day and "train hard" but don't get results. Once your body gets used to the pace, you're no longer improving. Interval workouts mix things up, raise your heartrate and get your body to develop different energy systems. You need to teach your body to deal with lactic acid buildup and push through your comfort zone mentally and physically, in order to see continued progress. Switch it up between going hard over short distances and going longer with lower effort.

4) I'm a huge fan of cross training. Find something other than paddling that you enjoy doing—for me it's mountain biking, trail running, Nordic skiing, yoga and CrossFit. Not only will you feel the physical rewards, but you'll also experience mental benefits as well. I love the break from the water because then I'm eager to get back into paddling again.

5) If you have the luxury of training on different bodies of water, do it. Flatwater training is important for working on stroke technique, consistent intervals and endurance. Open ocean work helps in understanding current, tides and chop and improves balance. SUP surfing is super fun, aids in stability, turning and dealing with fast-moving water. Downwinding helps you handle bumps, move better on your board and take advantage of wind. Trying all aspects of SUP will help with overall physical and mental fitness, skill and lasting enjoyment.

ATHLETE PROFILE
MIKE EISERT

AGE: 55
BASED IN: Laguna Niguel, California
SPORTS: SUP, outrigger canoeing, rowing, sprint kayak

CAREER HIGHLIGHTS: Gold medalist at the Molokai Hoe World Championships, Queen Lili'uokalani race and K-2 and K-4 Nationals, silver in the K4 at the US Olympic Festival, 2nd place in Hawaiki Nui Va'a

BRINGING UP GENERATION SUP: This is the first crop of paddlers who can learn from the founding fathers like Laird Hamilton and Dave Kalama, coaches from other disciplines and the experiences of today's younger pros like Kai Lenny. A lot of these kids have grown up in the ocean doing junior lifeguarding, playing water polo and swimming, so they're raring to go when they get on a SUP board. Canoeing and kayaking have had centers of excellence and expert coaching for years and we're now starting to see that trickle down into standup. You start to see the positive impact of deliberate and intentional programming when you have juniors like Shae Foudy breaking through into the senior ranks. As Kai said after he coached one of our sessions recently, "These kids are going to be doing things we didn't even know were possible by the time they're my age."

COACHING CHARACTER: The technique, race strategy and ocean safety work we do is very important, but we want to help our kids become well-rounded young men and women of character. By showing up consistently, even on days they're tired, have a ton of homework or don't feel good, they're learning the importance of dedication and consistency. They also need to display teamwork and camaraderie even when their teammates are annoying the

heck out of them, and learn that doing your best is as or more important than being the best. These are life lessons that will hopefully set these kids up well for later in life, whether they become pro watermen and women or not.

INTENTIONAL PRACTICES: Just putting in 10 miles a day isn't going to get the kind of results you want. We focus a lot on stroke fundamentals, work on every kind of turn you can imagine and get comfortable coming in and out of the surf. When there's a race coming up we'll practice starts and drafting, and add in some speed work for the shorter contests. The mental side is just as important. When I paddled sprint canoe, missing a stroke was the difference between a medal and being in the middle of the field. A coach taught me that I needed a verbal cue that I could use as a reset button. So every 5 strokes, I'd say "Go!" to myself. I'm teaching our juniors this, as it helps them maintain focus during races and makes it easier for them to overcome falls and other issues you come across in competition.

MIKE EISERT'S TOP 3 TIPS FOR COACHING JUNIOR AND BEGINNER PADDLERS

1) Most SUP athletes, both pro and recreational, typically set the paddle with their bodies, hence the localized, mid-back hinge effect and lack of rotation. Ultimately, hunching over and not rotating into the catch and then counter-rotating through the pull phase is a recipe for an injury-prone junior athlete, especially as they begin to train and race more.

2) The bottom arm has to remain straight at the catch and through the pull phase until the exit position. Otherwise, power is minimal and efficiency is diminished. Missing the catch—pulling before the blade is fully submerged—creates slippage and encourages the athlete to bend his or her arm immediately in the pull phase. This is highly inefficient and places too much stress on the biceps and shoulders.

3) Paddle with the big muscle: your body. With repetitive motion endurance sports such as SUP, paddling with your entire body is

the only way to create the torque/power needed to drive the board through the water as SUP boards are the most inefficient with the most drag of all paddle sports. The arms and legs should simply be levers used as connectors to your core, which ultimately creates all the power needed to succeed with each stroke through rotation and counter-rotation.

ATHLETE PROFILE
CARTER JOHNSON

AGE: 42
BASED IN: Sausalito, California
SPORT: Surfski

CAREER HIGHLIGHTS: Set Guinness World Records for farthest distance paddled in 24 hours on moving and flatwater and course records at the Texas Water Safari, Yukon River Quest, MR340 and 2 Dam Days races

DON'T SLEEP ON NUTRITION: No matter how much training you do or how long you paddle, most people are unaccustomed to paddling at night. You have to make sure that you can continue to focus when it gets dark and be aware of your surroundings so that you keep a good pace going and avoid obstacles and other boats. It's also essential that you maintain your nutrition and hydration. Your body may not be used to taking in food and fluids at night, but you still need to keep yourself topped up so you have enough energy. I set a timer so I know to consume enough calories and water every 30 minutes or so. Engineered products like gels and powders don't work for me, so I know to eat real foods like cheese and sausage instead. But that's a personal thing—just find what works for you and do it.

DON'T LET THE STROKE BECOME YOUR ENEMY: Whether you're in a sprint or in a week-long expedition, on flatwater or a rushing river, technique is everything. If you're getting your stroke right, the big muscle groups are doing the work, the load is balanced and you feel like you can keep going on and on forever. But as soon as your form begins to break down, you start overusing the smaller muscles and your body eventually lets you know with aches and pains in weird places. You also start to learn that getting your boat up to speed and keeping it there requires just the right amount of effort. After you

hit that sweet spot, it will take a disproportionate amount of exertion to get the boat to go faster, and that's not going to be sustainable for long.

GET YOUR MIND RIGHT AND YOUR BODY WILL FOLLOW: A lot of people tell me that they zone out during distance races. While it can be helpful to play games in your head to get through the end of a long paddle, I take the opposite approach to letting the mind drift. It feels like I need to stay engaged in every moment and every stroke. This particularly comes into play when the light starts to fade, as your senses tend to tone down their alertness. At these times I'm focusing extra hard on what's going on around me and getting ready to react to something instantly, like an obstacle in the river. And, at the end of the day, I always try to remember that paddling isn't about records or wins—I do it because I like to go out on the river with my friends and have fun. Someone who likes reading makes sure they go through a lot of books. For me, that's paddling: it's what I do.

CARTER JOHNSON'S TOP 3 TIPS FOR LONG PADDLES

1) You'd think that elite paddlers would be the best suited to longer races, but in fact some of them—Olympians and world champions included—have real pacing issues. They're used to going all out over short distances and so aren't accustomed to being below 80 percent intensity. This means they often burn out in the first couple of hours. Instead, you need to find a comfortable cadence that you can maintain for a long time. It's better to start out slow and make it to the finish than to go out hard and fade quickly.
2) An efficient stroke is important, but you can also be efficient in other ways. One is by being well organized and working out a detailed plan with your crew. You can lose a lot of time at checkpoints and so should have your support boat packed with several small bags that can be easily handed to you each time you stop. Otherwise, you're going to struggle to make up all that lost time late in the race.
3) Many first time racers try to ignore chafing seams, small leaks or

WATERMAN WISDOM: TIPS FROM THE PROS

other issues because they think they'll lose time by attending to them. Actually, this can be a big mistake because small problems usually become big ones if you leave them alone. It's better to deal with an issue as soon as you notice it so that you minimize its impact. This will actually save you time in the long run.

ATHLETE PROFILE
JONAS LETIERI

AGE: 33
BASED IN: Cabo Frio, Brazil
SPORT: SUP

CAREER HIGHLIGHTS: 2nd place at the Brazilian Triple Crown (in which he was the only adaptive athlete), was the first adaptive paddler to win a heat at a major US SUP event (the Payette River Games), became the first double arm amputee to finish Molokai 2 Oahu, carried the Olympic Torch at the 2016 Rio de Janeiro Olympics, finished 4th at the 2016 King and Queen of the Sea and won Most Awesome Award at the Salt Lake Tahoe race

LIVING TO SURF: Growing up, surfing was everything to me. Then in a moment, everything changed. I was volunteering for a building project at my church and a giant surge of electricity sent thousands of volts into my hands. I should be dead. When I woke up in the hospital, surgeons had amputated both hands and most of my forearms. Though I was in a lot of pain, I was grateful that God had spared me. A lot of people said I'd never surf again, but I knew in my heart that I would return to the ocean. My parents believed in me and encouraged me in this dream, as well as helping me adapt to the new challenges I now faced. As I could no longer pop up on a surfboard, I began looking for another sport that would get me back out on the water and found SUP.

THE IMPACT OF INNOVATION: As I couldn't grip a traditional standup paddle, I needed a new design that would allow me to control the shaft and apply torque. My father helped me find someone to craft a paddle with 2 rings. Then I met Jim Terrell from Quickblade at Brazil's Battle of the Paddle and he told me he'd come up with a better design. The paddle I had allowed me

WATERMAN 2.0

to SUP surf and do distance paddles, but as I had to try and grip the top of it, my arms quickly fatigued. Jim gave me his new version at the 2015 Payette River Games and I could tell a big difference right away. It gave me way more control and I could paddle a lot longer without getting as tired. Then he created an even better paddle that was tailored to my body the following summer. I'm privileged to have a custom designed paddle from the best paddle maker in the world.

THE POWER OF COMMUNITY: When I first got back on the water I was so joyous and felt so blessed. But I didn't know how other people would view me. So I was surprised by how much encouragement I've received from everyone I've encountered—in the lineup, at events and on the beach. One of my main champions is SUP legend Anthony Vela. He not only supported me, but also introduced me to Jim Terrell and Mark and Kristina Pickford, who sponsored me for the Payette River Games.

I never dreamed that I would be racing against the best athletes in the sport, and to win a heat at Payette was overwhelmingly emotional. Then Jimmie and Anthony helped me and my father come over to the US again the next year, which enabled me to not only race, but also live my dream of SUP surfing in California. Candice Appleby has also been amazingly supportive. I'm so thankful to this wonderful community for embracing me.

ATHLETE PROFILE
NICK TROUTMAN

AGE: 29
BASED IN: Rock Island, Tennessee
SPORT: Freestyle kayak

CAREER HIGHLIGHTS: Gold medalist at the 2009 World Freestyle Championships, became the first person to do a complete descent of the Rio Alseseca and Rio Jalacingo, 5-time national champion, winner of the World Cup and Pan Am Championships, 3rd at 2016 GoPro Mountain Games

Sibling (in-law) Rivalry: For a long time EJ [Eric Jackson] was my primary training partner, but as soon as Dane had been in the senior ranks for a couple of years, he took over. We're both very competitive, but at every event we try to help each other succeed. We'll be talking the whole time about the best lines, giving tips on equipment tweaks and trying to bring out the best in each other. It's amazing to have your training partner rooting for you from the bank, even though he wants to medal or place just as badly as you do.

PASSING THE TORCH: I'm heavily involved in the Keeners program, which helps juniors improve their kayaking skills. When my friend Joel Kowalski and I were 15, it was the greatest thing ever to go to a weeklong camp where you just kayak your heart out every day. Stephen Wright has done an amazing job with the program and each day is purposeful. On Mondays and Tuesdays, the kids run the Ottawa River. It's one of the best in the world for freestyle, so they get a chance to really show their stuff.

On Wednesdays we take them through head to head and timed races. On Thursdays we desensitize them to heavy water by taking them to the biggest hole on the river. It's actually really safe, but seems scary the first time and once the kids come out the other side they feel ready to handle anything.

WATERMAN 2.0

Our freestyle competitions are on Fridays. It's not about who wins, but each camper reaching their goals—doing a certain spin or staying in the water feature for the whole time.

ARE YOU SITTING COMFORTABLY? If you're going to be out on the river all day, you'll be miserable if you don't make your boat as comfortable as possible. You've got to figure out the best seat height and make sure you've got a boat and paddle that you can deal with for several hours. Shoes are another thing many people overlook. You don't want something with a big heel because it will alter your foot mechanics and make your feet sore.

I like to use neoprene socks or booties, or sometimes a lightweight and flexible water shoe that has a thin and soft sole. As you won't be getting on and off the water a lot, you should pack snacks. I usually stuff a couple of Kind bars in a pocket of my lifejacket. When you're getting splashed in the mouth and face, it tricks your body into thinking you aren't thirsty, but you can quickly become dehydrated. You need to make sure you sip water regularly.

NICK TROUTMAN'S TOP 6 TIPS FOR WHITEWATER PADDLING

1) Learn to read it. Whitewater can be intimidating when you don't understand it. Learn how the currents are flowing and how they interact with obstacles in the water, how to identify where rocks are and how to navigate the water properly. Learning to read whitewater is like learning to read music—it seems daunting, but is quite simple and intuitive.
2) Start with a friend. It will be easier to learn and stay motivated and you'll have more fun if you've got someone to paddle with. You'll teach each other if you learn together.
3) Take your time going up the classes of rapids. There is nothing "badass" about jumping into Class V whitewater before you're ready, injuring yourself and needing someone to rescue you. Paddle the type of whitewater that is appropriate for your skill level.

4) Know who you are paddling with. You are a team while paddling whitewater and you are only as strong as the weakest link. Understand the skill level of the people you paddle with.

5) Never stop learning. Whether you are a beginner or seasoned veteran, you will always be able to learn from someone better, get in more practice and spend more time scouting rivers. You can always advance your skills no matter how good you think you have become.

6) Stay safe! This is probably the most important tip, and a bit of a combination of them all. Know what you are getting into and make sure you have the appropriate equipment such as proper footwear, flotation, helmet and throw rope. Remember you're a unit when paddling whitewater, so you need to stay safe and be ready to save your friends as well. Make sure to learn about the river in advance to minimize any dangers that could occur before they happen.

ATHLETE PROFILE
NOA HOPPER

AGE: 21
BASED IN: San Diego, California
SPORTS: SUP, flatwater and whitewater canoeing and kayaking

CAREER HIGHLIGHTS: Won 7 medals at the USA Canoe/Kayak Sprint National Championships, won the mixed SUP relay in the Molokai 2 Oahu World Championships, claimed 1st place in the junior technical division at the 2016 Pacific Paddle Games

KEEPING IT FRESH ON THE WATER: In the weeks leading up to USA Canoe and Kayak Nationals, I'd never tried C1 or sprint canoeing. Jim Terrell told me I should take a crack at both because he thought I should challenge myself. I only had time for 9 or 10 practice sessions in the sprint canoe, but somehow made the final and finished fifth. It was also the first time I'd paddled with Paul Chevalier in the C2, but we clicked immediately and claimed the title. Trying new things means I'm never bored on the water.

THE IMPORTANCE OF MENTORING: Before M2O in 2015, I wasn't sure about whether or not I was going to race. Candice Appleby talked me into it and told me she'd be my partner in the relay. Thanks to her experience we won the division. Danny Ching was also a big help and gave me a lot of tips during a long downwinder a few days before the race, even though he'd already put in more than 20 miles in his OC1 that morning. Training with Chuck Glynn and the San Diego Canoe and Kayak Team coaches has also been hugely beneficial.

CONCENTRATING ON CONSERVATION: My Dad took me to Asia when I was a kid and I was shocked to see rows of shark fins in the markets. It ignited a fire inside of me to educate people about sharks and the need to protect them. I'm determined to balance being a professional waterman with a career in marine conservation.

LEARNING ON THE JOB: So many of the greatest paddlers and surfers have been lifeguards, and working at the tower in Del Mar with seasoned guards is teaching me so much more about the ocean. It's only going to help me when I'm training and racing because I'll be able to read the water better.

NOA HOPPER'S TOP 5 TIPS FOR SUP CROSS TRAINING

1) Flatwater canoe and kayak practices go year round and vary between long, slow sessions and short, fast intervals. Both disciplines engage other muscles because you have to emphasize your rotation, legs and core differently than in SUP.
2) C1 (Olympic canoe) is the closest discipline to SUP in that you're extending and planting your paddle to pull forward, but with C1 you paddle on one side only. It really helps you become efficient at high stroke rates and you can't miss a stroke or someone will overtake you.
3) I look at outrigger paddling as a mash-up of kayak paddling and SUP. It requires lots of leg strength and core rotation and the practices can develop different energy systems as we do everything from low rate distance work to short "wall-to-wall" sprints.
4) SUP surfing is another great way to work on speed as there's lots of sprinting to catch the waves followed by long slow pulls to get back out to the lineup. It also helps develop the balance and coordination you need to do well in whitewater. Longboard surfing is a good way to unwind, too.
5) Water polo really enhances my coordination and increases my aerobic capacity, which helps with SUP distance racing. SUP is an individual sport, so it's also nice to be part of a team and get to practice, hang out and travel with the guys.

ATHLETE PROFILE
SEAN PANGELINAN

AGE: 31
BASED IN: San Diego, California
SPORTS: C1 sprint canoe, dragon boating, SUP, outrigger canoeing

CAREER HIGHLIGHTS: Made the semi-finals of the 2008 Beijing Olympics, won the silver medal at 2008 Oceania Championships, was a member of the USA Dragon Boat Team, was an assistant coach for the USA Outrigger San Diego Team, founded The Fit Lab in San Diego

OLYMPIC EXPERIENCE: It was a great honor to represent Guam at the 2008 Olympics and I had an amazing time in Beijing. The main thing I'd change if I could do it over again was the way I prepared. My coaches were from Eastern Europe and training camp was like being in the military—up at the crack of dawn, everything regimented and disciplined. It didn't matter that I'm not at my best early in the morning or what I wanted to eat. Everything was decided for me. I wish it had been tailored more to me and my body and preferences, but I'm still very thankful to have gone to Beijing and made it to the semi-finals.

THE IMPACT OF DAILY MOBILITY: If I'm too busy training clients at The Fit Lab to get a hard session in myself, I still need to spend at least a few minutes mobilizing. I know my own weaknesses—lack of internal shoulder rotation and a tacked down t-spine from years of paddling—and so I target those areas regularly. It makes a huge difference in my stroke and if I skip a day I'm tight and sore. Being a waterman or woman is all about getting out on your boat or board, but I wish I'd had MobilityWOD back when I was competing as I know I'd have achieved more. Now that I'm planning to get into more Olympic lifting, SUP and CrossFit competitions, mobility is a must.

WATERMAN 2.0

TRAINING SMARTER: It's frustrating to see people writing that get-ups, kettlebell swings, snatches and clean and jerks don't do anything for you as a paddler. I know from my college degree and keeping up with the best strength and movement coaches that these exercises improve your shoulder integrity, teach you to explosively hinge at the hips and develop all the major muscle groups you utilize while paddling. And moves like this aren't just for beginners—I've seen some of the best watermen and women add power and become more durable by changing up their gym routines.

SEAN PANGELINAN'S TOP 5 TIPS FOR NUTRITION

1) Eat enough to match your activity level. A lot of athletes have a caloric intake that's far below their minimum needs and then wonder why they're losing weight. It's important to take in the right blend of protein, healthy fats and slow burning carbs to fuel your workouts and races and then recover afterwards. Take into account your age, body composition, genetics and fitness goals when creating the right nutrition plan for you.

2) Hydrating adequately before, during and after exercise is key to regulating body temperature, digestion and nutrient transport. Avoid the temptation to chug water right before a race or training session as your body can't process high volume during activity and if the fluids don't have the right blend of electrolytes, you're putting yourself at risk. If you feel the need to drink a lot before you hit the water, your hydration strategy needs to change.

3) Top up fluid levels during longer races lasting more than an hour. While you don't want to gulp large amounts, take regular sips of a mix containing electrolytes—sodium, potassium, manganese and magnesium—and make sure you replenish with branched chain amino acids soon after the race so your body goes into repair mode. Be wary of "sports drinks" that have excess sugar and improperly balanced sodium and potassium levels. What you drink can also boost your immune system. I start each day by drinking water with

lemon and sea salt, and drink a lot of green tea. It might be a coincidence, but I haven't had a cold in over a year.

4) You've got to rest to maximize your nutrition intake. If you're overtired, your body isn't going to properly absorb the nutrients you're putting in or effectively flush out waste products. To adapt to your training stimulus and recover adequately from hard sessions and races, you must sleep well, mobilize often and create conditions that will help you relax. Otherwise, you're just going to limit your progress.

5) Trust in your preparations and stick to what you know. If you've dialed in your nutrition and hydration plan well in advance of a race, believe in it and don't try any last-minute experiments. Also stick to clean, additive-free foods that you know your body will process well in the days leading up to a competition. When you're in a new place it's fun to try new foods, but there will be time for that after your competition. You don't want that spicy curry coming back to haunt you during the race!

ATHLETE PROFILE
JOE JACOBI

AGE: 48
BASED IN: La Seu d'Urgell, Spain
SPORTS: Canoe slalom, C2

CAREER HIGHLIGHTS: Gold medalist at the 1992 Olympic Games in slalom doubles canoe, 8th place at the 2004 Olympic Games, 3rd place overall at the 1989 Canoe Slalom World Cup Series, 5th place at the 1989 Canoe Slalom World Championships, 6-time World Cup medalist in doubles and singles canoe, 10-time US national champion in multiple disciplines

MEANINGFUL MORNING PRACTICE: I've realized that just as one bad, unhealthy habit is likely to lead to others, so too do a few good, healthy habits have a knock-on effect. That's why when I was trying to come back to health I recognized the importance of how I start the day. Every morning, no matter what I'm going to do later on, I dedicate 1 hour to quiet time. This includes yoga, meditation and writing 10 ideas on a certain topic, a habit I got from Tim Ferriss's interview with James Altucher. If I feel like the routine is becoming too routine, I'll switch it up by adding something like a cold shower. These might seem like small things, but when I look at big things I've done in the past few years like my recent paddle from Cuba to Key West with Carter Johnson and some other friends, it's the small daily habits that have empowered me to reach for big things.

MOVING WELL TO MOVE THE BOAT: To move your craft of choice as efficiently and effectively as possible, you've got to align with forces greater than yourself. A lot of people get obsessed with the relationship between their paddle and the water, and you can't ignore that because where those meet is a crucial energy transfer point. But the paddle blade is

such a small surface, whereas the boat is a much bigger one. That's why I tell my students to prioritize the water-to-boat relationship. To do this, you've got to think about how you can capture energy from the water. In the 1992 Olympics my partner and I were the only crew with a combined weight less than 300 pounds. The German powerhouses next to us were about 375 pounds and determined to win by pounding their paddles and defeating the river. The only way we could beat them was to do the opposite and dance with the river using the efficient stroke we'd honed by practicing the basics every day. But you can only maximize your technique if you move well and have the positional capacity and range of motion in your torso, spine and shoulders to take advantage of that water-boat relationship. Otherwise, you're making compromises and all that hard work isn't going to pay off.

GO SLOW TO GO FAST: Because the Olympic events are such intense sprints, most people assume we spend all our training time going all out in whitewater. But that's not the case at all. To be successful at the highest level, you've got to love the process and enjoy the steps it takes to become the best you can be. For me, that meant a lot of time breaking things down into parts

on slow, flatwater. You become obsessed with how you're interacting with your boat, your paddle and the water, trying to find the slightest advantage that will help you and your partner move a bit faster than your rivals. When I get in or on a new craft, such as a SUP board, I'm not trying to apply that elite speed so I can feel satisfied that I went fast. Instead, I go back to basics, slow down and really put some thought into how I can get more from what's around me so I have to do less.

365

ATHLETE PROFILE
SHAE FOUDY

AGE: 19
BASED IN: Dana Point, California
SPORT: SUP

CAREER HIGHLIGHTS: Won Female Breakthrough Performer at the 2015 SUP Awards and 2016 Pacific Paddle Games, 2nd place overall at the 2016 Pacific Paddle Games, 3rd place overall at the 2017 Pacific Paddle Games, won the Race the Lake of the Sky and Santa Monica Pier events, won the 2016 Quiksilver Waterman's Festival

GOING FROM GROM TO PRO: Candice Appleby got me into standup and it's been amazing to learn from her and other accomplished women who've achieved so much. It's important for me to share these lessons and my own experiences with kids at The Paddle Academy and on the beach because the only way we can keep growing this sport is for the pros to give freely and pass on what has been given to us to the next generation.

DANA POINT CULTURE: I'm blessed to have grown up with access to Doheny State Beach, the open ocean and the harbor right outside my front door. It was the birthplace of competitive SUP with Battle of the Paddle and the waterman culture is everywhere. Being taught to surf by my family and then having great coaches and mentors like Mike Eisert to guide me has been huge, and I take what I've discovered about reading the ocean to every contest I enter.

OVERCOMING FOOD ALLERGIES: I'm allergic to dairy products, eggs and gluten, which makes it difficult to fuel for hard training and competition. I decided that the best path was going vegan and got a lot of criticism for

WATERMAN 2.0

it. It can be challenging to get enough protein, but I combine plant-based sources and protein supplements to make sure I'm getting what I need. The real key is eating clean, which helps me perform my best and makes me feel great day to day.

SHAE FOUDY'S TOP 5 TIPS FOR GROMS

1) Start off by getting into a training regimen. I suggest paddling 3 times a week and cross-training on your off days. Remember that you're still growing, so get plenty of rest to recover adequately.
2) Find the flaws in your paddling technique. You can do this by looking at videos of pros and comparing their stroke to yours or having a coach analyze your stroke. Work on changing a small thing in your technique one day at a time until you correct it. Then see what's next.
3) Face the things that frighten you and consciously decide to conquer them mentally and physically. Whether it's a wave or going up against better competition, face it with confidence and know you can do anything when you put your mind to it.
4) Find people in your community who also enjoy SUP and train with them. When I workout in groups I tend to push myself much more than when I'm on my own. It is more fun and encouraging, too.
5) Once you decide you want to dedicate yourself to standup paddling or any other discipline, never forget to have fun. It's not a job!

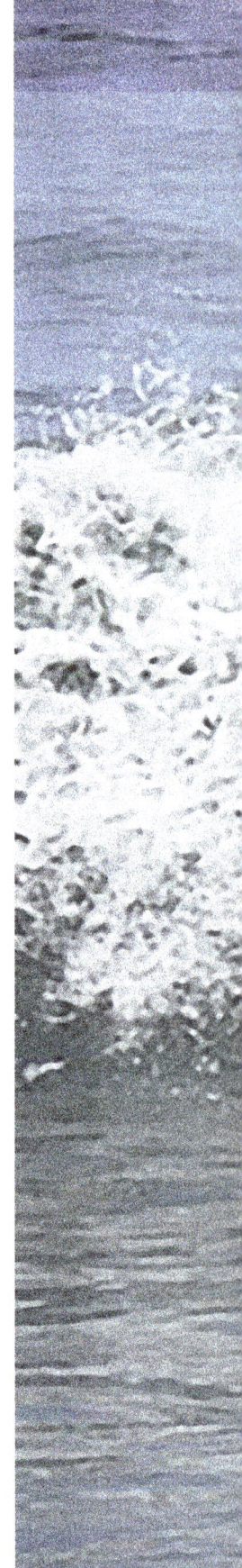

ATHLETE PROFILE
SHANE PERRIN

AGE: 42
BASED IN: St. Louis, Missouri
SPORT: SUP

CAREER HIGHLIGHTS: Broke world record for miles paddled in 24 hours, first SUP athlete to complete the Texas Water Safari, La Ruta Maya and the MR340 races

TO ST. LOUIS AND BEYOND: I wanted to find a unique way to celebrate the 10th anniversary of my kidney transplant and settled on something that hadn't been done before: paddling 340 miles down the Missouri River on a SUP board. When I showed up, a lot of racers laughed at me and said I'd never make it. But by the end, these same doubters saw that I'd finished and many became advocates.

I had no intention to do any more races, but the organizers of La Ruta Maya contacted me and asked me to come race in Belize. So I went and after paddling through the jungle, I thought, "Maybe I can make something of this." People at the Texas Water Safari were placing bets on where they thought I'd die or quit on the course, but I managed to get through and made a lot of new friends. Now I just want to show others that a SUP board is a viable craft for long distances.

LIFE LESSONS ON THE RIVER: Going into the MR340 my only goal was to make it to the finish without messing myself up. But it became more than just survival—it taught me a lot about what I was capable of if I truly pushed myself. There have been so many times that my body is just done and is screaming at me to stop. But I've been able to steel myself mentally and push on, and have learned that if I can just keep my attitude in check, I'll be alright.

THE KEEP STANDING PROJECT: I never set out to be an inspiration for anyone, but somehow Nathan Woods heard my story and it inspired him to paddle 160 miles up the Willamette River. When I found out he's missing half of one leg, I was amazed—he has overcome so much more than me. So I told him I'd paddle with him. In the year that followed, we kept coming across amazing against-the-odds stories and so decided to start interviewing them for a podcast. I take something valuable from each one of these heroes, and if I can offer them advice for their expeditions, I do it freely. I didn't have any endurance SUP athletes to consult when I did my first long paddle, so I'm glad to be that resource for others.

SHANE PERRIN'S TOP 4 TIPS FOR SUP EXPEDITIONS

1) If you're new to expeditions I'd recommend starting with a supported trip. A support crew can help with re-supply, moral encouragement and dealing with unforeseen challenges such as storms. However, the support team should be an aid and ultimately you're responsible for your own success or failure and completing or abandoning an expedition. Pre-planning goes a long way and will help you be successful.

2) Do your research on what gear to take and what to leave behind. Err on the side of taking more than you think you need and make sure you have a board that can support it. You'll be traveling a little heavier, but that's better than being under-provisioned. Ultra-light expeditions are fine once you've refined your gear needs over many trips, but going too light in the beginning can result in a bad experience or failed expedition by having to cut the trip short.

3) A common mistake new distance paddlers make is to eat a normal diet at home and through training and then bring salty or sugary,

easily packable foods with them on the trip. Your body tends to like to revolt anytime you introduce something unfamiliar. Protein and energy bars work great in a pinch, but if that's your main source of nutrition on your trip, your body will have fun tormenting you from all the sugar. Bring plenty of toilet paper and electrolyte replacements! Have a good balance of foods your body is used to prior to the trip.

4) For self-supported trips you should have someone who's experienced with expeditions advise you on planning details such as primary and secondary routes, nutrition, water, first-aid, sleeping arrangements, gear and supplies. Always have a trip plan and share it with at least one reliable source who lives nearby, such as a friend, family member or spouse. Check in with this designated person at set times and if you don't, have them alert the authorities. A SPOT tracker transmits your location every 10 minutes. It also has a help button that can contact the Coast Guard, who you should send a float plan to in advance.

ATHLETE PROFILE
JUDE TURCZYNSKI

AGE: 59
BASED IN: Sacramento, California
SPORTS: OC1, surfski

CAREER HIGHLIGHTS: Founded Huki Outriggers and Surfskis

ERGONOMICS MEETS PADDLING PERFORMANCE: When I first started building boats, I recognized that body position and balance are essential in making the boat go faster, and that the boat design itself can influence that balanced positioning. Existing surfski designs made the catch zone too wide, so my goal was to narrow it so the paddler didn't have to reach so far out to the side. In the ski, we've also put the seat as low in the boat as possible. Foot position is also important. We want the feet to be low in the boat in both the OC1s and surfskis. More advanced paddlers will be more comfortable with their feet closer to their seat, whereas beginners or intermediate paddlers will want a bit more room in between.

Everyone has a different torso-to-arm-length ratio, but the goal for the "typical" paddler in having a low seat and low feet is that they can maintain an organized torso throughout the stroke and end each stroke with their pinkie touching the top of the water. We feel that's the most efficient finish position. We want every level of paddler to feel comfortable, so their boat is less tippy than that of a competitive racer. The goal is to achieve stability without reducing glide, so that each paddler can apply most of their power most of the time.

BUILDING BETTER BOATS: My driving force when I started building boats full-time in the late 80s was to do something I loved and could get paid for. But

I also saw an opportunity to move boat design forward. You have to create a nice looking craft, of course, so that it's appealing to people, but it also has to perform well on the water because the design is based on sound principles. When I brought my first 2-man canoe to the 1990 World Sprints, the Tahitian paddlers told me they'd never seen a design tailored to sprinting.

At the time, a lot of people were concerned with the boat's surface-to-water area, so you had a lot of these big, flat hulls because that's what was supposed to be the most stable. I thought I could build a narrower, sleeker hull that had enough flat areas to provide stability but would create less drag. The result was the S1-X. In the surfski, that wide catch zone was being used to add volume. I believed you could still enable the paddler to balance their boat, but change the design to provide them with a much narrower catch entry. That was the critical concern: maintaining stability without compromising hull speed.

BEWARE FADS: You see a lot of design fads come and go in boat and paddle design. While there's more than one design that will produce a fast boat, not every new idea is an improvement. Several times wide-tail canoes have become popular, with the thinking being that it will help improve an OC1's pick up and get you surfing a wave earlier. This design has cropped up in the 80s, mid-90s and again recently, but I think each time we've seen that it didn't really lead to better surfing or a faster boat. Another trend is the reverse bow, which I'm not convinced about. On the paddle side, we've seen experimentation with bends and double bends, but to me, that increases the actual shaft length and so introduces more flex. Some people might need that in a paddle, but you don't want to lose too much energy during each stroke. I think the traditional design—straight shaft, offset blade—is more energy efficient and lends itself to faster and sustainable paddling in any craft.

JUDE TURCZYNSKI'S TOP 3 TIPS FOR PADDLING COACHES

1) The ideal stroke for an advanced paddler is a short, efficient one that generates a lot of power each time the blade goes into and through the water. But a lot of beginners simply don't have the strength or power to move their boat with such a stroke. So if they need it, let them start off with a longer stroke and aim to shorten it as they become more proficient.

2) It's important to choose the right boat for a paddler's skill level, as a beginner in a narrow boat is going to be tippy and will focus too much of their energy on their balance, while an advanced paddler will be slowed down by a bigger, more stable boat. But in the end, the boat is just the platform and the stroke is everything. So it's essential that coaches are teaching the correct mechanics early on, before they add in speed or power.

3) Don't overlook the grip. The point that the paddler's hands meet the shaft is where they mold to their tool and connect themselves to the boat and water. Beginners tend to have a death grip, which leads to fatigue. It's better to teach a more relaxed grip so your smaller fingers are barely touching the shaft. Many paddlers find it's easier to achieve this with an oval-shaped shaft.

ATHLETE PROFILE
CHUCK GLYNN

AGE: 30
BASED IN: San Diego, California
SPORT: SUP

CAREER HIGHLIGHTS: Gold medalist for Team USA at the 2015 ISA World Championships and silver medalist at the 2014 ISA World Championships, 11th place at Molokai 2 Oahu in 2016, 8th place at the Carolina Cup in 2016, 7th place at the 2016 Hanohano Huki Ocean Challenge, board shaper for Laird Standup

BREATHE TO BEAT THE BONK: For a few years I really struggled in the second half of longer races like the Carolina Cup and Molokai. I'd bonk hard about 90 minutes in and start feeling dizzy and woozy. I always assumed that it was a nutrition thing, so I started trying different tactics for how I fueled before and during the race. Then I attended an XPT Life session with Laird Hamilton, Gabby Reece, Kelly Starrett and Brian Mackenzie and learned how much breath control can center you. During the 2016 Carolina Cup I again started feeling light-headed. Instead of panicking, I dropped back from the pack for about 10 minutes and just focused on my breathing and timing it with my stroke. Once I'd found my rhythm again, I caught back up and got close enough to the leaders to be in a sprint finish with Connor [Baxter]. Because of the breathing, I overcame the bonk and picked up 7 places.

TECHNIQUE IS KING: To me, having solid paddling technique is the key to longevity in your chosen sport. Even when my coach and I do a hard interval session, my form has to stay the same when I increase my stroke rate. If it starts to deteriorate, then we're done for the day. You see some of the young guys who just focus on how fast and hard they can go. Maybe you can get

away with that at the start and end of a race, but if going quickly with poor technique becomes a habit, you default to it. That's why you're seeing paddlers in their early 20s battling chronic injuries already. To make sure I don't fall into the same trap I do at least a couple of sessions at a slower pace each week, just focusing on my form and making sure I'm distributing force to all the major muscle groups rather than overusing 1 or 2.

My coach also has me do tempo work with a metronome so I get into a good, sustainable rhythm. This can vary by the type of board you're using on any given day, but it's important to find your ideal cadence and stick with that in training and competition. You might lose a little bit of speed in the middle of the race, but that's usually when everyone's in a pack anyway, so as long as you stay in touch with the leaders you'll be OK. If you're paddling smoothly and efficiently, you're also going to have something left for a hard sprint at the end of the race, which can make all the difference.

BUILDING PHYSICAL AND MENTAL RESILIENCE: Another important thing I learned from Laird and Brian was the power of combining hot and cold. It definitely improves my recovery and also makes me mentally tougher, particularly the ice. Your body gets used to freezing, but it's your mind that suffers in that ice bath. I take that toughness into competition with me. I've also learned to better match my off the water training to the type of race that's coming up. So before a shorter, faster contest I'll do some quick mountain bike runs because I feel like the up and down of the terrain is the best kind of interval training you can do, and it gets me ready for an intense effort on race day. Before a longer race, I go road biking instead, as that more constant, sustained effort mirrors what I'll face in a course race or downwinder. It's just a case of knowing what kind of preparation works best for the specific challenge.

photo by Johann Meya

ATHLETE PROFILE
TRAVIS BAPTISTE

AGE: 21
BASED IN: Kihei, Maui
SPORTS: SUP, outrigger canoeing, SUP surfing

CAREER HIGHLIGHTS: Won stock division of Molokai 2 Oahu 3 times in a row (14' board), won Breakthrough Performer of the Year at the 2014 SUP Awards

TRANSFERABILITY: When the SUP race season winds down in late fall, I start doing a lot more surfing. I also like to compete in outrigger races with my canoe club, which are usually 6-man contests. The competition is really fierce among Hawaii's canoe clubs and working with 5 other guys to propel the boat helps the power and rhythm of my stroke. This directly translates when I get back on my SUP board. For standup I do a lot of downwinders so that I peak at Molokai.

A SOLID FOUNDATION: Since I started doing CrossFit a couple of years ago I've noticed a huge difference in my power output and strength. People often forget the involvement of the legs in SUP, and doing squats, cleans and box jumps have given me a solid foundation whether I'm surfing, doing a channel crossing or anything in between. I also don't get as fatigued on downwinders or during races because I push myself so hard at the gym.

REST AND RECOVERY: I've always been a big sleeper and am usually in bed by 9 PM. For the past few years I've been juggling school, training and racing, and so coming home to relax has been my sanctuary. Now that I'm lifeguarding and going to college I'm still really busy and am worn out by dinnertime. If I didn't get enough rest, I'd be a wreck.

WATERMAN 2.0

FUELING RIGHT: When I first started CrossFit, I found I was actually losing weight because of the extra calorie burn. So I increased the amount of protein I'm getting at each meal. Most of the time it's from whole foods like fish, chicken and turkey, but I also add whey protein to smoothies to keep my intake high throughout the day. If I get too far below my "fighting weight" it hurts me on the water, so I need to make sure I'm getting enough fuel to repair and get stronger.

TRAVIS BAPTISTE'S TOP 5 TIPS FOR OPEN OCEAN RACING

1) Everyone wants to bolt off the line at the start of a distance race, which is one of the worst things to do as you need to be smart about how you spend your energy. At the beginning of a long race it is important to get a good start, but you have to be careful not to go too hard and burn out.

2) Make sure you dial in your supplements, food and drinks. During a long distance race you need to look at your energy levels like the fuel gauge on a truck and never let the needle dip below 60 percent. Make sure you know when to refuel and experiment with different supplements to see what works best for you.

3) Don't try anything new on race day. Stick with your familiar routine of what you like to eat for breakfast, what you eat right before and during the race and what liquids you drink. You don't want to change any of this on race day because your body will expect what it knows.

4) When it comes to a race like the Molokai 2 Oahu channel crossing, there is no paddle run I can do that will simulate exactly how the channel will be. To prepare adequately I try to train in all conditions that I could experience out there so I'm ready for wind and chop, bumps, flatwater—anything.

5) 2 big things to focus on the week before the race are recovery and carb loading. As you've done lots of training you might be sore and tired, so it's essential to fully recover before the big race. You also need to make sure your body has plenty of carbs so it has the energy to go the distance.

photo by Johann Meya

ATHLETE PROFILE
TRAVIS GRANT

AGE: 35
BASED IN: Honolulu, Hawaii
SPORTS: SUP, outrigger canoeing

CAREER HIGHLIGHTS: Won the Molokai 2 Oahu race 3 times (SUP twice, OC1 once), #1 in SUP World Rankings, won the 2012 ISA World Championships technical race title, Battle of the Paddle and Carolina Cup champion and Performance of the Year at the 2015 SUP Awards

MAKING THE MOST OF THE OFFSEASON: The winter before the last race season I hardly set foot on a SUP board. Instead, I entered a lot of canoeing races—OC1 and OC6—all over Hawaii, and did a lot of my training in these boats. As your center of gravity is lower you can really pull hard, and that gave me a good power base by the time the SUP races started up again in the spring. To be your best, you can't just stick to one board or boat.

GUTTING IT OUT AT MOLOKAI: I like it when things get rough and choppy, so the lack of wind at M2O 2015 didn't really favor me. But I was able to go out pretty strong and hold Kai off when he made

his move. In the end, it just came down to who had the most left after slogging across the channel for 5 hours and luckily I kept going long enough to pull out the win.

REFUELING BETWEEN EVENTS: I prefer to get my nutrition from real food, but when I'm on the road or between events I usually drink a UB Super protein shake to make sure I'm getting everything I need in one go. It's also important for me to stay hydrated, especially on days when I have a couple of races. Some of the events are really close at the finish, particularly in the shorter races. So it's important to refuel correctly so I can keep at it and save something for the last couple of hundred meters.

TRAVIS GRANT'S TOP 3 TIPS FOR BECOMING A MORE ADVANCED PADDLER

1) If you're fighting, digging a hole or throwing a ball, you need to be in a strong, stable position that provides a platform to perform the task well. It's the same when you're paddling. You need to be in the equivalent of a fighting stance—feet slightly staggered, knees bent a little and solid from your feet up.
2) Try this drill to ensure you're used to engaging your core before you even get on your board. On the beach or on grass, get into a staggered stance and reach out with your paddle. When you reach full extension as if you were about to dig the blade into the water, squeeze your abs. This will protect your lower back as you rotate your trunk.
3) As important as your board is, your paddle is an essential bit of kit. You want a paddle that you can knife into the water, is light enough for a fast swing and, most importantly, is appropriately sized for your body. Tennis players wouldn't use a second rate racket, so make sure you get the right paddle. After a few thousand strokes, you'll really notice a difference.

RESOURCES

To help encourage your continuous improvement, we've put together some resources that provide valuable information on movement and mobility, training, equipment and more.

MOBILITYWOD
www.mobilitywod.com
Get daily mobility videos and in-depth episodes, webinars and interviews with experts and top athletes. Plus, find physical therapists, chiropractors and other orthopedic professionals in your area and interact with our online community.

POWER SPEED ENDURANCE
www.powerspeedendurance.com
Learn more about Brian Mackenzie's high quality training approach that can help you meet your performance goals in less time and breathe optimally to achieve the physical, cognitive or emotional states you want to be in.

XPT LIFE
www.xptlife.com
Laird Hamilton and subject matter experts like Gabrielle Reece, Dr. Andy Galpin and PJ Nestler provide a practical waterman training and lifestyle blueprint.

TUNE UP FITNESS
www.tuneupfitness.com
Find more help for your soft tissues and fascia, courtesy of Jill Miller.

RESOURCES

OSMO NUTRITION
www.osmonutrition.com
Discover hydration supplements designed for efficacy by Dr. Stacy Sims and her team.

PADDLEFIT
www.paddlefitpro.com
Check out Brody Welte's systemic approach to improving your paddling and land-based fitness.

KALAMA KAMP
www.kalamakamp.com
Learn more about waterman legend Dave Kalama's unique paddling experiences across the globe.

FUNCTIONAL MOVEMENT
www.functionalmovement.com
Extensive movement knowledge from Gray Cook and his team.

ROGUE FITNESS
www.roguefitness.com
Your online superstore for all things mobility and strength training.

JACKSON KAYAK
www.jacksonkayak.com
Home of the boats built by legendary kayaker and canoer Eric Jackson, which his world champion kids, Emily and Dane, and son-in-law, Nick Troutman, help run.

QUICKBLADE
www.quickblade.com
You'll know why founder Jim Terrell is dubbed "The Mad Scientist" when you dive into the creative process behind his paddles.

WATERMAN 2.0

BARK PADDLEBOARDS
www.joebark.com
Learn more about the paddleboard designs from the legendary California shaper.

THE PADDLE ACADEMY
www.thepaddleacademy.com
If you live in SoCal and have kids who are into paddling, look no further than Mike Eisert and his fellow coaches to take them to the next level.

WATERMAN'S LANDING
www.watermanslanding.com
If you're heading up to Lake Tahoe, be sure to go and train with Jay and Anik Wild.

SUP ST. LOUIS
www.supstlouis.com
The Arch isn't the only thing to see in St. Louis. Check out one of endurance paddler Shane Perrin's classes as well.

THE FIT LAB
www.thefitlabsd.com
Train with Olympian Sean Pangelinan at his San Diego HQ.

DR. KELLY STARRETT is the author of *The New York Times* bestsellers *Becoming a Supple Leopard* and *Ready to Run* and *The Wall Street Journal* bestseller *Deskbound*, all of which have revolutionized how coaches, athletes, and everyday humans approach performance as it relates to movement, mechanics, mobility, and the actualization of athletic potential. Kelly is also the co-founder of San Francisco CrossFit and MobilityWOD.com, where he shares his innovative approach with millions of coaches and athletes around the world. Kelly believes every human being should know how to move and be able to perform basic maintenance on themselves.

Kelly is a lifelong paddler. He began whitewater kayaking at age 12 and went on to paddle whitewater slalom canoe on the US Canoe and Kayak Teams. He also led the U.S. Men's Extreme Whitewater Team to two national titles and participated in two World Championships. Kelly has competed in the Molokai 2 Oahu (M2O) crossing twice – once in an OC1 and once on a surfski. He has paddled with several Bay Area outrigger canoe clubs and loves to surf and stand up paddle.

PHIL WHITE is an Emmy-nominated writer and the co-author of *Game Changer* and *59 Lessons* with Fergus Connolly, *Unplugged* with Dr. Andy Galpin and Brian Mackenzie, and *The 17 Hour Fast* with Dr. Frank Merritt. He's a frequent contributor to *The Inertia* and *SUP the Mag* and collaborates with a select group of partners such as TRX, Onnit, XPT, and Train Heroic to tell compelling stories that improve performance and change lives. When not writing about himself in the third person, Phil enjoys SUP, hiking with his wife and two sons in Colorado forests, and a nice pint of stout. Start a conversation with him at www.philwhitebooks.com or via all major social media outlets @PhilWhiteBooks.

Lightning Source UK Ltd.
Milton Keynes UK
UKHW05f0507140918
328824UK00003B/32/P